A Century of North American Stock Markets

"Michael Szanto's A Century of North American Stock Markets is an impressive and engaging contribution to the study of financial markets. He combines deep historical research with practical financial insight, shedding light on how North American equity markets evolved and continue to influence today's global economy. What I appreciate most is how clearly he connects complex economic developments with real-world consequences. It's not just an academic work—it's a story of how institutions, innovation, and regulation have shaped modern finance. Michael's experience in markets comes through on every page, making this book both informative and enjoyable to read."

—Sandesh Mouli, *Founder, Ignite23 VC & Partner, Redwood Collective Ventures*

"In his highly anticipated book, Dr. Michael J. Szanto simplifies the complex world of securities markets. His detailed analysis is grounded in historical case studies, presenting unique insight into the dynamics of securities markets. His work is a must-read for undergraduate and graduate students of business, economics, political science, and finance. It is also for anyone seeking a better understanding of market structure and regulatory change."

—Hanna Samir Kassab, PhD, *Associate Professor of, Political Science and Security Studies at East Carolina University*

"Combining technical expertise with narrative prose, Szanto's book makes a unique contribution to economic history. The detailed analysis of the financial system closely examines the motives of market drivers to take risks and policy regulators to address risks over time. Broad in its sweeping scope to survey the history of the past century, this book engages academic scholars, business practitioners and the greater general readership. Spanning a century - from the rise of early regulation after the Great Depression and the fast pace of globalization at the end of the Cold War to technology opportunities brought on by new emerging technologies - the book is important reading to understand the twists and turns in the intervening decades. In addition to the depth of knowledge of U.S. markets, another focus on Canada provides a deep dive into the merits of this financial system. Szanto's book is a welcome wealth of valuable information at a time when markets continue to change at an accelerating pace. This book shows how far financial markets have come and makes the reader wonder what comes next."

—Beverly Barrett, *Lecturer, Bauer College of Business, University of Houston*

Michael J. Szanto
Miami, FL, USA

ISBN 978-3-032-22418-7 ISBN 978-3-032-22419-4 (eBook)
https://doi.org/10.1007/978-3-032-22419-4

This Palgrave Macmillan imprint is published by the registered company Springer Nature Switzerland AG.
The registered company address is: Gewerbestrasse 11, 6330 Cham, Switzerland

Acknowledgments

This book would not have been possible without the support, guidance, and encouragement of many people. I would like to take this opportunity to express my heartfelt gratitude to everyone who contributed to this endeavor.

Academic Guidance

I wish to extend my sincere thanks to my advisors and instructors, whose expertise and insightful feedback were invaluable. Steve Ralph, Isabella Figueroa, Alexis Fernandez, Doreen Yamamoto, and Lilian Yaffe gave me the guidance I needed to finish my PhD. Lisa Baker was always there to help me find the research resources I needed. I am thankful to all the members of the committee for my dissertation, which was the main inspiration for this book: Bruce Bagley, Roger Kanet, Joseph Ganitsky, Ambassador Ambler Moss, and Alex Horenstein. I owe particular thanks to Dr. Bagley for impressing upon me that I had to finally get my dissertation done and Dr. Kanet for always being there for me, even when he was at the hospital.

Colleagues and Friends

A special thank you goes to my colleagues and friends for their collaboration, constructive criticism, and moral support. I met so many wonderful people at the University of Miami and elsewhere that I cannot name them all. However, I do have to mention, in particular, Suzanne Loftus,

Jonathan Rosen, Melanie Goergmaier, Luba Adler, Diana Mazel Pittarelli, Steve Simon, Natalie Ghosn, Maria Campbell, Jimmy Wong, Beverly Barrett, Sara Hoffen, Diana Soller, Dina Moulioukova, Sabrina Taldone, Melissa Myers, Jennifer Solnik, Hannah Podlevsky, Ronen Nazarian, Doron Feinsilber, Uri Man, Lois Katz, and Paoulina Bourova. Additionally, nobody pushed me more to do this book than Hanna Kassab. Most of all, thank you, Yadira, for your patience and support as I worked on this book.

Editorial Support

I deeply appreciate the support and assistance of the Palgrave editors, particularly Tula Weiss.

Additional Support

In addition I would like to thank everyone else who contributed in ways both big and small. Your kindness and assistance are truly appreciated.

Thank you all for being part of this journey.

Personal Thanks

Finally, I am most grateful of all to my parents. I will always be super proud of my dad who came to this country as an immigrant and devoted his career to medicine and medical education. My dad and his colleague, Arthur Schneider, must have set a record for the number of Best Professor Awards at Rosalind Franklin University. Above all, I dedicate this book to my mother, Anna Winterman Szanto, who came to this country also as an immigrant with her family having absolutely nothing and always feeling so thankful for the blessing of having made it to America. I know my mom would have really loved reading this book.

Contents

CHAPTER 1

Introduction: A Century of North American Stock Markets

Introduction

This book takes the reader through roughly a century of North American stock market history. It traces the roots of the modern stock market to the Gilded Age, a time where steel, oil, trains, and skyscrapers made their mark on the United States. The book goes on to explore the key figures of the early stock market including Jay Cooke, Anthony Drexel, J. Pierpont Morgan, and Jacob Schiff. It explores how the Bankers Panic of 1907 led to the Pujo Committee investigation led by Samuel Untermyer of the so-called Money Trust and paved the way for the creation of the Federal Reserve. It looks at how major American companies like General Electric were created by a process known as Morganization. Morganization referred to Pierpont Morgan's strategy of streamlining and merging firms in industries often creating either monopolies or near monopolies. It explores how new twentieth-century technologies like the automobile and the radio fueled the explosion of the stock market and American economic optimism.

The book explores how the Federal Government under first Herbert Hoover, but even more so under Franklin Delano Roosevelt (FDR), responded forcefully to the events of the 1929 stock market crash followed by the devastating economic depression. A key figure is Harvard Law's Felix Frankfurter who effectively assembled FDR's Brain Trust for Securities Laws being drafted: John Landis, Benjamin V. Cohen, and

M. J. Szanto, *A Century of North American Stock Markets*,
https://doi.org/10.1007/978-3-032-22419-4_1

Tommy "the Cork" Corcoran. Congress and the FDR administration settle upon a disclosure-based regulatory system with the foundational 1933 Securities Act, not following the lead of states like Kansas whose "Blue Sky Laws" followed a merit-based system empowering government officials to reject securities offerings purely on the basis of discretionary findings of riskiness. This is likely for the best given that decades later the State of Massachusetts blocked its residents from taking part in the initial public offering (IPO) of Apple in 1980. A later federal law would preempt such state actions for Nasdaq-listed stocks.

The book reviews the early days of the Securities and Exchange Commission (SEC) including looking at Joseph Kennedy's role as first chairman of the SEC, effectively launching the Kennedy Political Dynasty, though one could argue that the real foundation of the Kennedy Dynasty comes earlier from Joseph Kennedy's swashbuckling days hustling and manipulating markets on Wall Street during the 1920s. Progressive reformers looked at Joseph Kennedy's leadership at the SEC with some trepidation given his appointment looked a lot like having a wolf guarding the henhouse. For the most part, however, his brief but historic chairmanship is widely viewed to have been a success. The passage of the Maloney Act of 1938 would allow for the creation of the National Association of Securities Dealers (NASD) to oversee the over-the-counter (OTC) market for stocks. The NASD would become an absolutely vital American financial institution which would launch the revolutionary Nasdaq marketplace in 1971. The Investment Advisers and Investment Company Acts of 1940 would create the regulatory underpinnings of today's investment management and advisors, which mutual funds and exchange traded funds operate under today.

Not many years after World War II, the boom stock market of the 1950s would take off. It was fueled by the rebound in military spending due to the Korean War combined with the global nature of the Cold War, the rise of suburbia, the growth of home ownership, and a ravenous demand for cars and modern appliances. Sydney Weinberg, who had started out as a janitor at Goldman Sachs, would lead the IPO of Ford Motor Company, the largest in history. The Ford deal would cement Goldman's restored place as a leading bank on Wall Street that it has held to this day. The 1950s bull market combined with the rapid growth of the middle class would drive a rapid expansion in retail demand for American stocks. The New York Stock Exchange (NYSE) heavily advertised to Americans that stock ownership offered the opportunity to take part in the rise of great businesses. Mutual funds would provide an opportunity for Americans to invest in a very diversified manner, but their steep fees and questionable marketing tactics also attracted a lot of controversy and increasing scrutiny from the SEC and Congress.

After a brief downturn in 1961, the bull market resumed for the rest of the 1960s. Certain glamour stocks attracted disproportionate buyer interest. The Nifty Fifty, in particular, were stocks that seemed to be impossible to lose with. This market exuberance that had more than a passing resemblance to the Roaring Twenties was also referred to as the go-go years on Wall Street. Certain mutual funds that chased the hottest stocks of the day came to be known as go-go funds. The most famous of these was Fidelity's Capital Fund, managed by the charismatic Gerald Tsai. The other major market development of the 1960s was the rise of the conglomerates. Companies like Radio Corporation of America (RCA) and International Telephone & Telegraph Corporation (ITT), who were originally telecommunications firms, evolved into aggregators of a wide assortment of companies in numerous often unrelated industries. The conglomerateurs sometimes not only came from humble backgrounds but also at times had little education. The key skillset in building a massive colossus at times was simply the ability to sell a lot of debt and equity. The leadership of these corporate goliaths would typically brag of their superior management capacity, but often the growth amounted to little more than financial engineering and very creative accounting. Prominent conglomerates United Technologies and General Electric would survive into the early 2000s with this type of structure, but they were unique. The 1970s, 1980s, and 1990s consisted very often of the unwinding of existing conglomerates.

The booming market of the 1960s overwhelmed the financial infrastructure of the markets. Stock trading still depended on the mailing of physical stock certificates, which ultimately unraveled into the mess known as the Paperwork Crisis. In 1973, the Depository Trust Corporation (DTC) was created transforming a stock trade into a book entry instead of a cumbersome feat of overworked paper pushers. Before the creation of the DTC, stock certificates often got lost or stolen. Both the American Stock Exchange and the NYSE as well as the regional exchanges had not yet significantly digitized their operations with the Computer Age only starting to impact Wall Street. Institutions represented by mutual funds, insurance companies, corporate pensions, and trust companies started to overtake retail investors as the main buyer of stocks. Their sheer scale required them to utilize newly developed block trades to maneuver in and out of their positions. Gus Levy at Goldman Sachs with his partner Robert Mnuchin became one of the first to truly master this business.

The 1963 Special Study on the Securities Markets specifically funded and authorized by Congress revealed for the financial markets a road forward. The study recommended greater automation of the markets, which became crucial for the continuing functioning of NYSE and The American Stock Exchange (AMEX) with the explosive growth of trading volumes driven by growing institutional trading. The NASD responded to the SEC's insistence on building a computer network for trading data first by hiring the management consulting firm Arthur D. Little to determine the feasibility. Chicago defense contractor Bunker Ramo ultimately got the contract to build what became the Nasdaq market. The centralization and computerization of the OTC market allowed the Nasdaq to grow into the major rival to the NYSE. Still not a fully developed exchange by modern standards in the 1980s, the Nasdaq struggled to gain the same respect from investors and regulators as the traditional exchanges chiefly the NYSE and AMEX. When Apple had its IPO on the Nasdaq, the state of Massachusetts would not even allow its residents to take part. Black Monday in 1987 revealed how the Nasdaq despite its seeming sophistication still depended on the market makers actually choosing to pick up their phones in order to allow trades to go through. High-flying tech and telecom companies like Microsoft, Intel, Apple, and MCI would lead the Nasdaq to become the hottest American stock market in the 1990s.

In the 1990s and the 2000s several Canadian firms also started to attract major investor interest in the United States. Imax offered a whole new cinema experience for audiences around the world. Nortel Networks, a firm that had evolved from the original equipment manufacturer for Canada Bell, grew to have one of the largest market valuations in the world. However, Nortel's efforts to aggressively compete against Lucent and Cisco led to it getting horribly overextended, and it blew up in what bordered on a massive accounting fraud. Blackberry revolutionized mobile email and for a time led the world in producing personal digital assistants (PDAs) for business but ultimately was crushed by the advent of Apple's iPhone. More recently, Lululemon and Shopify have been breakout Canadian stock stars on American markets. Lululemon beginning with yoga apparel practically launched the global trend of wearing athleisure. Shopify continues to be a leader in building e-commerce sites. The Toronto Stock Exchange's efforts to rival the NYSE and the Nasdaq in the past decade has fizzled as major Canadian firms like Lululemon and Imax, once cross listed, have delisted from the Toronto Stock Exchange. A proposed transatlantic merger between the Toronto Stock Exchange and the London Stock Exchange was foiled by Canada's all-powerful banks but had offered to potentially create a more global exchange. Canada remains the only major economy not to have a national securities regulator as a result of the Supreme Court striking down every effort to create one.

CHAPTER 2

Origins of the Modern Stock Market

The modern US financial system and stock markets emerged during the Gilded Age after the Civil War. Industrialization led to the rise of the steel, petroleum, and railroad industry. Many of the leading titans of industry later came to be known as robber barons as a result of a book written by Matthew Josephson in 1934 with that title.[1] Andrew Carnegie became the leading steel producer, while John Rockefeller ultimately dominated the US oil industry, and Cornelius Vanderbilt became the leading railroad tycoon. By the turn of the twentieth century, Wall Street increasingly overshadowed Philadelphia in finance, and the New York Stock Exchange (NYSE) had completely overtaken the Philadelphia Stock Exchange. The two leading investment banks were JP Morgan led by Pierpont Morgan and Kuhn, Loeb, and Company led by Jacob Schiff.[2]

The New York Stock Exchange

The New York Stock Exchange traces its existence back to the 1792 Buttonwood Agreement signed by 24 founding stockbrokers. The origins of the Philadelphia Stock Exchange are even older. Philadelphia's early status as the financial capital of the United States was demonstrated by the fact that both early central banks chartered by Congress were based in Philadelphia. However, after President Andrew Jackson torpedoed efforts to renew the bank's charter in 1836, the United States would not again

M. J. Szanto, *A Century of North American Stock Markets*,
https://doi.org/10.1007/978-3-032-22419-4_2

have a central bank until the Federal Reserve Bank of 1913 nearly a century later. The development of the financial markets in Philadelphia took off with George Washington's fundraising for the American Revolution. One of the first public works raising funds in Philadelphia was the historic Philadelphia and Lancaster Turnpike.[3] In 1765 the exchange began its life as the London Coffee House, created by local printing magnate William Bradford. Unlike Bradford's archrival in the printing business, Benjamin Franklin, Bradford was always hostile to the British.[4] It should be no surprise then that the London Coffee House would play a pivotal role in the American Revolution. In the late part of the nineteenth century, the Philadelphia Exchange operated in the Merchants' Exchange Building. Leading American financier Stephen Girard had actually organized the building to house another exchange that ultimately went defunct.[5] In 1952 the National Park Service took over the building and continues to maintain the iconic building as a historic landmark. Around the time of the Civil War, Jay Cooke, often considered America's first investment banker, established his bank in Philadelphia. The unraveling due to overextended bets of Jay Cooke & Company greatly contributed to the Panic of 1873. Another important Philadelphia firm was Drexel & Company founded by an Austrian immigrant artist named Francis Martin Drexel. His son Anthony Drexel, the founder of Drexel University, took over the firm. At the urging of American banker Junius Morgan, Anthony Drexel took in Junius's son, Pierpont, founding Drexel, Morgan, & Company in New York City in 1871. This firm would come to be eventually named JP Morgan and take on an astounding level of dominance not just on Wall Street but throughout America's rapidly expanding industrial economy. The move of Drexel from Philadelphia to NYC reflected the Big Apple's ascendancy over Philadelphia.

The New York Stock Exchange moved to its current location in 1865, but the current southern part of its headquarters was built in 1903. The stock ticker, a specialized form of telegraph, was deployed in 1867 allowing information from the exchange to be shared throughout the country.[6] The original firm that produced the stock ticker was the Gold and Stock Telegraph Co. founded by inventor Edward Callahan. Callahan's firm would quickly merge with one of Thomas Edison's firms. Telephones were brought to the exchange in 1878. In the nineteenth century canal and railroad companies led but would then be joined by steel, mining, and commodity companies. Union Pacific, for example, was first listed on the NYSE in 1870. Another significant company traded on the exchange by the turn of the twentieth century was Chicago Gas, Light, & Coke Co. which started by selling gas for lighting but then expanding into gas for heating and stoves as well. Chicago Gas evolved into today's People's Gas. By the turn of the twentieth century, the New York Stock Exchange had firmly overtaken the Philadelphia Stock Exchange as the leading stock market in the nation. The ascendancy of the NYSE mirrored NYC's rise as the unrivaled financial center of the United States. An additional building addition was constructed in 1922 increasing both the trading floor and the offices.

Curb Market

The main rival to the Big Board was the Curb Market. Traders known as the curbstone brokers would assemble on Broad Street in Manhattan with initially no formal requirements or regulation for the traders. The Curb Market essentially operated what would today be called a junior market. Companies that were not yet ready or able to be listed on the NYSE could trade on the Curb and even hope to graduate to the NYSE on a future date. E.E. Mendels known as the "Father of the Curb" led the effort to somewhat formalize the arrangement into what came to be known as the Curb Market Association.[78] Operating outside in all weather became a powerful tradition, and traders came to recognize that maintaining its ostensibly informal nature helped them elude moves by the state of New York to begin to regulate them. Ultimately recognizing the need to formalize the organization and activities as well as grow respectability, it moved into a newly constructed building in 1921. The Curb Market (later renamed the American Stock Exchange) would stay there for the rest of the twentieth century.

John Pierpont Morgan

John Pierpont Morgan (Pierpont) grew up in an illustrious family. His uncle, James Pierpont, was even the composer of the song Jingle Bells.[9] Pierpont's uncle had probably only intended the song to be about sleighing and paying his own bills, but the song's history has attracted some controversy in recent years because of its early adoption by racist minstrel shows. Pierpont had been nurtured by his banker father, Junius, to know and thrive in the banking industry. His father, Junius, had been a partner in a British merchant banking firm, George Peabody and Company, and gave him his start working in New York as the representative of Junius. He ultimately went on to establish his own firm that came to be known as JP Morgan. Morgan's takeovers and restructuring of companies and even entire industries became such a pervasive force in the US economy in the late nineteenth century the term morganization was coined to describe it. Pierpont's success at consolidating control over the New York Central Railroad by gaining the right to act as the agent of the British investors became the model for morganization throughout his later career. Often, they basically amounted to outright monopolies or at least overwhelmingly dominant firms which challenged the intent of the Sherman Anti-Trust Law. Examples of these consolidated firms organized by Pierpont are General Electric, Western Union, and US Steel. This would ultimately make him run afoul of Teddy Roosevelt's trust-busting efforts.

Kuhn, Loeb, and Company

Kuhn, Loeb, and Company was founded by Abraham Kuhn and Solomon Loeb in 1867. They were German Jews that were a part of an immigrant community that called itself "Our Crowd."[10] On the one hand this generation of German Jews faced the discrimination of the dominant Anglo-Saxon bankers in major US financial centers like Wall Street. On the other hand, many of them had actually come to America already experienced with what in many ways was Europe's more advanced banking sector. Another major nineteenth-century Jewish German investment bank had been J. & W. Seligman and Company, which was a major financier of the railroads. Perhaps a reflection of the anti-Semitism of the time, a national scandal occurred when Florida hotel owner, Henry Hilton, did not allow Seligman founder Joseph Seligman to stay at his hotel in 1877.

At Kuhn, Loeb, no other partner would ever match the towering figure of Jacob Schiff. Jacob Schiff had effectively married into the firm through his wife Therese Loeb. Under Schiff, Kuhn, Loeb, and Company was only rivaled by JP Morgan. In fact, the rivalry between JP Morgan and Schiff got so intense between Schiff and Pierpont that in 1901 their fight over the control over Northern Pacific Railroad almost crashed the American stock markets. Morgan's massive purchases of Northern Pacific Stock led to a catastrophic short squeeze, leading to traders on the wrong side of the market for Northern Pacific to start liquidating positions in other companies. However, Schiff and Pierpont Morgan often could and often did cooperate. In fact, in the end only close cooperation between Morgan and

Schiff could end the market crisis of 1901. In order to save the market, Schiff and Morgan had to coordinate a way to bail out those with badly losing short positions. Amazingly, Jacob Schiff and Kuhn, Loeb, and Company are names largely forgotten by the public despite Schiff's enormous contributions to charities from the American Red Cross, Boy Scouts of America, to the American Jewish Committee.[11]

Citibank

At the turn of the twentieth century, the largest commercial bank in the United States was what is now named Citibank. From 1891 to 1909, the president of Citibank was James Stillman. Stillman led an expansion of Citibank that resulted in it becoming the largest in the United States, and he led Citibank to be the first American bank with foreign branches.[12] Citibank had infamously bad timing opening a branch in Moscow in 1914 weeks before the Bolshevik takeover. Citibank's early twentieth-century branches in Cuba, Haiti, Argentina, and Brazil have received a lot of critical scrutiny in recent decades. For example, Citibank played a role during the Woodrow Wilson administration in inspiring a military occupation of Haiti by US Marines. Under Stillman, Citibank worked closely with the Rockefellers and Kuhn, Loeb, and Company. Stillman's ties to Rockefeller were further cemented by marrying two of his children to close relatives of the oil magnate. Stillman was also able to capture a large number of balances from the federal government. Citibank worked with Jacob Schiff to fund the restructuring of the Union Pacific railroad company.

Theodore Roosevelt's Trust Busting

Theodore Roosevelt becoming president was the result of an unlikely sequence of events. Roosevelt proved himself to be a progressive reformer with his service in the Civil Service Commission and then through his leadership as New York City Police Commissioner. Roosevelt played a key role in modernizing the Federal Civil Service into a professional apolitical work force. The modern-day New York City Police Force was highly shaped by his defining oversight. Like his cousin, Franklin Delano Roosevelt (FDR), Roosevelt's time as governor of New York gave him a chance to raise his national profile and learn the ropes on the key economic issues he would later need to deal with as president. His adversaries in the business community maneuvered to have him chosen as vice president only to marginalize him. Instead, the assassination of President McKinley led to him becoming president. Under Theodore Roosevelt the Bureau of Corporations, the predecessor of the Federal Trade Commission, was created to study American big business.[13] In 1906, Theodore Roosevelt's Justice Department sued Rockefeller's Standard Oil for violating the Sherman Trust Act eventually leading to the dismemberment of the monopoly.[14] The seminal legal case was built on the research conducted by the Bureau of Corporations. Today's ExxonMobil is a direct descendant of Standard Oil of New York and New Jersey, and Chevron is the continuation of Standard Oil of California. Agencies like the Bureau of Corporations and its successor the Federal Trade Commission would serve as early incubators for a system for administrative laws and processes that today characterize the modern Securities and Exchange Commission (SEC) on the federal level as well as state securities administrators.

Goldman Sachs

Goldman Sachs was founded by Marcus Goldman, the son of a poor Jewish Bavarian farmer.[15] Unlike many of the other leading nineteenth-century German Jewish investment bankers at firms like Selinger and Kuhn, Loeb, who were often born into successful banking families in Europe, Marcus Goldman's family were basically simple peasants. He started out as a street peddler in Philadelphia but then set up shop in Manhattan in 1869 as a seller of IOUs, the predecessor of today's commercial paper. He took in, as his partner, his son-in-law, Samuel Sachs. For decades all the key partners would come out of the two families. Marcus's son Henry would prove to be the most innovative and resourceful of the partners. As a relatively smaller Jewish firm, Goldman Sachs largely found itself locked out from major industrial clients, but Henry Goldman badly wanted to expand into the underwriting industry. The fact that some of the key players in retail were Jewish helped, but the challenge laid in proper valuation. Traditionally publicly traded stocks were largely valued based on capital assets, which were really light in the retail industry. Henry pioneered the use of price to earnings ratio in order to leverage the expectations of future earnings to sell stock offerings.

In 1906 Henry Goldman would pull off his first major initial public offering (IPO) for the United Cigar Manufacturers.[16] In order to raise additional capital, he partnered with his childhood friend, Philip Lehman, at Lehman Brothers. Lehman Brothers was a historically southern firm focused on financing cotton but also had a very rich source of financial capital. The Goldman Lehman partnership would last for nearly a decade. One of the biggest IPOs to result from this partnership was of the Sears Roebuck Company. The President of Sears, Julius Rosenwald, was a family friend of the Goldmans. The funding raised by the Goldman Lehman partnership allowed the Chicago-based Sears Corporation to grow into the Amazon of its day. The magnificent rise of Sears that would one day lead to the construction of the world's tallest building in Chicago would not have been possible without the work of Henry Goldman. Julius Rosenwald also was a stellar philanthropist singlehandedly funding the Chicago Museum of Science and Industry and greatly supporting the University of Chicago. Much of his great generosity today has been forgotten only due to Rosenwald's extraordinary level of humility. Rosenwald was very devoted to supporting organizations devoted to bringing equality and equity for African Americans.[17]

Studebaker

Another example of new clients cultivated and developed by Henry Goldman was Studebaker. Studebaker had originally been a German immigrant horse wagon and carriage business in what is now Maryland that dated all the way back to the 1740s. The family founder, Peter Studebaker, had learned his craft in his native Germany. Peter's son, John, would ultimately move to South Bend, Indiana, and it would be John's five sons who would formally found the company in 1852. The last of the five founding fathers, John M. Studebaker, would die in 1917. By the late 1890s, Studebaker was the largest manufacturer of horse-driven vehicles and soon after the turn of the twentieth century was rapidly transitioning to the production of automobiles.[18] In 1909 Studebaker purchased Michigan-based Everett-Metzger-Flanders company greatly expanding its automobile production. In 1911, the merged company was reorganized as the New Jersey-based Studebaker corporation, and it was listed on the NYSE as well as the Chicago and Detroit stock exchanges. The IPO was handled by both Lehman Brothers and Goldman Sachs and led by Henry Goldman. Henry Goldman would be added to Studebaker's Board of Directors. Studebaker's existing relationship with the British government allowed it to quickly gain a lot of war-related business after the outbreak of World War I.

Woolworth

Woolworth was a five-and-dime discount store publicly listed through Henry Goldman's underwriting in 1912. Frank Winfield Woolworth had been rejected by more traditional Wall Street underwriters who were turned off by his five-and-dime stores. Woolworth had pioneered and mastered the business model for discount stores that maintained low margins but also managed to sustain high volume.[19] He had opened his first store in 1879, and by 1909 Woolworth had expanded to the United Kingdom ultimately leading to a large subsidiary overseas.[20] In 1912 he was able to obtain agreement of all of the owners in his syndicate of stores to merge their firms into his creating a large discount chain for a historic NYSE listing. The IPO was underwritten by Goldman Sachs, Lehman Brothers, and British Kleinwort, Sons & Co but led by Henry Goldman. In 1913 partly using the proceeds from the Goldman-sponsored IPO, the discount store chain built the famous Woolworth building which for more than 15 years would be the world's tallest building. Today Foot Locker is the American successor organization to Woolworth, and technically its NYSE-listed issue is the same one initially underwritten by Goldman, Lehman, and Kleinwort back in 1912. Other retail firms brought public by Goldman were both Macy's and Federated Department Stores.

The Departure of Henry Goldman

The outbreak of World War I would create one of the first existential crises for Goldman Sachs. As a child, Henry Goldman had spent a lot of time in Germany and felt very close to his family's home. Very much unlike the Sachs family and even much of his family, he felt very compelled to side with Germany. Samuel Sachs had developed a very strong relationship with the British firm Kleinwort, Sons & Co, which had been able to provide a steady stream of funding for deals in the United States, which was increasingly threatened by Henry Goldman's troubling political views. Even worse, the feelings of the Sachs family grew stronger once the United States joined the war and their own children started to serve in the US military. Henry Goldman was forced out by the Sachs family, leading to a rift between the two families that has lasted to this day.[21] Henry Goldman is said to have died a broken man after the Nazis took over Germany.[22]

General Electric

One of the leading entrepreneurs in the early electrification of the United States was Thomas Edison. Thomas Edison is most famous for mastering the incandescent light bulb. In the 1880s Edison also would engage in a struggle against the alternating current transmission promoted by his rival inventor, George Westinghouse. George Westinghouse had gotten his start designing and manufacturing railway air brakes and then had gone on to become a leader in alternating current infrastructure. In order to design the key alternating currency infrastructure, Westinghouse had taken in Nikola Tesla, a former protégé of Edison. In 1889 Drexel, Morgan & Co. financed the creation of the Edison General Electric Company consisting of several of Edison's electric firms. A subsequent merger with Thomson-Houston Electric Company also underwritten by Drexel, Morgan & Co. led to the creation of today's General Electric in 1892.[23] This purchase solidified General Electric's manufacturing of the equipment for alternating current transmission, which had by then proven undeniably to be more robust than direct current. By 1896 General Electric was included by the Dow Jones company in its original Industrial Index of 12 companies.[24] The Westinghouse Air Brake Company continues to produce various components of trains to this day. After the turn of the twentieth century, the Westinghouse Electric Company increasingly focused on building the generators for large electric production plants. Today it is a leading builder of nuclear reactors and is owned by Canada's Cameco and Brookfield Corporation.

The Steel Age

One of the most important companies created by Pierpont Morgan's effort to consolidate firms was US Steel. The core of the firm was purchased from Andrew Carnegie for nearly a half a billion dollars in 1901 securing for Carnegie massive wealth. Pierpont combined Carnegie's Steel Empire with Federal Steel and National Steel to create a giant controlling 2/3 of American steel production at a time that that steel was critical for many of the innovations of the day from modern bridges to skyscrapers. Carnegie's Steel Empire came out of the Scottish immigrant having been the first entrepreneur to master the Bessemer process to mass produce steel. Carnegie, however, got his start working as a telegraph messenger boy in 1849. His first big steel project was providing the superstructure for the Eads Bridge that spanned the Mississippi River by St. Louis.[25] US Steel was the first firm to be valued at a billion dollars in the currency of the time. The headquarters of US Steel was placed in the Empire building in 1901 (not to be confused with the Empire State Building) and remained there till 1975. It was a fitting home for US Steel given the building represented a state-of-the-art steel-framed skyscraper.[26] The modern for the day elevators were built by Otis Worldwide. In the 1850s Elisha Graves Otis had transformed the dangerous unwieldy lifts used in factories and warehouses into a trendy ride up into the sky in both residences and retail establishments. His sons took over after his untimely death from diphtheria, but his sons would go on to make the firm a global leader in elevators. In 1870 Lord & Taylor installed an Otis elevator in their Broadway store.

Bankers Panic of 1907

A key turning point in the financial history of the United States was the Bankers Panic of 1907. The financial crisis was partly preceded by a costly earthquake in San Francisco in 1906 but was largely caused by a failed attempt led by F. Augustus Heinze to corner stock of United Copper through the Curb Market. Heinze had attempted to trigger what would be known today as a short squeeze, but he had overestimated the number of shares he could gain control of. This botched effort led to a run-on banks and trusts associated with Heinze particularly the Knickerbocker Trust. The resulting panic quickly started to spread to unaffiliated banks and financial institutions posing a systemic threat to the overall US economy. Banks in New York had formed the New York Clearing House, which had limited loaning services for banks but did not extend credit to trusts. Pierpont Morgan in conjunction with other leading financiers and bankers as well as the New York Clearing House was able to engineer a bailout that stopped the unraveling of New York-based banking and financial institutions. JP Morgan effectively had to step in and act like a central bank, since none existed in the United States. Morgan had also orchestrated funding from major institutions for credit for stock investors. The New York Clearing House also stepped in with 100 million dollars in loan certificates injecting critical liquidity into New York City's financial system. Lost among the public was the unprecedented concurrent intervention and action by the US Treasury Department, resulting in an exaggerated public perception that JP Morgan had singlehandedly acted to rescue the US economy. This exacerbated existing fears about JP Morgan's undeniably massive power over the US economy. The enormous levels of economic control exerted by JP Morgan and other titans of the day came to be known as the money trust. A great unsung hero of the crisis however was Theodore Roosevelt's Secretary of Treasury, George Cortelyou. Cortelyou had managed to come up with $25 million from what was rather limited federal coffers to deposit with NYC banks.[27] John D. Rockefeller deposited $10 million more into Citibank. All of these collective actions to inject liquidity in the system acted to curb the tide of panic. Had this model been better followed by President Hoover, President Franklin Roosevelt, and the later-created Federal Reserve System in the 1930s, the Great Depression probably would not have persisted throughout the decade. Amazingly there is near consensus today that had the Federal Reserve System acted as Pierpont Morgan and his contemporaries had back in 1907 shortly after the NYSE stock market crash in 1929, the spree of bank failures in 1931–1933 and the subsequent lost economic decade could have been averted.

The Pujo Committee

The main response by Congress to the perceived powerful and even dangerous money trust was the formation of the Pujo Committee, which was authorized by bill sponsored by Republican Congressman Charles Lindberg in 1912. The investigation initially overseen by Louisiana representative Arsène Paulin Pujo was led by counsel Samuel Untermyer. Untermyer most famously questioned Pierpont Morgan, but the Pujo Committee also investigated other key financial leaders including Jacob Schiff, Paul Warburg, James Stillman, and William Rockefeller. Friends and family of Pierpont Morgan blamed his death on the stress of the hearings and his feelings of anger of what he felt was a lack of gratitude for his orchestrating bailouts of the US economy. A series of articles in *Harper's Magazine* written about the money trust by leading social activist and Woodrow Wilson supporter, Louis Brandeis, later got compiled into the book *Other People's Money and How the Bankers Use It*. Calls by Brandeis in the book to impose greater transparency, oversight, and regulation over the financial sector would have a major influence over FDR's later New Deal legislation. In many ways, the Pujo Committee would function as a rehearsal for the even more famous Pecora Commission a couple decades later.

The Federal Reserve Act

Back in 1907 an emergency Republican bill Aldrich-Vreeland Act had included the commission of a National Monetary Commission in addition to all the efforts to stabilize the national currency and banking systems. The National Monetary Commission was led by Republican Senator Nelson Aldrich, who led a delegation to various European capitals, revealing how deficient America's banking and financial system was in comparison. It was clear that the United States needed a currency that was both stable but also elastic, while the banking system needed to be backed up by more robust reserves. Aldrich organized a secret meeting of leading figures in banking at Jekyll Island to devise the creation of a central bank for the United States. The vision that prevailed at Jekyll Island was largely that of Paul Warburg of Kuhn, Loeb.[28] In 1912 the Republicans lost the White House and both houses of Congress. Suspicions of the New York money trust and of European-styled central banks only grew, preventing Aldrich's bill from ever being passed in its original form. The ultimate Federal Reserve Act sponsored by Congressman Glass and supported by Democratic President Woodrow Wilson however largely mirrored the Aldrich Plan with a few minor modifications intending to ensure that bankers did not end up completely controlling the Federal Reserve System. Congressman Glass also altered the Aldrich Plan by making the Federal Reserve System decentralized hoping to bolster regional banks across the country.[29] Instead to Glass's consternation, banks across the country tended to invest their money in New York City banks and financial institutions which later helped to fuel the 1920s Stock Market bubble. By the 1920s local banks across the country would loan money to NYC money bank centers like Citibank and Chase, who would then loan the money to brokers to fund margin loans.

Federal Trade Commission

In 1914 Congress passed the Federal Trade Commission (FTC) Act. The FTC absorbed the previously created Bureau of Corporations and was intended to prevent unfair or deceptive trade practices. That same year Congress passed the Clayton Antitrust Act to expand and broaden the federal government to broaden the existing anti-trust powers under the 1890 Sherman Antitrust Act. The FTC would serve as a prototype for administrative governance which would shape the functioning of the future SEC. For the first year after the 1933 Securities Act was passed, the FTC oversaw and enforced the new federal securities regulations. However, the agency faced distrust from Wall Street, lacked the necessary industry expertise, and already had very broad responsibilities. John Landis, a key figure in drafting the 1930s securities legislation and an early administrator of the SEC, had spent a year as commissioner of the FTC.[30]

Blue Sky Laws

The first real effort at government regulation of the securities industry began at the state level, and Kansas led the way in 1911 with the first legislation to regulate the investment industry. This law and the numerous others passed by other states largely modeled on the Kansas statute have come to be known as the "Blue Sky Laws." There has been some debate about the exact original meaning behind the phrase Blue Sky, but it is generally understood to be a reference by the Kansas State Banking Commissioner Joseph Norman Dolley's view that some stock offerings in the state were built on nothing more than thin air. The Securities Act passed in Kansas was "merit based" giving the state banking commissioner broad-based discretion to approve or reject new securities offerings. It was part of the national progressive movement that was epitomized by the reforms of the Theodore Roosevelt administration. Within a couple years 21 other states had passed comparable legislation. The merit-based nature of most state securities acts would contrast later with the disclosure-based philosophy of later federal securities laws passed as part of FDR's New Deal legislation and reflects what is considered to be a more paternalistic approach. The North American Securities Administrators Association (NASAA) was launched in Kansas in 1919 offering a forum for state securities administrators and their respective Blue Sky Laws.[31]

The 1921 Martin Act in New York provides powerful authority to the attorney general to carry out civil and criminal prosecutions for fraud, but it was little used until the leadership of Elliot Spitzer in 2001. It was sponsored by assemblyman Louis Martin granting attorneys general broad investigatory and civil enforcement power but did not add criminal penalties for the Martin Act until 1955.[32] The most noteworthy early use of the Martin Act was by NY Attorney General Albert Ottinger against the Consolidated Exchange also known as the Little Board. The Consolidated Exchange had been formed in 1885 by the merger of two smaller exchanges. The exchange had a strong enough business that it was able to build a larger headquarters selling its original location to the Knickerbocker Trust.[33] The Little Board offered a potential competitor to the New York Stock Exchange, but failures of major affiliated brokerages coupled with the aggressive regulatory scrutiny by Ottinger led to the Exchange's shutdown. Ottinger's aggressive action against the Consolidated Exchange was part of a broader campaign against abuses that included his shutting down so-called bucket shops—dodgy establishments for speculating on stock price moves that amounted to no more than gambling halls if not outright frauds. Albert Ottinger would narrowly lose to FDR in the 1928 gubernatorial election dashing hopes of what would have been the first Jewish governor of New York.

Investment Bankers of America (IBA)

Between 1919 and 1921 a number of acts were drafted by Congress intending to create federal securities regulation largely based on the British Companies Act, but they were all defeated with the help of the IBA, except for a couple notable exceptions. The 1920 Transportation Act gave the Interstate Commerce Commission the right to regulate the issuance of railroad securities.[34] Bank stocks were also often overseen by bank regulators. Still even in the Roaring Twenties, bankers understood they would not be able to keep regulators away forever. If you cannot beat them, you might as well join them. At the annual 1923 Investment Bankers of America conference held in St. Petersburg in 1923, the organization called for the creation of a uniform securities law to be adopted by all the states of the Union. The IBA had been created in 1912 to establish and maintain standards in American investment banking and now exists as the Securities Industry and Financial Markets Association (SIFMA). The founders of the IBA had considered instead simply forming as a section of the much larger American Bankers Association but ultimately chose to set up their own independent organization.[35] The IBA also sought a centralized organization for evaluating securities and storing information. At this time the IBA firmly opposed a federal securities law. Finally, delegates at the 1923 conference expressed grave concern about the growing real estate bubble in Florida seemingly a problem in virtually every decade of the past century.[36] In the 1920s and 1930s, investment banks were often considered and referred to as private banks, because they had historically been formed as private partnerships and had not engaged in any advertising or marketing in order to obtain new clients.

Jack Morgan

Jack Morgan was Pierpont Morgan's son, but he was never really able to fully fill his oversized shoes. Jack graduated from Harvard in 1889 and took over the family firm in 1913 when his father died while vacationing in Rome. He was able to preside over leading fundraising for loans to Russia, France, and the United Kingdom. Morgan Jr. benefitted in his leading role in wartime financing from the fact that Jacob Schiff was morally opposed to supporting the Russian government, which was directly responsible for the massacre of Jews in horrific pogroms. Schiff was long an advocate for stronger relations with Japan.[37] In fact, Schiff is famously known for almost singlehandedly financing Japan's upset military victory over Russia.[38] At the time, Schiff's actions were popular among Americans who disliked Russia's bullying of Japan and its murderous rampages against Jews. Similarly, Henry Goldman's sympathy for his family's native Germany undermined Samuel Sachs's efforts to get Goldman Sachs behind United Kingdom. This helped to open up a major opportunity for Jack Morgan. JP Morgan became the sole underwriter for both France and Great Britain during the war. JP Morgan gave massive loans to Russia, France, and Great Britain. The House of Morgan also earned huge commissions as the official purchasing agent of the British government.[39] JP Morgan's oversized role in financing World War I would help maintain the firm's dominant role in American finance all the way up to the 1929 stock market crash. Unfortunately, his activities supporting the allied war effort also caught the attention of German spy Erich Muenter, who was able to shoot Jack Morgan twice at this home in New York.[40] Fortunately, JP Morgan Jr. was able to quickly recover from his wounds. Over time much of the operational control of JP Morgan would be assumed by Thomas Lamont.

World War I would help drive the American industries that would lead to the Roaring Twenties. The United States became a major supplier and creditor to the Western Allies in World War I. War production helped America perfect aspects of mass production including assembly lines. The carefree nature of the 1920s was in part a reaction to the brutality Americans faced both from the trench warfare of World War I for those who served and the even more widely devastating Spanish flu pandemic. Cars, radio, airplanes, and even electrification were all boosted by war efforts. The United States emerged as the leading economic power also because of suffering less devastation than the European nations that were forced to fight the war on or at least near their home territory. The rapid decline of the British Empire and lack of American willingness to step up and later play a leading economic and political role globally would help pave the way for a global economic depression and World War II a mere decade later.

Notes

1. Josephson, Matthew. The Robber Barons : The Classic Account of the Influential Capitalists Who Transformed America's Future, HarperCollins Publishers, 1962. ProQuest Ebook Central,
2. Charles R. Geisst. (2001). The Last Partnerships: Inside the Great Wall Street Dynasties. McGraw Hill.
3. Landis, C. I. (1916). The First Long Turnpike in the United States (Vol. 20, No. 8-10).
4. Vitiello, D., & Thomas, G. E. (2010). The Philadelphia Stock Exchange and the city it made. University of Pennsylvania Press.
5. Barnes, A. W. (Ed.). (1911). History of the Philadelphia Stock Exchange, Banks and Banking Interests. Cornelius Baker.
6. Broad Expansion of Stock Ticker: Approximately 12,700 in Use in the Country, Compared with 7100 Five Years Ago. (1927). *Barron's (1921-1942), 7*(52), 8.
7. Centennial Journal: 100 Years in Business --- Curbs Come to an Outdoor Market, 1908. (1989, Feb 17). Wall Street Journal
8. FATHER OF THE CURB DEAD.: EMANUEL S. MENDELS, JR., ELEVATED TRADE AND ROUTED DISHONEST BROKERS. (1911, Oct 18). New York Times (1857-1922)
9. Payne, L. (2002, Dec 15). LOCAL SLEIGH RACES INSPIRED `JINGLE BELLS': [THIRD EDITION]. Boston Globe
10. Birmingham, S. (1967). "Our crowd"; the great Jewish families of New York. ([1st ed.]). Harper & Row.
11. Cohen, N. W. (1999). Jacob H. Schiff: A Study in American Jewish Leadership. UPNE.
12. Burr, A. R. B. (1927). The Portrait of a Banker: James Stillman, 1850-1918 (Vol. 25). Duffield.
13. Johnson, A. M. (1959). Theodore Roosevelt and the bureau of corporations. The Mississippi Valley Historical Review, 45(4), 571-590.
14. Rostow, E. V. (1970). Monopoly Under the Sherman Act: Power or Purpose. J. Reprints Antitrust L. & Econ., 2, 45.

15. Schulman, D. (2023). The Money Kings: The Epic Story of the Jewish Immigrants Who Transformed Wall Street and Shaped Modern America. Vintage.
16. Fisher, J. B. (2010). When money was in fashion: Henry Goldman, Goldman Sachs, and the founding of Wall Street. Macmillan.
17. Diner, H. R. (2017). Julius Rosenwald: Repairing the World. Yale University Press.
18. Erskine, A. R. (n.d.). History of the Studebaker corporation. Chicago, Poole Bros.
19. Pitrone, J. M. (2003). FW Woolworth and the American Five and Dime: A Social History. McFarland.
20. Hawkins, R. A. (2009, May). The Influence of American Retailing Innovation in Britain: A Case Study of FW Woolworth & Co., 1909-1982. In Proceedings of the Conference on Historical Analysis and Research in Marketing (Vol. 14, pp. 118-134).
21. Ellis, C. D. (2008). The partnership: the making of Goldman Sachs. Penguin.
22. McDonald, J. G. (2007). Advocate for the Doomed: The diaries and papers of James G. McDonald, 1932-1935 (Vol. 1). Indiana University Press.
23. Israel, P. (2024). Thomas Edison: A Reference Guide to His Life and Works. United Kingdom: Rowman & Littlefield Publishers.
24. Sechel, I. C. (2014). FROM THE HISTORY OF STOCK MARKET INDEXES. Managerial Challenges of the Contemporary Society. Proceedings, 7(2), 113.
25. Brown, J. K. (2024). Spanning the Gilded Age: James Eads and the Great Steel Bridge. JHU Press.
26. Hugh McAtamney & Company, New York. (1913). The Master Builders: A Record of the Construction of the World's Highest Commercial Structure. The Company.
27. Bruner, R. F., & Carr, S. D. (2023). New Lessons from the Panic of 1907. Financial History, (146), 18-21
28. Lowenstein, R. (2016). America's Bank: The Epic Struggle to Create the Federal Reserve. Penguin.
29. Fink, M. P. (2019). The Unlikely Reformer: Carter Glass and Financial Regulation. University of Virginia Press.
30. Landis, J. M. (1966). The administrative process. Yale University Press.
31. Goodkind, C. G. (1976). Blue Sky Law: Is There Merit in the Merit Requirements. Wis. L. Rev., 79.
32. Poon, A. (2017). AN EXAMINATION OF NEW YORK'S MARTIN ACT AS A TOOL TO COMBAT CLIMATE CHANGE. Boston College Environmental Affairs Law Review, 44(1), 115–115.

33. NEW BROADWAY SKYSCRAPER.: PLANS FOR KNICKERBOCKER TRUST BUILDING AT EXCHANGE PLACE. (1907, Aug 18).
34. BAKKER, G. (2001). Edwin J. Perkins, Wall Street to Main Street. Charles Merrill and Middle Class Investors (Cambridge: Cambridge University Press, 1999
35. Parrish, M. E. (1970). Securities regulation and the New Deal. Yale University Press.
36. (1925, Dec 08). Bankers Preparing Strong Law to End 'Blue Sky' Issues. *New York Times*
37. Schiff, J. H. (1910). Peace and Friendship with Japan. The Advocate of Peace (1894-1920), 72(11), 268-268.
38. Best, G. D. (1972). Financing a foreign war: Jacob H. Schiff and Japan, 1904–05. American Jewish Historical Quarterly, 61(4), 313-324.
39. Burk, K. (1988). A Merchant Bank at War: The House of Morgan 1914–18. In Money and Power: Essays in Honour of LS Pressnell (pp. 155-172). London: Palgrave Macmillan UK.
40. Holt Is Muenter, Say Associates: Student Friend Tells Of Fugitive Harvard Professor's Return Under New Name. Others Recognize Picture New York Detectives Working On The Theory That The Two Men Are The Same. Holt Is Muenter, Say Associates. (1915, Jul 05). New York Times

CHAPTER 3

Stock Market Boom, Bust, and Federal Response

Roaring Twenties

The Roaring Twenties was generally characterized by rapid technological and economic growth in the United States. However, the decade had begun with a fairly short recession, then known as the Depression of 1920–1921. The economic contraction likely was caused by a combination of lingering effects from the 1918 Spanish flu pandemic, a wind down of military efforts after the conclusion of the Great War, and an overly tight monetary policy by the Federal Reserve Bank of New York. After the conclusion of this recession the economic downturn was replaced by strong steady economic growth leading to a very vibrant stock market. Economic growth was fueled by the explosion of new technologies from refrigerators to cars. The United States became a global industrial powerhouse that was unrivaled by any other world power. The rocket fuel that powered the meteoric rise of stock market prices was easy access to margin credit and the increasing participation of the wider population in various stock markets. One of the most outsized figures in the booming stock market of the 1920s was Joseph Kennedy. Rejected by the New York Protestant-dominated investment houses, he set off to make an enormous fortune though at times by means that may appear ethically questionable. The excitement for stock trading reached such a high level that E.F. Hutton & Co. set up a special radio room on the German SS Bremen for investors to trade while at sea.

M. J. Szanto, *A Century of North American Stock Markets*,
https://doi.org/10.1007/978-3-032-22419-4_3

The giant in the securities trade in the United States in the 1920s remained the New York Stock Exchange (NYSE). This was a position the exchange had fiercely fought to maintain over a century including through the devastating American Civil War. In order to attract the highest-quality most liquid issues, the NYSE maintained listing standards far beyond any state's Blue Sky Laws. At this time, some of the smaller riskier firms preferred the less stringent requirements found at exchanges like the Chicago Exchange.[1] However, regional exchanges could not really compete with the New York Curb Exchange, because of its proximity to the NYSE and to Wall Street firms.

Radio Corporation of America

One of the most iconic firms during the 1920s was Radio Corporation of America (RCA), which quickly became the glamour stock of the period. For the past hundred years in every bull market there always seemed to be a few stocks that only went up and attracted endless amounts of investor money. In the 1960s they were known first as glamour stocks then the Nifty Fifty. Then in the 1990s they were the Dot Coms. During the 2010s they were the FANG Stocks, and so far in the 2020s they have been the Marvelous Seven stocks. Like with most of these later glamour stocks, RCA was a combination of innovation, seeming endless potential mixed with speculative excess and a bit of a bubble. The infamous stock pools of the 1920s often acted to bid up RCA stock price.

RCA originated as the American subsidiary of the British Marconi Wireless Telegraph Company. Guglielmo Marconi was the Italian inventor of the wireless telegraph equipment famously used by the doomed Titanic to radio for help. The technology developed by Marconi was the foundation of modern-day radios and television and formed the basis for his Marconi Company in the United Kingdom. During World War I, the US Navy seized the American assets of the Marconi Company and after the war did not want to relinquish the assets back to the British. The US government forced the sale of the assets to General Electric, which would spin off the company into what would become one of the most traded and widely held stocks of the 1920s, Radio Corporation of America.[2] RCA became the dominant leader in radios and launched the country's first radio network, the National Broadcasting Company (NBC).[3] RCA developed the technology for black and white television in the 1920s and would go on to also create the American standard for color television in the

1940s.[4] Amazingly, the RCA Laboratory in New Jersey in the 1960s would also later invent liquid crystal display (LCD) screens but would fail to ever bring to market a commercially viable product. [5]

Charles E. Mitchell

No other figure epitomized the bubbly fervor surrounding the 1920s US stock market than Charles Mitchell of National City Bank of New York (often referred to and now known as Citibank). Mitchell known as Sunshine Charlie was probably the main pioneer of commercial banks creating security affiliates to skirt federal and state laws prohibiting banks from selling securities or even having branches across state lines. Mitchell started Citibank's investment affiliate, National City Company, in 1916 and went on to also become president of Citibank in 1921. Mitchell created an aggressive nationwide securities sales machine selling out of Citibank branches in New York as well as National City offices across the country.[6] Perhaps, more than any other figure in the United States, he promoted speculative investing in the stock market by the wider public. By feeding a mania that led to a bubble and ultimately a crash combined with his extraordinary level of income for the time, Mitchell ended up becoming the poster boy for Wall Street greed.[7] National City Company became a major inspiration for Congress later implementing a stronger division between commercial and investment banking. In 1933 Mitchell was arrested and tried for tax evasion but acquitted on all charges. He was forced to settle with the federal government for a million dollars on civil charges.

The Investment Trust

In the 1920s the predecessor to the mutual fund came into being tapping into the popular demand to buy stocks but offering the public the opportunity to have their investments professionally managed. Investment trusts were a financial intermediation vehicle originally developed in Great Britain in the nineteenth century. British investment trusts already had their own day of reckoning by the turn of the twentieth century in the form of the 1890 Barings Crisis that led to recessions in both Great Britain and in the United States. The fallout from the crisis exposed weaker less reputable investment trusts in England.[8] Most trusts in the 1920s were closed end, meaning that shares could only be bought and sold on the open market, resulting in less transparency and security. One variant, the unit investment trust, at least offered greater clarity by only investing in a fixed portfolio of securities. Open-ended trusts were pioneered by companies in Boston like State Street Investments, where investors could have their shares redeemed or issued on a daily basis at a clearly determined net asset value.[9] With virtually no regulation, there was little to enforce the moral obligations that ought to come with this fiduciary responsibility. Investment trusts could be highly leveraged, high fees charged, and not have proper diversification. The 1936 Revenue Act acted to preserve the investment company industry by granting conduit treatment for dividends and capital gains thereby preventing triple taxation but ended the exemption for regular corporate dividends.[10]

Goldman Sachs Trading Corporation

The departure of Henry Goldman created a terrible deal making vacuum for Goldman Sachs. In 1918 Sachs family member Arthur recruited Harvard classmate Waddill Catchings to Goldman. Catchings led the initial public offering (IPO) of what is today Kraft Foods. However, more significantly at the end of 1928, Catchings had launched the Goldman Sachs Trading Corporation (GSTC) which was listed on the New York Curb Exchange. It would turn out that Goldman Sachs had heaped not only layers of leverage on its funds but also multiple layers of profits for itself. Under Catchings, Goldman Sachs had really sunk to a real low forgetting its roots under founder Marcus Goldman to always dedicate the firm to the interests and well-being of the client.[11] The fact that GSTC had been separately incorporating from the partnership was the only thing that spared the partnership and the Sachs family from financial ruin. The losses by GSTC during and after the stock market crash represented most of the losses suffered by the entire investment trust industry. The failure of the GSTC not only nearly destroyed Goldman Sachs but left it dealing with costly lawsuits for years to come. Catchings was forced out with Walter Sachs overseeing the dissolution of the investment trust and Sid Weinberg taking over the firm for decades to come. Walter Sachs is also historically significant as one of the founders of the National Association for the Advancement of Colored People (NAACP). Walter's brother, Paul, worked with Julius Rosenwald to support the National Urban League, another organization that advocates for African Americans. At this trying time, the legendary Sidney Weinberg, who had started at the firm as an assistant janitor, took over as senior partner in 1930. Weinberg dropped out of junior high at the age of 13 to work. As an early supporter of Franklin Delano Roosevelt (FDR) and his New Deal, Weinberg was awarded a key position on the Business Advisory and Planning Council. This was followed by him serving in a key position on the War Production Board. It was Weinberg's service in these key government councils that established strong relationships with the leaders of America's largest corporations that would serve Goldman Sachs extremely well for the first two decades after World War II. Weinberg is singlehandedly credited with saving the firm culminating in Goldman's underwriting of the Ford IPO in 1956, then the largest one in history.[12]

Herbert Hoover

Herbert Hoover was elected president in 1928 by a very decisive vote. Today, Hoover is viewed in an overwhelmingly negative manner, but it can actually be argued that he was one of the most qualified people to ever run for president. In 1914, Hoover had organized the Commission for Relief in Belgium to get food to help those threatened with war-imposed starvation. Democratic President Woodrow Wilson had appointed Hoover as his director of Food Administration during World War I to ensure the reliable production and distribution of food during the war. After the war Hoover ran the American Relief Administration formed by an act of congress to provide food to struggling Europeans. In 1920 FDR approached Hoover about running as the Democratic candidate for president, but Hoover decided to join the Republican Party instead. In the lead up to the 1929 market crash, Hoover failed to heed numerous warnings of a growing stock market bubble or take adequate action to address the growing danger.

Once the stock market crash had occurred, Hoover never fully accepted the severity or the potential for enduring fallout. He excessively blamed short sellers and overseas investors, rather than recognizing fundamental problems with the stock market, banking system, and even the real economy. Even so he did take some significant steps intended to revive the economy. The Reconstruction Finance Corporation was formed by the Hoover administration to give out loans to help revive lending and investing. After FDR's 1932 election victory, President Hoover became increasingly bitter that President-elect Roosevelt would not work with him more to try to right the American economy. Nevertheless, the March 4, 1933, inauguration of FDR represented a major passing of the torch for American politics. Franklin Delano Roosevelt promised the Americans particularly the poor, disadvantaged, or recently laid off a fundamentally New Deal. His presidency would represent the birth of the American administrative state and herald in the enactment of the foundations of US securities regulation.

Samuel Insull

In 1932 one of the largest early corporate collapses during the Depression was of the Insull Empire. Samuel Insull was an English immigrant who had gotten his career start in America as a personal secretary for Thomas Edison. Insull took part in first the founding of the Edison General Electric and then ultimately today's General Electric, which was heavily financed by the Vanderbilts and J.P. Morgan. Insull moved to Chicago and started utility companies that were merged to become Commonwealth Edison. ComEd is still one of the largest utility companies in the United States. However, Insull had assembled a complex scheme of interwoven holding companies that would ultimately collapse. Insull remains a highly controversial figure to this day. On the one hand he appeared to have been an extraordinary magnanimous philanthropist of the day caring greatly for both his own employees and the community as a whole. Insull was singularly responsible for the creation of the Lyric Opera of Chicago, including the iconic Lyric Opera House that continues to be its home. On the other hand, when his financial empire collapsed leaving many average shareholders, many of whom were his own employees with enormous losses, many accused him of fraud and market manipulation.

Insull fled to Greece but was arrested overseas and brought back for trial in Chicago. A specific act of Congress was passed to legally allow his arrest overseas, bypassing the need for extradition. The case revolved around accusation of mail fraud, but he was acquitted by a Chicago jury of all charges. Today opinion remains divided about Insull. Some view him as the innocent victim of the 1929 Crash and the Great Depression. Others view him as the victim of his own overconfidence, hubris, and even naivete. Congress as well as federal and local prosecutors took the view that he was little more than a deliberate stock manipulator and fraudster. The views of Insull defenders that his downfall was the result of the manipulations of New York bankers may have actually been partly fueled by antisemitism. Sociologist Georg Rilinger notes that Arthur Anderson's contemporaneous audit of Insull's empire firmly establishes it really was a Ponzi scheme, which is ironic given Arthur Anderson's later role in covering up the massive fraud at Enron, which would result in the dismantling of the storied accounting firm at the turn of the twenty-first century.[13]

The Pecora Commission

In 1932 the United States Senate Committee on Banking and Currency launched what has become known as the Pecora Investigation or the Pecora Commission. It was spearheaded by Ferdinand Pecora, the New York County district attorney. Pecora was actually the fourth attorney hired as chief counsel by Republican committee chair Senator Peter Norbeck. A unique development was that the Senate Republican leadership also chose Democratic Senator Glass to lead the key subcommittee that oversaw the process. Pecora was an unlikely foil for powerful Wall Street originally being a poor Sicilian immigrant who had completed his law degree at night school. The 1932 election resulted in the Democrats winning both houses of Congress, but FDR encouraged Democratic Senator Fletcher to allow Pecora to continue his investigation. The whole process has come to be identified with Ferdinand Pecora and his charismatic interrogation of famous witnesses.[14] Pecora was greatly empowered by the fact that 1933 was the height of the banking crisis. The failure of the private Bank of the United States added fuel to the fire that threatened to burn down the entire American banking system. The hearings took on an absolutely theatrical quality which reached its peak with the subpoena issued to Jack Morgan and his partners.[15] In the course of the hearing Senator Glass tried to restrain Pecora's questioning of JP Morgan Jr., at which point Pecora melodramatically threatened to quit. Glass accused Pecora of creating a circus. Famously, the next day Ringling Circus snuck in a circus performer and had her sit on the shocked Jack Morgan's lap.[16] Pecora's aggressive questioning of Jack Morgan invoked images of the contentious testimony of his father at the Pujo Investigation over two decades before. The revelation that Jack Morgan and other Morgan partners had not paid income taxes in recent years did not sit well with the public. The private bankers like J.P. Morgan were a source of particular suspicion, though strangely the subsequent federal regulations would leave private banking largely exempt from government scrutiny. Undoubtedly, private banks like the House of Morgan continued to serve a useful role in the American economy. University of Virginia Law Professor and former dean Paul Mahoney has found a lot to criticize about the hearings.[17] Despite what Mahoney views effectively as grandstanding, he felt that much of the criticism aimed at the Wall Street establishment was exaggerated and the subsequent government response misguided and counterproductive. On the other hand, the opportunity to confront the power brokers of Wall Street made the Sicilian immigrant a role model and inspiration for Italian Americans.

The New Deal

The revolutionary federal securities legislation began with President Franklin Delano Roosevelt's New Deal agenda. The phrase originally came from the title of an article in the New Republic by FDR advisor, Stuart Chase. In Roosevelt's acceptance speech for the nomination for president at the Chicago Democratic Convention, he called for "a New Deal for the American people."[18] The very rapid set of actions by the Roosevelt Administration and the Congress after FDR was inaugurated the following March 4, 1933, came to be known as the First Hundred Days. Included in the rapid-fire first round legislation was the Emergency Banking Act and the Securities Act of 1933. The Emergency Banking Act offered struggling banks greater assistance from the Federal Reserve system. However, the legislation that would prove to have the most lasting impact was the Glass-Steagall Act of 1933. In addition to creating the Federal Deposit Insurance Company (FDIC), it forcibly separated commercial banking from investment banking as well as from the brokerage business. The largest flaw in the US banking system contributing to the prolonged economic downturn would never be addressed throughout the 1930s. The Federal Reserve followed the Real Bills Doctrine which was procyclical in nature, and rather than mitigate the effects of financial crises and economic downturns, it only served to exacerbate them.

In response to Glass-Steagall, JP Morgan chose to concentrate on commercial banking and end investment banking activities. The investment bank Morgan Stanley was newly formed in 1935 by Jack Morgan's son, Henry, and JP Morgan partner, Harold Stanley. Morgan Stanley would continue to be viewed as continuing the tradition of the House of Morgan along with the original JP Morgan. JP Morgan would incorporate in 1940 and then list publicly on the NYSE in the 1942 ending its days as a secretive friends and family firm. Notably NYSE member firms would not be allowed by the exchange to be public companies until the 1970s setting apart JP Morgan from the large Wall Street firms. By listing on the exchange, JP Morgan was forced to make quarterly reports giving maximal transparency. Its newly public stock would give the firm the capital it needed to thrive well into the second half of the twentieth century and beyond.

The experts that Roosevelt enlisted to develop and push through his New Deal program came to be known as the brain trust. The original brain trust was led by Columbia University professors: Raymond Moley, Rexford Tugwell, and Adolf Berle.[19] Moley was a law professor and an expert on criminal justice. Moley had been a supporter of FDR as governor of New York but later would go on to become a critic of FDR and a leading conservative Republican thinker. Adolf Berle was a pioneer in corporate law, and Tugwell was an economics professor and an advocate for industrial planning. Meanwhile, the National Conference of Commissioners on Uniform State Laws devised the Uniform Sales of Securities Act of 1930, which was the first serious attempt to harmonize state securities regulation, but it was never widely adopted. The later work on the new securities legislation and their implementation would be dominated by professors and former students from Harvard Law School largely selected by Harvard Law professor Felix Frankfurter who would later be appointed by FDR to be a supreme court justice. Frankfurter himself was a protégé of Supreme Court Justice Louis Brandeis, who heavily guided Frankfurter in his legal and political activism.[20] Louis Brandeis was a longtime critic of big American bankers and long advocated for far greater transparency. It was at the request of Louis Brandeis that Wall Street magnate Jacob Schiff had funded Frankfurter's position at Harvard. Felix Frankfurter's general liberal outlook led him to be one of the founders of the American Civil Liberties Union.

The Securities Act is also known as the Truth in Securities Act reflecting its focus on required disclosures and was inspired by the English Company Act. Roosevelt originally enlisted former FTC chairman Huston Thompson to draft the first federal securities regulation bill, but what he created was a bit of a mess and firmly rejected by the powerful Congressman Sam Rayburn. Most controversially it introduced a high level of merit regulation, which would have put the federal government in the position of deciding which stock issues would be good investments for the public. Thompson was an attorney that had begun his adult life as a college football coach before going on to be assistant attorney general under President Wilson. Sam Untermeyer had also taken an early stab at devising the legislation, but his ideas had evolved very little since he had served on the

Pujo Committee. Different visions of how federal securities regulation appeared. One side was led by the NYSE who feared a heavy-handed or even excessively socialist federal government would meddle to such an extent not only to badly harm profits on Wall Street but also to effectively ruin what was a critical national asset for capital formation. The efforts of the NYSE to stop or weaken federal securities regulation was led by the NYSE president, Richard Whitney.[21] On the other side were those who had a deep distrust of Wall Street and strongly sought strong federal controls reining in the excesses of greed and too often the double dealing and deceptive business practices exposed by the Pecora Investigation. What is clear in retrospect is that the NYSE would not have been able to once again flourish unless its opaque nature was ended and strong effective regulation and rules enacted that would regain the trust of the investing public.

The drafting of the version of the 1933 Securities Act that ultimately passed Congress was led by Felix Frankfurter. For the task of drafting the securities act, Frankfurter recruited James Landis, a colleague at Harvard Law, attorney Benjamin V. Cohen, and civil servant Thomas Corcoran who would all work out of the Carlton Hotel in DC. All three men had been former students of Felix Frankfurter at Harvard Law and were nicknamed Frankfurter's hot dogs.[22] Corcoran had gotten his start in DC clerking for Oliver Wendell Holmes and had been appointed by President Hoover to the Reconstruction Finance Corporation despite having been a lifelong Democrat. Cohen had made a lot of money with a fortuitous investment in Chrysler, which made accepting government work very easy. Their bill was formally sponsored by Representative Sam Rayburn, who was chairman of the key Committee on Interstate and Foreign Commerce. Rayburn would go on to be the longest-serving Speaker of the House. The bill's imposition of mandatory disclosure was fervently opposed by the Investment Banking Association of America which exists today in the form of the Securities Industry and Financial Markets Association (SIFMA). As significant drafters of the Securities Act, Benjamin Cohen would be the target of anti-Semitism and Thomas Corcoran the victim of anti-Catholicism.

Notably the NYSE had already begun to require listed firms to provide financial statements audited by independent public auditors back in 1932. The Senate had actually passed the very different version of the securities act written by Thompson. However, Rayburn was able to get the Conference Committee to largely adopt the House version that was drafted by Landis, Cohen, and Corcoran. In 1939, FDR would later appoint Felix Frankfurter to fill the seat for retiring Louis Brandeis.

1934 Securities and Exchange Act

The subsequent 1934 Securities and Exchange Act created the Securities and Exchange Commission. The drafting of the bill was overseen by Cohen, Corcoran, and Landis—the team behind the Securities Act of 1933. They were assisted by Telford Taylor, the attorney who would go on to be the lead prosecutor for the High Command Case against leading Nazi generals following the international Nuremberg Trials. The Exchange Act bill was brought before both houses by Representative Sam Rayburn and Senator Duncan Fletcher. While the 1933 Securities Act required disclosure at the time of registration, the 1934 Exchange Act required quarterly and annual disclosures. William Douglas, a law professor at Yale Law School previously at Columbia Law School, had been a key critic of the 1933 Securities Act, arguing that it had needed to go much further. The initial two pieces of legislation are known for their conservative nature in that it largely preserved the status quo in America's stock markets while at the same time bolstering transparency. The creation of the SEC was a concession to Wall Street, which deeply distrusted the progressive-minded staff of the FTC. Wall Street understood that a specialized securities regulator would have much closer ties and even sympathies with the brokerage and investment banking industry. The United States has gone on to gain enormously however from having an agency with staff with so much extensive expertise in the securities industry. Like many other specialized agencies, the SEC has had to balance being policeman and also being facilitator. The SEC would move into the old headquarters of the Interstate Commerce Commission on Pennsylvania Avenue down the street from the White House and across the street from the Federal Power Commission. Overall, the SEC has played a major role in establishing and maintaining the dominance of the American capital markets. Very significantly, Congress in the 1936 Amendments to the Securities Exchange Act gave the SEC the power to grant unlisted trading privileges (UTP) of NYSE-listed stocks to the regional exchanges. This is the real beginning of Congress and the SEC working to create a national competitive marketplace for equities in the United States.

Ferdinand Pecora and James Landis served as two of the SEC's first commissioners, and Joseph P. Kennedy presided as the agency's first chairman. When asked to explain his rather questionable choice of Kennedy as the country's first top securities regulator, he responded that "took a thief to catch a thief."[23] Wall Street's suspicions of the new regulatory regime was reflected in *Businessweek*'s choice to place James Landis on the cover of *Businessweek* rather than Joseph Kennedy, the new chairman. Landis was viewed as an antibusiness progressive New Dealer. However, Kennedy himself turned out to be a very aggressive and relentless regulator but only stayed at the helm for a year before being replaced by Landis as chairman.[24] Pecora only stayed on with the Commission for 6 months before joining the New York Supreme Court. During Kennedy's 1 year at the SEC, Landis and Kennedy had developed a close working relationship. The SEC under Kennedy quickly began to enforce the requirement for all exchanges and publicly traded securities to be registered with the Commission. Both the problematic Boston Curb Exchange and the disreputable New York Mining Exchange were closed down. William Douglas from Yale Law School was another major leader in the development of federal securities legislation and regulation. Douglas' interest in the interaction of law and business led him to the creation of a program at Yale Law School, where the law students would take classes at Harvard Business School.[25] Douglas was part of the Legal Realism movement at Yale Law School which sought to integrate law with the other social sciences and viewed law from a broader social context rather than as fairly abstract rules. In 1936 FDR appointed William Douglas to the Securities and Exchange Commission, and in 1937 Douglas became the third chairman of the SEC. The new disclosure requirements also exposed the embezzlement of the former president of the NYSE, Richard Whitney. Whitney would end up pleading guilty to embezzlement and sent to Sing Sing. While Whitney had already been replaced by Charles Gay as president when his malfeasance had been uncovered, Douglas and the SEC still pressured the NYSE to modernize its governance. William McChesney Martin was appointed as the first professional paid president of the Big Board.

Public Utility Holding Companies Act

The Public Utility Holding Companies Act (PUHCA) was passed in 1935 giving the federal government unprecedented authority to regulate an entire industry entirely overseen by the SEC. This act was prompted by the collapse of the Insull Empire that was based in Chicago and the fact that half of utilities were owned by just three holding companies. Insull was not the only bad apple among big utility players. Wilbur B. Foshay's firm had spectacularly gone bust in 1929, and Howard C. Hopson's massive utility would be forced into bankruptcy by the SEC under the powers of the PUHCA in 1940. Two FTC investigations of the electric industry, one begun in 1924 and another started in 1928, helped shaped the drafting of the act. The nature of the sweeping utility legislation granting the SEC absolutely extraordinary powers over the industry came in part from the experiences of FDR as governor of New York. The constitutional defense, and ultimately enforcement of the PUHCA, would heavily depend on the work of William Douglas as Yale law professor, SEC commissioner, and ultimately SEC chairman. Benjamin Cohen once again played a major role in devising and drafting the legislation.

The goal of the PUHCA was to limit the concentration and centralization of power in utilities in the country and in this sense was the continuation of trust busting begun by President Theodore Roosevelt. While the PUHCA bestowed upon the SEC greater powers with utilities than any other industry, it was part of a much broader program of federal intervention in utilities that also included creation of the Tennessee Valley Authority and the Federal Power Commission (FPC). While the Tennessee Valley Act was passed in 1933 by a Democratic Congress, the power of the Federal Power Commission to regulate interstate electricity transmission largely took shape in 1930 Hoover era legislation. Granting oversight and enforcement of PUHCA to the SEC rather than to the FPC was a surprising choice but reflected the stature that the SEC had quickly achieved in DC. Congress created what was described as a "death penalty," the power to dissolve utility holding companies that the SEC determined did not make economic sense but stopped short of outright banning them.

The Maloney Act

In 1938 the US Congress passed the Maloney Act which amended the Securities Exchange Act of 1934. Amazingly, few outside of the field of securities law have ever heard of this law making it appear seemingly obscure. However, the reality is in fact entirely different. The passage of the Maloney Act in retrospect was the day the American investing world had changed, except nobody actually realized it at the time. Ostensibly it was a very minor building block placed on top of the four securities laws already discussed in this chapter. As previously discussed the Exchange Act allowed bourses like the New York Stock Exchange to police themselves. Maloney allowed for that power to be extended to the over-the-counter market allowing for the creation of the National Association of Securities Dealers (NASD).[26] It would have been easy to have seen the creation of the NASD as a nonevent of interest only to very dedicated accountants and attorneys or perhaps just the brokers who would fall under its regulation. The reality could not be more different. The NASD became the primary regulator for brokers and would ultimately create the Nasdaq.

The National Industrial Recovery Act (NIRA) would have made the codes from the Investment Bankers Association of America for fair competition and trading practices legally binding, but in 1935 the Supreme Court struck down the NIRA as unconstitutional. The Investment Bankers Code Committee had been successfully organized and had devised a code for the industry. The 1938 Maloney Act was an amendment to the 1934 Exchange Act that would allow for the creation for the self-regulatory organization for the over-the-counter market similar to what was lost with the striking down of NIRA. The bill was named for the chairman of the Senate Banking Committee, Francis Maloney. The Investment Bankers Conference was formed in 1936 to salvage and retain the work done by the Code Committee but only gained the force of law with the passage of the Maloney Act in 1938 and was officially registered under it as the National Association of Securities Dealers (NASD) on August 7, 1939.

The Investment Advisers and Investment Company Acts of 1940

The PUHCA Act had required the SEC to conduct a 5-year study of investment trusts and companies led by SEC Commissioner Robert Healy. The Investment Company Act was drafted by David Schenker, Alfred Jaretzki, and Warren Motley. In 1940, the US Congress passed both the Investment Company Act and the Investment Advisers Act, largely placing investment firms and advisors marketing to retail investors under federal regulation. Exemptions from the Investment Company Act and the Investment Advisers Act have largely been for wealthy sophisticated investors and institutions. A firm or individual doing business in only one state may be exempt from federal regulation, but state officials and administrators increasingly had the wherewithal to regulate and monitor those intrastate activities. The Investment Advisers Act largely eliminates performance fees for advisors serving retail clients understanding they potentially incentivize overly aggressive and speculative conduct. The Investment Advisers Act established a fiduciary responsibility for the advisor that distinguishes them from brokers that is on par with doctors, lawyers, and accountants. The Advisers Act relied on the courts to develop and define the nature of the fiduciary responsibility of advisors. The Supreme Court even held in *SEC v. Capital Gains Research Bureau* that the mere failure to disclose a conflict of interest could constitute fraud under the statute.[27] The ambitions of the FDR administration were curbed in 1940 by what had become a Congress very skeptical of the New Deal reforms. Democratic losses in both the House and the Senate during the 1938 midterms allowed for a coalition of Southern Democrats and Republicans alarmed by what they perceived as FDR's federal power grab. The botched effort by FDR to try to stack the Supreme Court in 1937 certainly did not help matters. Congressional skepticism of the New Deal agenda at this time led to narrower regulation that relied more on principles rather than rules and enforcement by courts as opposed to administrative action. Yet in drafting the Investment Company and Investment Advisers Acts FDR's brain trust had once again succeeded in creating an additional robust securities regulatory framework even if somewhat limited that would survive the test of time. The 1940 Investment Company Act remains the governing legislation for the regulation of mutual funds and exchange traded funds to this day.

Philadelphia Headquarters

In 1942 the growing demands placed on the federal government by World War II led to many government agencies being moved out of DC with the SEC temporarily relocating to Philadelphia. However, the location of the headquarters did not affect much SEC operations given that the bulk of enforcement actions were conducted out of regional offices. The most important work that came out of headquarters during a time somewhat jokingly referred to as the Philadelphia Exodus is Rule 10b-5, the fundamental basis of today's restrictions against insider trading as well as many forms of stock manipulation. Rule 10b-5 represented a sea change in the nature of the SEC's role in that it was principles based, not ruled based. It extended the Commission's oversight role to transactions and not just registration. It became the fundamental basis for enforcements against insider trading and other pernicious forms of stock manipulation.[28] The SEC would not move back to DC until 1948. By spending its formative years in Philadelphia rather than NYC or DC, the agency was able to cultivate its rather independent and professional nature that would allow it to play a major role in the evolution of the securities markets in the United States. In a way it was fitting for the still young watchguard of our securities markets to spend many of its early years in Philadelphia, our country's first financial capital.

Notes

1. White, E. N. (2013). Competition Among The Exchanges before the SEC: Was the NYSE a Natural Hegemon?. *Financial History Review, 20*(1), 29-48.
2. Woolley, S. (2016). The Network : The Battle for the Airwaves and the Birth of the Communications Age (First edition.). Ecco.
3. Bilby, K. W. (1986). The general : David Sarnoff and the rise of the communications industry (1st ed.). Harper & Row.
4. Lyons, E. (1966). David Sarnoff, a biography. ([1st ed.]). Harper & Row.
5. Gross, B. (2018). The TVs of tomorrow : how RCA's flat-screen dreams led to the first LCDs (1st ed.). University of Chicago Press.
6. Mitchell, L. E. (2008). The speculation economy: how finance triumphed over industry. Berrett-Koehler Publishers
7. Morris, E. (2015). Wall Streeters: the creators and corruptors of American finance. Columbia Business School Publishing.
8. Hutson, E. (2005). The early managed fund industry: Investment trusts in 19th century Britain. *International Review of Financial Analysis, 14*(4), 439-454.
9. llen, D. G. (2015). Investment Management in Boston: A History (1st ed.). University of Massachusetts Press.
10. Jaretzki Jr, A. (1940). The Investment Company Act of 1940. Wash. ULQ, 26, 303.
11. Baldwin, A. (2015). WADDILL CATCHINGS. In A. Baldwin (Ed.), Heroes & Villains of Finance: The 50 Most Colourful Characters in the History of Finance (pp. 74–77). John Wiley & Sons, Incorporated.
12. Baldwin, A. (2015). SIDNEY WEINBERG. In A. Baldwin (Ed.), Heroes & Villains of Finance: The 50 Most Colourful Characters in the History of Finance (pp. 106–109). John Wiley & Sons, Incorporated.
13. Rilinger, G. (2019). Corporate Conspiracies and Complex Secrets: Structure and Perception of the Insull Scheme in 1930s Chicago. *American Journal of Sociology, 124*(4), 1043–1089.

14. Morris, E. L. (2015). Wall Streeters : the creators and corruptors of American finance (1st ed.). Columbia University Press.
15. The Man Who Will Question Morgan. (1933, May 21). *New York Times.*
16. Special to THE NEW YORK TIMES. (1933). Glass And Pecora Battle as to Goal Of Morgan Inquiry: Senator Hotly Demands Purpose As United Corporation Financing Is Revealed. Pecora Draws Applause Pay of $255 a Month No Incentive to Remain, He Says -- Fletcher Defends Him. HUGE UTILITY STOCK DEAL Purchase Price $12,000,000 Under Market -- G.H. Howard Tells of Morgan Warrants. Battle As To Goal Of Morgan Inquiry. The New York Times, 1.
17. Mahoney, P. G. (1999). The Stock Pools and the Securities Exchange Act. *Journal of Financial Economics*, 51(3), 343-369.
18. 1932 Democratic National Convention. (n.d.). Www.youtube.com. Retrieved March 23, 2022, from https://www.youtube.com/watch?v=-mqWhDwAFmk
19. Tugwell, R. G., & American Council of Learned Societies. (1968). The brains trust. Viking Press.
20. Dawson, N. L. (1980). Louis D. Brandeis, Felix Frankfurter, and the New Deal. Archon Books.
21. Mackay, M. (2014). Impeccable Connections: The Rise and Fall of Richard Whitney.
22. Mendelson, W., & Frankfurter, F. (1964). Felix Frankfurter. Reynal.
23. Kennedy, D. M. (2009). What the new deal did. *Pol. Sci. Q.*, *124*, 251.
24. chie, D. A. (2013). James M. Landis: Dean of the Regulators. Harvard University Press
25. Robert W. Gordon, "Professors and Policymakers," in Anthony T. Kronman, ed., History of the Yale Law School (2004).
26. ARW. (1960). The NASD. An Unique Experiment in Cooperative Regulation. Virginia Law Review, 1586-1600.
27. SEC v. Capital Gains Research Bureau. (1972). Northwestern University Law Review, 67, 574–575.
28. Bromberg, A. R., & Lowenfels, L. D. (1967). Bromberg and Lowenfels on securities fraud (2nd ed.). Shepard's/McGraw-Hill.

CHAPTER 4

Postwar Boom Market, Rise of Mutual Funds, and the Age of the Conglomerates

The postwar economy was characterized by rapid economic growth driven by technological advances, growing demand for cars and houses, and the rise of the suburbs. The stock market, which had long been relatively stagnant, finally took off before its excesses inevitably caught up with it. Mutual funds would rapidly expand offering everyday Americans an easy opportunity to affordably diversify their stock investments. Unsustainable investment fads and abusive fee practices would undermine the credibility of the mutual fund industry and force Washington to step in with additional protective regulation. During the 1950s and 1960s, trading markets gradually shifted from catering primarily to retail investors to being dominated by institutional players such as mutual funds, insurance companies, pension funds, and university endowments. Wall Street would become enamored with the idea of the conglomerate, companies built on seemingly unrelated divisions but offering high levels of diversification.

Mutual Fund Industry

As the American economy surged forward, stock investing expanded beyond traditional instruments. One of the most transformative innovations was the mutual fund, which provided everyday investors with more accessible and diversified tools for long-term investment. Early mutual funds emerged in the Boston area, rooted in a long-standing tradition of

M. J. Szanto, *A Century of North American Stock Markets*,
https://doi.org/10.1007/978-3-032-22419-4_4

trust companies shaped by the region's Puritan values—frugality, saving, and future-oriented investing. Many of these firms, such as Welch & Forbes, originally began as law practices. A critical legal foundation for mutual fund development came from the 1830 Harvard College v. Amory decision, in which Justice Samuel Putnam articulated what became known as the "Prudent Man Rule," allowing trustees to invest in common stocks—a practice restricted in many other states at the time.[1] In 1924, the Massachusetts Investors Trust (MIT) launched the first publicly traded open-end mutual fund, which continues to operate today. MIT functioned somewhat like a modern index fund, broadly investing in the market.[2] Open-end funds issue new shares in exchange for investor capital and redeem shares on demand, returning funds to investors who cash out. In 1969, MIT's management company was reorganized as Massachusetts Financial Services (MFS), which was acquired by Canada's Sun Life in 1983.

Boston remained a central hub for mutual funds into the 1950s. State Street Investment Trust, though not open to the public until 1927, quickly rose to prominence. Its original private investors retained significant ownership stakes for decades. By 1937, Harvard University had become its largest external investor. The relationship deepened when State Street founder Paul Cabot was appointed Harvard's treasurer in 1948. Cabot also benefited from his close friendship with Sidney Weinberg of Goldman Sachs. State Street managed the Harvard endowment until the creation of the Harvard Management Company. Much of Harvard's modern endowment success can be traced back to Cabot and State Street. The firm pioneered fundamental research for mutual funds, with analysts conducting on-site visits and rigorous financial investigations. State Street doubled the market's performance during the 1920s.[3] In 1958, George Bennett succeeded Cabot as CEO. It is worth noting that State Street Research, later acquired by MetLife, is distinct from State Street Bank, which would go on to become a major force in exchange-traded funds.

Incorporated Investors was the third major mutual fund to originate from Massachusetts. One of its founders, George Putnam, went on to found the George Putnam Fund in 1937.[4] A descendant of a storied New England lineage, Putnam was the great-grandson of Massachusetts Supreme Court Justice Samuel Putnam, who articulated the legal principle that became known as the "Prudent Man Rule." The Putnam family had long been among Boston's most prominent, producing leading lawyers, financiers, historians, and even figures involved in the Salem witch trials. Notable ancestors included Revolutionary War General Israel Putnam, a Massachusetts governor, and a president of Harvard University. In 1957, the firm launched the Putnam Growth Fund, and in 1963 it came full circle by acquiring Incorporated Investors. While most mutual funds at the time relied on stockbrokers to sell their shares, Putnam was an early adopter of in-house salesmen. In 1970, the company was acquired by Marsh & McLennan for $33 million.

The Wellington Fund

In 1928, the first balanced mutual fund, the Wellington Fund, was established in Philadelphia by Walter Morgan. Morgan's new fund mixed holdings in common stock with corporate and government bonds. John Bogle, who later would start the Vanguard Group, would later get his career start at Wellington beginning in 1951. Terrifyingly, Bogle had six severe heart attacks beginning in 1956, a few of which his heart appeared to stop until miraculously restarted with cardiopulmonary resuscitation (CPR). In 1958, John Bogle would launch for Wellington its first all stock fund originally named the Wellington Equity fund and then rebranded the Windsor Fund in 1963. In 1964 John B. Neff became the portfolio manager of the Windsor Fund. To catch up with the fad of go-go funds, Wellington acquired the hot Ivest Fund in 1966 through a merger agreement, which would prove to be Bogle's near downfall. The new Ivest "whiz kids" from Boston literally gained enough leverage over the Wellington board to fire Bogle.[5] In 1974 Wellington fired John Bogle as CEO, but he responded by persuading all of the mutual funds he managed to declare independence from Wellington, becoming the only mutual funds to be taken over by the investors leading to the creation of Vanguard, a mutual management firm.[6]

While the founder of Edward Jones was a deep skeptic of the value of mutual funds, American Funds was able to establish a formal relationship with the firm after his passing in 1968. Similarly, Merrill Lynch would go on to launch a major mutual fund business once Charles Merrill and Winthrop Smith had passed away. One unique mutual fund scenario was One William Street which was formed out of a private investment company for a number of Ford executives named Aurora Corporation. Early on many management firms for mutual funds were structured as trusts under Massachusetts law, but their importance has steadily declined as the firms have gotten large and increasingly based outside of Massachusetts.

Another unusual entrant into the mutual fund industry back in 1939 was Investors Syndicate, which had been formed back in 1894 as a very simple face amount certificate firm. By 1949 its Investors Mutual was the largest mutual fund in the United States. It renamed itself Investors Diversified Services and went on to sell itself to American Express in 1984. In 1958 Lehman Brothers joined the party by launching its own mutual fund. Another early mutual fund family was the Oppenheimer Funds. The brokerage firm was started by Max Oppenheimer, which Leon Levy took a job as chief research analyst. Leon Levy and Jack Nash then went on to found the Oppenheimer Funds. In 1982, the United Kingdom's Mercantile House acquired Oppenheimer along with its mutual fund division. In 1990, the insurance company Mass Mutual acquired Oppenheimer Funds for $150 million dollars reflecting the growing involvement of insurance firms in fund management and sales. In 2019, Invesco bought the mutual fund family.

Mutual Fund Regulation and Oversight

Critically the Revenue Act of 1936 had allowed dividends to flow through to shareholders of mutual funds without taxing the fund itself but rather the end investor. The argument that prevailed in the day was that whereas wealthy investors could afford to be directly invested in individual stock issues, it would be unfair to add on a third tax to middle class mutual fund shareholders. On the one hand, requirements to qualify for the exemption under the Revenue Act of 1936 imposed upon mutual funds safeguards that curbed speculative excesses from the 1920, and on the other the bill favored mutual funds by not including closed end funds with the exemption until the updated act passed in 1942. A Wharton study in 1962 commissioned by the Securities and Exchange Commission (SEC) challenged the early mutual fund industry with its conclusion that open-end funds had underperformed the market in the 1950s.[7] However, one could reasonably question how realistic it would have been for the average retail investor to assemble and maintain a "market portfolio" back then in an age when trade commissions were very expensive and there was no competitive alternative to mutual funds. In 1968, the SEC came out with Rule 22c-1 in which shares purchased would always be priced based on the subsequent closing preserving fairness to all mutual fund investors.

In 1952, the Teachers Insurance and Annuity Association (TIAA) started the first variable annuity fund, College Retirement Equities Fund

(CREF), beginning a whole new area of insurance.[8] As previously discussed, traditional life insurance is protection against dying too soon, and annuities are protection against dying too late or, in other words, running out of money. Fixed annuities guarantee a fixed income for however long the owner lives. Variable annuities simultaneously allow participants to also benefit from gains in underlying investments like stock. CREF nicely complemented TIAA traditional, which had been established in 1918. A decision by the SEC exempting qualified retirement plans from the 1933 Securities Act and the 1940 Investment Act initially allowed major insurance firms like Prudential Insurance into the field.[9] However, insurance companies expanding beyond this exemption led to insurance companies becoming one of the largest players in the funds industry. By the end of the 1960s insurance companies were registering with the NASD as well as their salesmen. Insurance companies launched their own mutual funds even while acquiring existing mutual funds. Insurance companies also continued to place much of their own investments into the stock market and in the 1970s would start purchasing seats on major stock exchanges.

Pension Funds

While mutual funds made investing more readily accessible to more Americans, the emergence and growth of pension funds was what really led to the institutionalization of the stock market. The consequence of this institutionalization will be explored in the next chapter. American industries took off in the 1950s fueled by ever-growing corporations, and pension funds had to evolve to provide for the future retirement needs of their growing middle-class ranks. Pension funds increasingly became one of the largest institutional investors in the stock market. The first pension fund was created by American Express in 1875, but pensions had come a long way by the 1950s. The American Telephone and Telegraph Company (AT&T's) pension fund was started in 1913 and long represented the country's largest pension fund.[10] Another one of the largest pension funds, the GM Pension Fund, was started in 1952 at the insistence of the United Auto Workers. The GM Pension Fund became the first one to invest in the stock market, a move most other pension funds would quickly follow. The president of General Motors (GM), Charles Wilson, recognized that to invest the retirement of employees in their own company would be grossly irresponsible given the consequences should the company fail.[11] Sears Roebuck's pension fund founded in 1916 had always relied on the company stock, but Wilson noted that most other retailers from that time had already gone out of business in 1950. Eventually, pension funds expanded beyond just stocks and bonds and moved into investing in more exotic investments starting with home mortgages.

The Keogh Act of 1962 opened the door for self-employed workers to set up their own individual plans.[12] While treated legally as individual accounts, the funds in them would also typically be managed by and large by institutions by one means or another. The large-scale investment of the retirement savings of American workers in the 1950s and 1960s into corporate stocks and bonds greatly boosted the amount of money flowing into American equities markets providing corporate America large amounts of financial capital and expand. American pension plans played a major part in making US public capital markets the largest and most dynamic in the world.[13] It is often forgotten by the everyday public to what extent retirement plans including old school pensions have funded private enterprise through stock exchanges, private equity funds, and venture capital funds.

Auto Stocks

Just as the rise of mutual funds and pension funds was expanding the players in the market, automobiles were driving economic growth, which would have a profound impact on stock market dynamics. The Eisenhower Interstate Highway Act of 1956 would fully enshrine the automobile as the primary means of transportation for Americans. This represented the largest government infrastructure project in American history to that point. The initial public offering (IPO) for Ford in 1956 conducted by Goldman Sachs also was the biggest ever in history. It was led by Sid Weinberg after many years cultivating Goldman Sachs's relationship with Ford. Ford paid Sid Weinberg a remarkably small sum for the whole affair, but Goldman Sachs got the prestige and recognition of being the lead underwriter even while strengthening the firm's existing relationship with Ford. Before the IPO the Ford Foundation and Ford family were the largest shareholders in the car manufacturer. Owners of Ford Dealerships were allowed greater allotments to buy newly issued shares. Sid Weinberg would assume the role of a director on Ford's Board of Directors.

General Motors emerged from World War II with a great deal of manufacturing capacity, but most of it had been regeared for the massive war effort. At the same time Americans had a strong demand for new features like automatic transmissions, power steering, and power brakes. General Motors at times was the largest company in the United States in terms of revenue during the 1950s. The subsequent equity raise by General Motors in 1955 brought in over 300 million dollars. The issuance was organized by Morgan Stanley and represented the largest follow-on public offering in history. GM needed the funds in order to help finance a major expansion of car factories. Raising money through issuing new common stock risks diluting existing shareholders, but that risk was mitigated by the buoyant GM share price combined with the issuance being done through a rights offering. A rights offering is where the issue offers existing shareholders the opportunity to buy new shares at a discount to the market. In this case, the GM shareholders had the option of also selling their rights to other interested buyers. Handling the large number of subscription rights offered was a massive nationwide endeavor at the time led by Morgan Stanley.

Tech Stocks

The gears of American industry were soon joined by the spark of new innovation. The 1950s and 1960s saw the birth of the modern tech sector represented by discoveries like the transistor. Some key electronics companies were already publicly traded like Radio Corporation of America (RCA) and Motorola, which had gone public in 1943. Texas Instruments (TI) went public on the New York Stock Exchange on October 1, 1953. TI had begun its corporate existence providing seismographs for the oil industry but later expanded into electronics resulting in the US War Department being its largest customer during World War II. With the advent of the transistor age, Texas Instruments quickly became a leader in digital circuitry, which it remains to some extent today with new products like DLP chips. Hewlett Packard (HP) had its IPO on November 6, 1957, a company famously started by Dave Packard and Bill Hewlett, two Stanford grads who famously started the firm in their garage in the late 1930s. HP's first big customer for their audio oscillator was Walt Disney for his classic animation Fantasia. Another new high-flying issue was Polaroid which also had its IPO in 1957 with its new instant photography cameras acting as rocket fuel for its stock.[14] Another extremely hot 1950s tech stock was Ampex, the main manufacturer of videotape recorders for television stations. The video recordings by Ampex were so good they earned an Emmy in 1957. The 1959 "Kitchen Debate" between Nixon and Khrushchev also got recorded by Ampex equipment.

In 1961, Sony would become the first Japanese company to be listed on the New York Stock Exchange in the form of an American Depositary Receipt (ADR). Tech IPOs continued throughout the 1960s with National Semiconductor getting listed on the New York Stock Exchange in 1969. That same year DARPA would launch ARPANET, the predecessor to the Internet. In 1969, Wang Laboratories founded by Chinese immigrant and Harvard grad An Wang started trading publicly on the AMEX. Most of the original funding for Wang Laboratories had come from selling Wang's core memory invention to IBM in 1955. By the time of Wang Laboratories IPO, the main product sold was the desktop calculator. Intel, the Silicon Valley pioneer of DRAM chips and microchips overall, would not go public until 1971.

Space Race

While the transistor revolution was changing the commercial world, a new frontier was capturing imaginations and investment dollars: outer space. In 1957 the surprise launch of Sputnik by the USSR and the subsequent missile race led to a frenzy in rocket and missile-related stocks. RCA was able to take part in this stock action as a result of the work being done by its RCA Laboratories in Princeton, NJ, and the creation of the Astro Electronic Products. On December 18, 1958, RCA's first satellite was launched becoming the world's first communications satellite. RCA also led the way in building weather satellites in the early 1960s. Rocketdyne provided the rocket engines for the Redstone missile, the first American ballistic missile to carry nuclear weapons. The far more versatile Jupiter intermediate nuclear missile also used Rocketdyne Rocket engines. Rocketdyne also was the main supplier of engines for Saturn engines. In 1945 General Tire & Rubber Corporation purchased Aerojet, which would power the colossal Titan ICBMS and a number of Apollo missions to the moon. General Tire & Rubber also remained a major supplier to General Motors. In the early 1960s, AT&T manufactured Telstar 1 and Telstar 2 satellites that served as experimental communications satellites. These were the first satellites to take part in transmitting television signals.

Conglomerates

While many investors were attracted by the promise of new technologies, others were driven to the rapid rise of conglomerates. These sprawling corporate empires, woven together through ambitious acquisitions, promised both growth and diversification—but not without risk. Aggressive takeovers powered with the currency of rocketing share prices led to the creation of goliath corporations. The architects of the conglomerates have come to be known as the conglomerators. Textron under Royal Little would get its start in acquisitions after the end of World War II partly in order to harvest tax losses. In some ways, by restricting himself to traditional industries rather than emerging new technologies, Little foreshadowed the rise of Warren Buffett and Berkshire Hathaway. While often viewed as the first modern conglomerate, Textron never reaped the rapid stock gains of the later more glamorous conglomerates. One of the first new style conglomerate emerged in 1954 when the Electro Dynamics Company using a loan from Lehman Brothers acquired a vacuum cleaner manufacturer named Litton Industries. Over the next 15 years Litton Industries led by Tex Thornton would take over a whole series of firms. By 1969 Litton was ranked the 40th largest American firm in terms of revenue by *Fortune Magazine*. Another major conglomerate founded in 1953 by brothers Jay and Robert Pritzker was the Marmon Group. The Marmon Group would be the largest holding of the Pritzker Family until they entered an agreement to sell it to Warren Buffet in 2008. Jay Pritzker is most famous for being one of the founders of Hyatt Hotel and the uncle of Illinois Governor J.B. Pritzker and former Secretary of Commerce Penny Pritzker. While the Marmon Group may have fit the mold of super aggressive 1950s and 1960s conglomerates, it was far better run and successful than the vast majority of the rest.

LTV

Another major 1960s-era conglomerate was Ling-Temco-Vought (LTV). LTV was started by James Ling, a master electrician who had failed out of high school. In 1955, Ling took public his electrical contracting firm, and in 1956 he expanded it by acquiring L.M. Electronics. In 1959, he took over Altec Lansing, an organization founded by former Western Electric engineers in 1927. Ling's merger in 1960 with Temco Aircraft entered the company into military manufacturing. In 1961, a hostile takeover led to absorbing Chance Vought aerospace into Ling's conglomerate. So important to Wall Street was business from LTV, Gus Levy himself served on its board. Another director on LTV's board, William H. Osbourn, was also a partner on the board of Lehman Brothers. At LTV's height it ranked 14th on the Fortune 500 ranking with a revenue of over a billion dollars. One of LTV's most famous divisions was Wilson Sporting Goods. As Ling's highly speculative big bets started to unravel as the economy turned against him, investor disillusionment with LTV helped to fuel the later overall market funk of the 1970s. One of the most long-lasting conglomerates, United Technologies, was formed under the leadership of Harry Gray, an alumnus of Litton Industries. Originally United Aircraft, under the leadership of Gray United Technologies, rapidly expanded with acquisitions like Otis Elevator and Carrier Refrigeration.

General Dynamics

One conglomerate that survives to this day is General Dynamics which originated as the Electric Boat Company. American subs were pioneered by inventor John Holland. In 1899 Isaac Rice merged the Holland Torpedo Boat Company with the Electric Launch Company to form Electric Boat Company. In 1900 the Electric Boat Company delivered the USS Holland, America's first operational sub, to the US Navy. In 1953 General Dynamics purchased Convair. A 1956 deal to supply Howard Hughes' TWA with new Convair jet airliners almost sunk the whole firm when Hughes failed to come up with the money leading to a record breaking over 400-million-dollar loss. In 1955, General Dynamics purchased telephone equipment manufacturer Stromberg-Carlson. In 1970 Stromberg-Carlson built Disney World's telephone system which would include Florida's first functioning 911 emergency service.[15] Conglomerates were often formed and grown by firms with high price-to-earnings (P/E) ratios purchasing targets with low P/E ratios, but this tactic sadly often amounted to little more than creative accounting. Investors would at times find that reported earnings growth in the conglomerates of the 1960s was little more than a mirage.

RCA

RCA, the pioneering company behind radio, the color television, telecommunications satellites, and the NBC television network devolved into an aimless conglomerate in the late 1960s. RCA was continuing its long list of inventions including the first LCD screens, but at the same time it was rapidly expanding into unrelated areas like its purchase of the Hertz Rental Car Company. A 1958 consent decree with the US Justice Department had a major effect on RCA by forcing it to share its key technologies with domestic competitors for free giving RCA an incentive to diversify through unrelated acquisitions and focus on royalties from overseas manufacturers like Sony and Phillips. At the same time RCA Victor was a leading record label competing with Columbia Records. Amazingly, RCA Laboratories under the leadership of David Sarnoff announced their development of (liquid crystal display) LCD screen technology, the dominant display technology in the early 2000s back in 1968. RCA's transition to becoming a conglomerate began with David Sarnoff's purchase of the book publisher Random House. As RCA's increasingly sprawling expansions after the son, Robert Sarnoff, took over completely diverted the company away from its attention to critical research and development in its core area of consumer electronics. RCA bought Hertz Rental Car, carpet manufacturer Coronet Industries, and golfing gear marketer Arnold Palmer Enterprises. RCA spent hundreds of millions of dollars in an effort to compete with IBM in computers, but this by and large proved to be a failed effort. In 1971 Robert Sarnoff sold RCA's computer division for $250 million to Sperry Rand.

International Telephone & Telegraph (ITT)

One of the most fascinating conglomerates to emerge in the 1950s and the 1960s was ITT. The origins of ITT began as Porto Rico Telephone, the major phone company for Puerto Rico, which had expanded into a major telecommunications service and equipment provider in both Europe and Latin America. ITT's expansion in telecom equipment manufacturing was exemplified in its 1952 acquisition of Chicago-based Kellogg Switchboard and Supply Company. It would be Harold Geneen who would transform this telecommunications-focused firm into a classic 1960s-styled conglomerate. Geneen had been a very highly regarded executive at Raytheon, but the CEO would not go along with his vision into a conglomerate somewhat inspired by Textron.[16] His 1965 attempted purchase of ABC Television failed, with the film company instead being purchased by Paramount Pictures. The Federal Communications Commission (FCC) had initially approved the deal, but it later got thwarted by the Justice Department. Divesting Cablevision after ITT's failure to acquire ABC proved to be a major blunder. Geneen had envisioned substantial synergies between Cablevision and ABC, but the cable company proved to be immensely valuable on its own under different management. Serious concerns had been raised about the potential meddling of ITT executives potentially meddling in news coverage, but the deal was scuttled by the Justice Department rather than the FCC in the midst of a public backlash against conglomerates.

ITT did successfully acquire a diverse range of businesses from Sheraton Hotels to Avis Car Rental to Wonder Bread. Buying Avis may have been Geneen's response to RCA's purchase of Hertz. ITT's purchased Educational Services would become ITT Technical Institute, a leading for-profit university largely disbanded for actions views as predatory by the Obama administration. ITT's takeover of Sheraton Hotels would end up becoming a major drain on ITT's overall finances, though by adding ITT to the name it became the highest profile subsidiary. At the time of the acquisition Sheraton was the world's largest hotel brand. ITT already operated 13 Holiday Inns at that point in time. Sheraton was historically significant for having the first automatic digital reservation system and for having created a chain of Motor Inns with free parking primarily near highways. Beginning with the hotel chain's location in Israel, Sheraton had expanded beyond North America. The 1968 purchase of Continental Baking gave ITT ownership of the company that made Wonder bread and Twinkies. ITT's purchase of Hartford Insurance in 1970 was then the largest corporate takeover in history. In response to an antitrust lawsuit by the federal government, ITT divested from assets including Avis.

Gulf & Western

Charles Bluhdorn started out running a car parts firm and would end up with one of the largest, most diversified companies in the United States. One of the most glamorous acquisitions by Bluhdorn was Paramount Pictures in 1966. This was followed with purchase of Desilu Studios, the television firm started by Lucille Ball and Desi Arnaz for *I Love Lucy*. Desilu would go on to produce *Star Trek*, *Mission Impossible*, and *The*

Untouchables. Under the ownership and leadership of Bluhdorn, Paramount came out with movies like *Love Story*, *The Godfather*, and *Chinatown*. The frenetic number of corporate acquisitions made by Gulf & Western in the 1960s was far too numerous to discuss here, but one other noteworthy and iconic acquisition worth mentioning is Sega Electronics. Bluhdorn was called by some the "Mad Austrian." Gulf & Western and Bluhdorn were major investors and supporters of development in the Dominican Republic, with his daughter going on to marry the former president of the Dominican Republic. The Gulf & Western business empire would not be able to survive long after Bluhdorn's unexpected death in 1983.[17]

Warren Buffett

Amid the corporate reshuffling of the era, a handful of individual investors quietly built legacies that would outlast even the largest conglomerates. Most notable among them was Warren Buffett, who saw opportunity not in size or hype but in value and discipline. In 1951 Buffett completed an MS in economics from Columbia giving him his opportunity to directly study under one of his key inspirations, Benjamin Graham. One of Buffett's first real jobs was working for one of Graham's partnerships back in 1954. However, by 1957 Buffett already ran three of his own partnerships. Charles Munger began his famous lifelong collaboration with Buffett in 1959. Warren Buffett's greatest returns of his career were probably back in the 1950s. His largest investment was in the insurance company Geico. Buffett merged all of his partnerships into a single Buffett Partnership and then took over the textile firm Berkshire Hathaway. Over time Berkshire was evolved into an insurance and reinsurance business at its core but also a type of conglomerate overall due to numerous acquisitions strapped on by Buffett in numerous industries over the years. Annual meetings for Berkshire Hathaway in Omaha, Nebraska, have become an annual pilgrimage for Berkshire shareholders, avid investors, and Buffett fans. In 1963, Warren Buffett began to invest in American Express during the fallout from the massive fraud perpetuated by Allied Crude Vegetable Oil Refining Company. In 1966 Warren Buffett purchased 5% of Disney after personally meeting Walt Disney but then made "the terrible mistake" of selling it the next year with only a 50% gain. Only 5 years later Disney would open the Magic Kingdom in Florida.

The Lion of Wall Street

Jack Dreyfus known as the Lion of Wall Street is also considered to have been one of the investment greats of the twentieth century. His eponymous fund had been originally started by John Nesbett in 1947. In 1951 Dreyfus purchased the Nesbett firm and renamed it the Dreyfus Fund. The Nesbett fund had been so incredibly tiny its founder had not even been able to support himself before he was bought out by Dreyfus. Under Jack Dreyfus, the fund expanded into one of Wall Street's leading mutual funds partly fueled by masterful marketing exemplified in its iconic use of a roaring lion running through Wall Street. The 1965 IPO of the Dreyfus Corporation made it one of the first publicly traded money management firms. Jack Dreyfus was a distant relative of Alfred Dreyfus, who was falsely accused of treason in France, in a case widely perceived as antisemitic in nature. His extended family in France remains prominent today and includes Seinfeld actor Julia Louis-Dreyfus. Jack Dreyfus somewhat controversially spent decades advocating for widespread use of antiepileptic drug phenytoin to curb depression and boost cognitive abilities. One of the biggest mutual fund scandals of the 1970s ended up revolving around Bernie Cornfeld, who had his start selling Dreyfus Funds shares to American expatriates overseas. In 1965, Howard Stern replaced Jack as the manager of the Dreyfus Fund though the firm would continue to use a lion as its trademark mascot well into the 2000s long after being purchased by Mellon Bank.

Alfred Winslow Jones

Another noteworthy investor of the time is Alfred Winslow Jones. Jones is considered by many to have been the first hedge fund manager. His life definitely differed from most financiers as he had worked as a journalist and served as a social activist nearly until his 50th birthday. It was perhaps his 1949 article for *Fortune Magazine* on technical analysis that stimulated his passion and interest in investing. Jones combined buying stocks on leverage with simultaneously shorting related shares. A fund that utilizes a strategy of offsetting long and short positions has come to be known as a long short fund. While Jones is not necessarily the first investment manager to utilize this type of strategy, he was definitely the first one to have coined the term "hedge fund." Jones also introduced the concept of a 20% performance fee, setting a precedent for extraordinarily lucrative compensation for hedge fund managers.[18] Brokerage houses lured by the tantalizing revenue for trade commissions were highly incentivized to give their best research and stock ideas to Jones, but concerns have been raised if some stock tips could have amounted to illegal front running.

Endowments

One of the earliest major not-for-profit foundations in the United States was the Ford Foundation, founded by Henry Ford's son, Edsel. Not-for-profit endowments really began to grow and expand upon their professionalization during the 1950s and 1960s. Key to their success however was their ability to continue to attract more private donations partly based on the exemptions granted under the Revenue Acts of 1913, 1917, and 1918.[19] Until 1974, Harvard's leading endowment was managed by State Street at which point it was turned over to the Harvard Management Company. The President of the Ford Foundation, McGeorge Bundy, began to encourage universities to more aggressively invest their endowment money. Yale responded by launching the Endowment Management and Research Corporation. Yale's investment fund also created a mutual fund, the Omega Fund, in order for the wider public to take part in its investments. The Omega Fund was heavily oversubscribed with the Yale investor managers limiting the total outside investment to $100 million.

Merrill Lynch

Just as institutional endowments began to adopt more sophisticated strategies, brokerage houses like Merrill Lynch were modernizing how everyday Americans accessed markets. Charles Merrill continued his vision of having an honest, scrupulous brokerage for the average American family. The firm continued to center around the values that Merrill firmly believed in. Due to Merrill's heart attack in the 1940s, Winthrop Smith handled many of the routine management tasks. Throughout the 1950s, Merrill Lynch grew itself as a leading brokerage on Wall Street while also expanding its "thundering herd" of financial advisors throughout the country. One of the major ways that Merrill Lynch prevented its brokers from unfairly exploiting their clients through churning was not to pay commissions for trades. In 1958, Merrill Lynch purchased the IBM 705 mainframe. Shortly afterwards, Merrill Lynch added the even more powerful IBM 7080. The New York Stock Exchange would not let members be incorporated until 1953. At the beginning of 1959, Merrill Lynch incorporated, transforming the 117 partners into major shareholders in the new corporation. During the same year Merrill Lynch sponsored an influential study at the University of Chicago that validated the potential of stock investing for the average American. This work evolved into the Center for Research in Security Prices, which still exists today. Merrill's unrivaled access to retail investors earned a major role in Goldman Sachs's underwriting of the Ford IPO in 1956.[20] Furthermore, Merrill Lynch's history of prudent management resulted in it being one of the few major Wall Street firms not to take part in the debt financing of Penn Central Railroad in 1969, sparing the firm from the pain of one of the worst financial collapses of the day. By 1961 Merrill Lynch could execute 7 million shares in a day and was the "largest single stockholder in nearly every publicly traded corporation in the United States." Not surprisingly, Merrill Lynch held onto $5 billion dollars' worth of stock certificates in its vaults.[21] Merrill Lynch's assumption of the US Treasury business of C.J. Devine and Company cemented the firm a major role in dealing in government securities.

Go-Go Investors

Yet not all investors were interested in steady, value-driven gains. By the 1960s, a new breed of "go-go" fund managers emerged, chasing rapid returns in high-flying growth stocks. It was an era of bold bets—and even bolder personalities. Fidelity's hiring of Gerald Tsai led to one of the first celebrity mutual fund managers. Tsai is credited with launching the "go-go" period by seemingly being able to jump on hot stocks for rapid gains. Tsai managed the Fidelity Capital Fund, which for a number of years very significantly outperformed the market. When Johnson passed up Tsai to lead Fidelity in favor of his son, Tsai left to form his own fund, the Manhattan Fund. While widely sought out by enthusiastic investors, the Manhattan Fund completely failed to replicate Tsai's previous success at Fidelity. In 1968, CNA Insurance purchased Tsai's management company that acted as the investment advisor for the Manhattan Fund and three other mutual funds.[22] The merger agreement also elevated Tsai to a high-ranking officer in the major insurance company for years to come. The overall nature of the aggressive momentum-focused style investing that took off in the 1960s would be detailed in the seminal work, *The Go-Go Years*, by John Brooks.[23]

Nifty Fifty Stocks

The Nifty Fifty were a group of glamour stocks that by the early 1970s consistently traded at a significant premium to the market. Some have argued that the plunge in the valuation of the Nifty Fifty stocks during the 1970s proved that they had been overvalued. Jeremy Siegel on the other hand argues instead their lows during the 1970s were simply the result of them being undervalued in the short term, but over the longer term they actually outperformed the market particularly value stocks.[24] They included tech stocks like IBM, Polaroid, and Texas Instruments and consumer products companies like Black & Decker, Kodak, and Gillette. One member of the Nifty Fifty, Walt Disney, ended up getting a major boost from the opening of Magic Kingdom in Florida on October 1, 1971. The most official listing of what was known as the Nifty Fifty was a group of top 50 stocks compiled by JP Morgan in 1972.[25]

Disney Corporation

Among the celebrated names of the Nifty Fifty, few captured the public imagination like Disney. From humble beginnings as a small animation studio, it became a cultural and business juggernaut—especially with the opening of its theme parks, which would redefine entertainment. The opening of the revolutionary new Disneyland in California in 1955 had expanded Disney beyond its roots as primarily a movie production house and animated studio. The cost of launching such a revolutionary new theme park forced Disney to take in partners to finance the construction of Disney Land. Future president Ronald Reagan was one of the anchors for the television broadcast of the opening day. Disney would eventually decades later acquire one of the key investors in Disneyland, ABC Television. The IPO for Walt Disney was led by Goldman Sachs in 1957.

By the mid 1960s, Disney was buying land in central Florida to build the world's largest theme park, which would first open in 1971. Disney World's proprietary phone company, the Vista-Florida Telephone System, would launch the first 911 service in the state of Florida. The system utilized advance touch tone dialing as a standard, when much of the country still had to rely on rotary dials. Vista would pioneer many innovations in telephony including being the first completely digital phone and company and the first one to use fiber optics. Vista soon became the phone servicer for other major campuses including Ohio University and the Mayo Clinic.

The opening of this new theme park would hint that a great deal of magic was still to come not only for Disney but for the United States as a whole over the next years. Disney may contribute to bringing people from all over the world together, but Disney World would be anything but small by theme park standards.

The bull run for the stock market that ran through the 1950s and 1950s was over. The 1970s would herald in both a very poor economy and a poor stock market. The heyday of conglomerates was over. Mutual funds would be nearly discredited for both questionable fee structures and mediocre results. Americans would feel defeated in Vietnam and in great social turmoil at home. Many were starting to wonder if the American Century had come to an end and if the US economy was no longer the leader of the world. Events in the 1980s and the 1990s would prove these concerns to have been greatly overblown. Still the 1970s were definitely far from a booming economic time. Yet as the next chapter will show, pivotal developments on Wall Street and throughout America's financial markets continued to advance at a breakneck pace during the 1970s. Even as disillusionment clouded the economic skies of the 1970s, Wall Street was laying the groundwork for a new financial age. The next chapter explores the revolutionary shifts that would soon redefine the stock market in America.

Notes

1. Higgins, M. (2024). The Unexpected Legacy of a Prudent Man. Financial History, (148), 16-19.
2. Allen, D. G. (2015). Investment Management in Boston: A History (1st ed.). University of Massachusetts Press.
3. Yogg, M. R. (2014). *Passion for Reality: The Extraordinary Life of the Investing Pioneer Paul Cabot* (1st ed.). Columbia University Press.
4. Martz, E. (2010). " Relationships, Relationships, Relationships": The Mutual Fund Industry's Mantra for Success from the 1940s Through the 1960s. essays in economic & Business history, 28, 57-72.
5. The Whiz Kids Take Over (Institutional Investor, January 1968). (2012). *Institutional Investor.*
6. Bogle, J. C. (2019). Stay the course : the story of Vanguard and the index revolution (1st ed.). Wiley.
7. Wharton School, United States. Securities and Exchange Commission, & Foreign Commerce. (1962). A Study of Mutual Funds (No. 2274). US Government Printing Office.

8. Fink, M. P. (2008). *The Rise of Mutual Funds: An Insider's View* (1st ed.). Oxford University Press.
9. Bartlett, J. W. (1966). Variable Annuities: Evolution and Analysis. *Stanford Law Review*, *19*(1), 150–166.
10. Chandar, N., & Miranti, P. J. (2007). The development of actuarial-based pension accounting at the Bell System, 1913—40. *Accounting History*, *12*(2), 205–234.
11. Drucker, P. F. (2013). *The Unseen Revolution: How Pension Fund Socialism Came to America*. Butterworth-Heinemann.
12. Campbell, T. C. (1963). Self-Employed Individuals Tax Retirement Act of 1962. *Fordham l. reV.*, *32*, 279.
13. Drucker, P. F. (2013). The Unseen Revolution: How Pension Fund Socialism Came to America. Butterworth-Heinemann.
14. Blout, E. (1996). Polaroid: dreams to reality. Daedalus, 125(2), 39-53.
15. Chapuis, R. J., & Joel, A. E. (1982). *100 years of telephone switching (1878-1978)*. Sole distributors for the U.S.A. and Canada, Elsevier Science Pub. Co.
16. Sobel, R. (1982). *I.T.T. : the management of opportunity*. Times Books.
17. Sobel, R. (1984). The rise and fall of the conglomerate kings. Stein and Day.
18. Morris, E. (2015). Alfred Winslow Jones: Financial Hippie. In Wall Streeters (pp. 201–222). Columbia University Press.
19. Reamer, Norton, and Jesse Downing. *Investment: a History*, Columbia University Press, 2016. *ProQuest Ebook Central*,
20. Smith, W. H. J. (2014). *Catching lightning in a bottle : How merrill lynch revolutionized the financial world*. John Wiley & Sons, Incorporated.
21. Smith, Winthrop H., Jr.. *Catching Lightning in a Bottle : How Merrill Lynch Revolutionized the Financial World*, John Wiley & Sons, Incorporated, 2014
22. Centennial Journal: 100 Years in Business --- Going to a 'Go-Go' With Gerald Tsai, 1965. (1989, Sep 15). Wall Street Journal
23. Brooks, J. (1973). The go-go years. Weybright and Talley.
24. Siegel, J. J. (1995). The nifty-fifty revisited: Do growth stocks ultimately justify their price? *Journal of Portfolio Management, 21*(4), 8.
25. By, R. M. (1974, Oct 03). Market Place: Are the Nifty Fifty Passe? New York Times

CHAPTER 5

Automation, Money Markets, Institutionalization, and the Creation of the Nasdaq

In many ways the 1970s might have seemed destined to be a total disaster for the US stock market. The decade began in the midst of a disabling paperwork crisis in which the major exchanges could not even keep themselves open throughout the week, the beginning of an economic recession, and a seemingly decade-long bear stock market. President Nixon resigned in scandal having committed crimes that appeared to threaten our very democratic system. The decade really seemed to only go from bad to worse. The American people bore the brunt of the Arab Oil Embargo, Saigon fell to the North Vietnamese Communists, and the US economy was increasingly gripped by a period of stagflation that started to seem like it would never end. In 1979, America's closest ally in the Persian Gulf, the Shah of Iran, was toppled, and the USSR launched a brutal invasion of Afghanistan.

Despite all of this, throughout the decade the US Congress, the Securities and Exchange Commission (SEC), and the exchanges were hard at work transforming and modernizing the markets into the structure that we have today. Pushed by the US Congress and the SEC, the exchanges introduced vital computerization and a centralized clearinghouse needed to handle the massive volume of stock trades. On May Day 1975, the New York Stock Exchange (NYSE) finally ended the anticompetitive system of fixed commissions, and a Consolidated Tape and a Consolidated Quotation System were created providing the whole

M. J. Szanto, *A Century of North American Stock Markets*,
https://doi.org/10.1007/978-3-032-22419-4_5

country with critical trading data. In 1971, the National Association of Securities Dealers Automated Quotations (Nasdaq) was launched bringing the most advanced computer technology of the day to the over-the-counter (OTC) market and linking all of the National Association of Securities Dealers (NASD) market makers throughout the country. Meanwhile, President Carter began a program of deregulation to revitalize the US economy and an arms buildup in response to Soviet aggression from the Horn of Africa to the Persian Gulf. Carter appointed Paul Volcker as chairman of the Fed, who is widely credited for later conquering the hyperinflation that plagued the United States. Carter was succeeded by President Reagan, who had an incredible ability to seemingly even inspire some of his worst critics with his infectious optimism that perhaps can only be explained by a bit of Hollywood magic. All of this would set the stage for both the great prosperity but also the excesses of the 1980s. This chapter will discuss the public and private efforts during the 1970s that led to the modernization of the US stock market backed by strong bipartisan support in Congress.

The 1938 Maloney Amendment

The Nasdaq is often viewed as the quintessential example of capitalism throughout the world. It is credited with financing some of the most epic, revolutionary firms from Apple to Microsoft to Google. Yet little known is the fact that from the very beginning much of the impetus for the creation of the Nasdaq came from the US federal government. The Nasdaq story begins with the relatively obscure legislation: the Maloney Amendment which was passed in 1938. To fully understand the context of the 1938 Maloney Amendment, one needs to quickly review a bit the securities laws passed by the Franklin D. Roosevelt (FDR) administration as part of his New Deal policies. These new federal laws introduced a role for the federal government for what had been left for the past couple decades to be the exclusive purview of the states. As discussed earlier in the book the groundbreaking 1933 Securities Act introduced the requirement of regular public disclosures for all federally registered publicly traded companies. This groundbreaking law set the standard for securities exchanges and regulators around the world. The 1933 Securities Act was followed by the 1934 Securities Exchange Act which most famously created the US Securities and Exchange Commission. However, equally important it codified the centuries-old tradition of the financial exchanges having their own self-regulatory organizations which henceforward would have the legal backing of the federal government granting them the status of quasi-governmental entities. This would even bestow upon them a certain measure of sovereign immunity that the federal government itself holds and would give their rulings the power of law. The trouble was back in 1934 most stocks were traded off exchange or "over the counter (OTC)." This rather haphazard system of stock trading depended on brokers calling each other by telephone and exchanging bids and offers while hopefully attempting to get a good price for their clients. While telephones first started to take off in some form in the 1890s, they were still considered state-of-the-art technology at that time. Telephones remained critical to stock trading well into the 1980s and even 1990s leading to the great hang-up during the 1987 stock market crash where Nasdaq market makers refused to even pick up the phone in order not to have to put through trades that would lose them money. Congress wisely passed the 1938 Maloney Amendment in an effort to bring a semblance of order to the over-the-counter stock market.

The Maloney Amendment allowed the broker dealers comprising the OTC market to form their own self-regulatory organization, the National Association of Securities Dealers (NASD), which was akin to those that oversaw traditional physical stock exchanges. The NASD would later be most widely known as the organization that also oversaw the licensing exams for stockbrokers until the 2000s. The emergence of this regulator of broker dealers as well as for off-exchange trading worked remarkably well. That was not entirely a surprise since it was in fact based on the self-regulatory mechanisms long used by exchanges for centuries. However, it still did little to address the chaotic nature of a completely decentralized market linked only by telephone. While trading in OTC stocks was known as the Second Market, the trading of NYSE-listed stocks by NASD-registered broker dealers came to be known as the Third Market.

The Push for Market Reform

The Special Study of the Securities Markets

In September 1961, Congress funded a project known as the Special Study of Securities Markets which would be headed by Milton Cohen and consist of a wide-ranging investigation of the securities markets. The Special Study was properly ordered in response to revelations of major corruption and double dealing on the American Stock Exchange. The Special Study would leave a roadmap for the creation of a national market system and the creation of national electronic networks for the transmission of pricing and trade data for stocks listed on exchanges as well as over-the-counter issues.[1] The SEC sought to severely curtail floor traders on the New York Stock Exchange, since they only traded for their own accounts. The Exchange members and particularly the floor traders themselves would always argue that floor traders added needed liquidity, but there was near consensus at the SEC that the floor traders did little more than exacerbate destabilizing rapid swings in stock prices. One of the major efforts emerging from this study was for the SEC to prompt the various major exchanges and markets to introduce greater automation and computerization of key market functions.

Early Automation Efforts

At every step, the SEC was constantly pushing the Big Board to expand automation and computerization. In response, the major exchanges led by the New York Stock Exchange and the American Stock Exchange would invest significant sums during both the 1960s and the 1970s implementing greater computerization and automation through the purchase of the most advanced computer technology of the time. The automation effort by the NYSE was led by John R. Bermingham, a veteran of ITT, while for the American Stock Exchange (AMEX) it was led by Donald R. Meng, a veteran of Radio Corporation of America (RCA).[2] In 1966 the Market Data System replaced the old convoluted human-driven system for entering NYSE trade data onto the tickertape.[3] The NYSE utilized IBM's new System 7010 which replaced the vacuum tubes with transistors. IBM worked with AT&T to create an information service accessible by telephone. The Market Data System also led to the automation of odd lot trading on the Big Board.[4] Virtually all of the automation of the exchanges was conducted by the Securities Industry Automation Corporation (SIAC), a company jointly owned by the NYSE and the AMEX. SIAC managed all of the computer systems of both exchanges. The automated data systems created by the NYSE and the AMEX facilitated the new Consolidated Tape, which was implemented by SIAC. In 1976, the designated order turnaround system (DOT) was created to automate routing of small orders for the NYSE. In 1970, the NYSE launched with great fanfare the Block Automation System to assist with block trades, but it was never widely adopted. Working with Bunker Ramo, the major stock options exchanges, the CBOE, and the AMEX created the Options Price Reporting Authority also built by SIAC.

Another outcome of the Special Study was a very firm recommendation that the NASD also automate its price data and create a mechanism for the electronic transmission of price data across the country. Stocks traded on the OTC market were tracked in reports compiled by the privately held firm the National Quotation Bureau, which were popularly referred to as the Pink Sheets. Pricing data was never recent enough to effectively trade on without calling around to many OTC brokers. Due to concern from Congress that the lack of transparency and clarity in price data can lead to confusion that can even be exploited by unscrupulous brokers, the 1964 Amendments to the Securities Acts required the NASD to develop a system for "fair and informative prices." The NASD hired a management consulting firm Arthur D. Little to determine the feasibility of creating a national electronic pricing network. Subsequently, Bunker Ramo, which produced trading screens for financial markets, was contracted to build the National Association of Securities Dealers Automated Quotations system (Nasdaq).

One area of trading that got completely streamlined during the 1970s was odd lot trading. Odd lots were stock orders involving less than 100 shares and were a key part to the involvement of small retail traders. Odd lot trading was dominated by a duopoly consisting of Carlisle & Jacquelin and De Coppet & Doremus leaving small-time investors with a fairly uncompetitive market. The odd lot markup was probably never itself great enough to significantly affect the returns of most small investors, but it was another reflection of how the NYSE tended to promote the interests of entrenched groups over the public at large. Carlisle & Jacquelin and De Coppet & Doremus had pioneered the business back in 1874, and little had changed in the dealing of odd lots since 1941.[5] The convoluted process for odd lot trades deprived many small retail investors of the ability to have their trades carried out on a timely basis. However, as the markets rapidly declined at the end of the 1960s, they were forced to combine. In 1975, Merrill Lynch effectively put this monopoly out of business by leading the way to handling on its own the odd lot transactions for its own clients without any additional markup. Merrill Lynch's takeover of odd lot trading for its own clients spelled the end of Carlisle De Coppet's century-old business as all the other major brokers followed suit.

Crisis and Innovation in the 1960s

Paperwork Crisis

By 1968 a growing paperwork crisis had gotten so bad that the New York Stock Exchange was forced to close every Wednesday to allow member firms the time for their back offices to catch up. The underlying problem was stock trading still depended on the physical shipment of paper stock certificates that were still typically required under state law. Organized crime was able to exploit the chaos to steal hundreds of millions of dollars of stock certificates. The forerunner of today's stock clearinghouses in the United States was the Stock Clearing Corporation established by the New York Stock Exchange in 1920 largely to streamline payments for stock transactions between members. The establishment of this clearing firm created a central counterparty for every transaction on the Big Board. The NASD hired Arthur D. Little to devise a plan to develop clearinghouses in Chicago and San Francisco in conjunction with the Chicago Stock Exchange and the Pacific Coast Exchange. The New York Stock Exchange created the Central Certificate Service (CCS) to handle the exchange of stock certificates and working with the AMEX jointly hired the Rand Corporation to further streamline the industry's back-office operations. The CCS was started working off three IBM 360 machines and loosely modeled after bank check clearinghouses.

One critique of a central depository for stock certificates was the fact that the Nazis had imposed it on the French stock exchange during their murderous occupation of France. The Nazis had mandated its use in order to better plunder Jewish assets as part of their genocidal campaign against European Jewry. However, developing a complete solution to the nation's paperwork crisis would ultimately require the coordination of the NYSE, AMEX, NASD, regional exchanges, and the New York Clearing House Association. The NYSE spun off the CCS, and it merged with the clearinghouses of the AMEX, the NASD, and the regional exchanges creating the National Securities Clearing Corporation in 1977.[6] The entire system would be managed by the Securities Industry Automation Corporation (SIAC) jointly owned by the AMEX and the NYSE despite the NASD originally having a deal with the Bradford Computer Company. Meanwhile broker dealers like Goodbody & Co. installed computer equipment from firms like Bunker Ramo to automate back-office tasks. Bunker Ramo was also the manufacturer of the widely used Telequote machine.

The paperwork crisis gave a strong advantage to Sandy Weill's CBWL, given its particularly strong back-office operations. Weill was able to parlay this advantage in order to build one of the largest brokerage houses on Wall Street. One particularly large acquisition by CBWL of Hayden, Stone & Company, was arranged by the New York Stock Exchange. Weill continued his pattern of opportunistic acquisitions throughout the 1970s until the firm later named Shearson Loeb Rhoades was only exceeded in number of brokers by Merrill Lynch.[7] Shearson Loeb Rhoades epitomized how the 1960s paperwork crisis followed by the 1970s bear market and the May Day ending of fixed commissions eventually led to a shakeout where the winners got bigger and sadly the losers faded into oblivion. In the end, the survivors came out that much stronger.

The Rise of Institutional Trading

Instinet

Rapid change was coming to the US equity market structure generally by the end of the 1960s. In 1969 the launch of Institutional Networks Corp. (Instinet) in Watertown Massachusetts by Jerome Pustilnik and Herbert Behrens to allow for institutions to trade large blocks of shares outside of exchanges with the use of market makers began the process of computerization in the Fourth Market. Autex and Institutional Networks Corporation (Instinet) created block automation systems on the eve of Nasdaq's launch, and the NYSE responded with its own Block Automation System. Block trades are typically defined as exchanges involving at least 10,000 shares at a time of any given issue. Instinet would eventually allow institutions to trade in large block trades of exchange-listed stocks off the Big Board even while protecting their anonymity. [8] The market was originally designed for institutional investors while excluding broker dealers and professional traders. The Sigma 5 computer powering this revolutionary trading network was built by world-leading Scientific Data Systems, a firm just purchased by Xerox. That same year Instinet was joined by another new firm, Autex, founded by Dr. Alan F. Kay. [9] Autex provided institutional users in 1969 a messaging service that was probably the world's first email system. Pustilnik had wanted Instinet to be a method for institutional investors to bypass brokers, but this concept proved to be flawed. As a result, despite Instinet's pioneering setup, it was little used until the 1980s. The big investor and institutional backer of Instinet was Weeden and Co.

Initially the SEC was concerned these new electronic networks could be vulnerable to market manipulation. [10] The SEC responded to the emergence of these alternative trading systems with a proposed Rule 15c2-10 that would effectively regulate them as exchanges but backed down, and then with a sleight of hand the issuance of no action letters allowed them to be regulated as broker dealers under the 1934 Act.[11] The SEC's leniency was intended to foster competition, though naturally the NYSE argued that these new trading venues posed a threat to the integrity of the markets.[12] The Chicago Board of Trade would test the SEC's refusal to compel these new networks to register as exchanges in the case of Delta Trading System, but the SEC's policy was upheld by the Seventh Circuit Appellate Court.[13] The competition for executing block trades for institutional clients between Instinet, Autex, and the NYSE Block Automation System (BAS) rapidly accelerated.[14] By eliminating the brokers in electronic transactions between institutions, Instinet and Autex had created what became known as the Fourth Market.[15] Soon even the "third market makers" who traded in listed stocks over the counter found these networks a useful adjunct to their existing tools.[16] The SEC's light hand on regulating alternative trading systems would persist into the early 2000s.

The Launch of the Nasdaq

On February 8, 1971, the NASD launched the National Association of Securities Dealers Automated Quotations (Nasdaq)—the world's first electronic quotation system. Very few likely realized the powerful capitalist forces that would be unleashed by this market or its revolutionary impact. Stock markets were no longer the sleepy esoteric private clubs once studied by Max Weber. Nasdaq absorbed most of the over-the-counter trading and brought down the spreads for the listed shares by improving transparency and liquidity. Initially only a system for recording and promulgating transactional and pricing information, it was not long before calls were made for it to be transformed into a full out exchange. The challenge in getting the NASD to take these groundbreaking steps is the majority of the seats on its board of governors had close ties to the New York Stock Exchange.[17] The NYSE initially strongly resisted the inclusion of exchange-listed stocks on the Nasdaq system. Despite the cross-linked membership and lack of total independence, the Nasdaq quickly encroached on the Big Board's turf by adding trading in listed securities in its very first year as a marketplace.[18] The SEC managed to sidestep whether this new marketplace should be regulated as an exchange by concluding that given that the NASD was already registered under section 15A of the 1934 Act, it was pretty much a moot point. By September trading on the Nasdaq had overtaken the half-century-old American Stock Exchange (AMEX) and had reached half the volume of the venerable New York Stock Exchange. There was no stopping the Nasdaq juggernaut. However, early challenges also appeared; numerous reports of fictitious quotations appeared where brokers did not honor their prices undermining the integrity of the market.[19] The early solution was to put in place a new NASD rule that forced market makers to honor those prices.[20]

The rapidly expanding communications and computer technology of the 1970s offered this newborn stock exchange the ability to rapidly reach new heights. The whole system had been built for the NASD by a Chicago-based military manufacturer named Bunker Ramo Corp. that had expanded into video display terminals for securities market players. Bunker Ramo was founded by George Bunker and Simon Ramo in 1964 through the acquisition of computer division of Thompson Ramo Wooldridge, Inc., by Martin-Marietta Corp.[21] Simon Ramo is known as the father of intercontinental ballistic missiles. After being absorbed by the Allied Corporation, Bunker's role in revolutionizing global markets has fallen into obscurity. However, Bunker Ramo was a major leader in trading technologies including terminals during the mid-1960s. Originally, its proposed Telequote IV service would have allowed for the transmission of actual orders, but AT&T and Western Union successfully fought it off by persuading the courts and the FCC that it would be an unlicensed communications service.

The genesis of the whole Nasdaq project came in 1964 when the SEC prompted the NASD to enlist management consulting firm Arthur D. Little for the role of overseeing the project to computerize the over-the-counter market (OTC). [22] This was part of SEC chairman Manuel Cohen's overall goal to computerize the securities markets as a whole. [23] Brokers were readily linked around the country to the Nasdaq allowing them access comparable to the specialists and brokers on the floor of the New York Stock Exchange. For some Nasdaq became the preferred platform to trade stocks in New York Stock Exchange-listed firms.[24] The New York Stock Exchange and its computing vendors and servicers would rapidly respond to this rapidly evolving threat. IBM was the lead supplier to the New York Stock Exchange and the member firms. With the establishment of the Nasdaq system, newspapers increasingly published the quotes for OTC stocks along with those listed on the NYSE and the AMEX.[25]

NYSE Members Going Public

Growing strains on the finances of many broker dealers at the end of the 1960s highlighted the weakness of partnerships and closely held corporations in raising capital. The first NYSE member firm to go public was Donaldson, Lufkin & Jenrette (DLJ). When DLJ first announced their intention to get listed, it went against the Big Board's standing rules and policies. The NYSE's prohibition against publicly traded members was partly intended to prevent institutions like insurance companies and pensions from gaining direct access to the market but also helped to maintain its clubby atmosphere. As the paperwork crisis was highlighted and the markets got increasingly computerized, relying on partners to come up with additional capital would prove to be woefully inadequate. Merrill Lynch, the country's largest broker dealer managed to be very well financed well even before going public. Unlike Merrill, many other NYSE firms had a lot of invested capital consisting of subordinate debt, which could be quickly withdrawn during difficult times.

The near instant success of the Nasdaq led to rapid growth. Far faster than expected the NASD started to move to take ownership of the computer network from Bunker Ramo who was still managing the system. The actual OTC trades were still executed on the telephone. Still, the Nasdaq quickly became a laboratory for the future world of electronic markets. The NASD grappled with how to best maintain an orderly stock market.[26] Changes needed to be implemented so that the market makers on the NASD could help ensure the liquidity and price stability for major listings provided by specialists on the New York Stock Exchange.[27] Bunker Ramo was not only a major computer manufacturer, but it had created in Trumbull, Connecticut, one of the country's first server farms.[28] The NASD had "seized upon the emerging technology of the telecommunications industry." In 1975 the NASD reached an agreement to purchase the computer system from Bunker Ramo for approximately \$10 million.[29] In 1976, the NASD took complete control over the computerized quotation system, and the Nasdaq was formally incorporated as a separate not-for-profit entity with a legal domicile in Delaware. This new corporation was devoted to creating and maintaining an orderly market in major over-the-counter stocks. Today Bunker Ramo is a completely forgotten firm, but its terminals and servers were part of a large national computer network that would define twenty-first-century stock exchanges and financial markets.

Registration of Brokers

In addition to the NASD's role in policing and regulating the over-the-counter market, it also served as the primary regulator for stockbrokers as a whole. As a result, the NASD took on the lead role for overseeing the examination and licensing for brokers and investment advisors. In 1974 the Series 7 General Securities Representative Exam for stock brokers was introduced through a collaboration between the NYSE and the NASD. The Series 63 Exam on the other hand was jointly developed by the North American Securities Administrators Association and the NASD for purposes of local state registration. The exam is used so that brokers can be registered in any US state they work in and largely tests knowledge on issues related to the Uniform Securities Act that today most states base their securities act on. The North American Securities Administrators Association (NASAA) and the NASD would later jointly develop the Series 65 Uniform Investment Adviser Law Exam in 1989 for investment advisor registration. Today stockbrokers wishing to also register as investment advisors can be credited with both the state registration exam and the investment advisor exam by taking the Series 66 which combines the two.

Martin Report

In 1971, the New York Stock Exchange commissioned William McChesney Martin to complete a report on the challenges facing the nation's securities markets and a vision for how the market structure should evolve over the coming decades. Martin had recently stepped down as the longest serving chairman of the Federal Reserve Board. His tenure as chairman had spanned nearly 20 years. The Martin Report portrayed the growing role of institutional investors and of technology as threats to an orderly and stable stock market. It advocated for a recentralization of trading on NYSE-listed firms and called for banning the trading of those firms off the exchange, which is known as the Third Market. The Martin Report would go on to be lambasted by Donald E. Farrar, the future director of the SEC Institutional Study, who effectively accused its recommendations of seeking to strengthen the NYSE's near monopoly on the trading of listed stocks.

SEC Institutional Study

In 1971, the SEC came out with its more extensive study focusing in on the role of institutional investors in the securities markets. The findings of the study starkly contrasted with the Martin Report noting the high fixed commissions faced by institutions and noting the challenges faced by institutions in placing large blocks with the current market structure. The institutional study called for greater competition and linkage between the markets. The institutional study took special note of the growth of hedge funds as well as offshore funds. It also investigated the growing integration of insurance, investment management, and brokerage services as well as studied an increasingly aggressive approach to enhancing performance on the part of institutions including mutual funds. An overzealous pursuit of performance was viewed to lead to unsustainable returns and sometimes excessive exposure to risk. One of the results of the study was to clearly identify the unfair burden placed on institutions by Wall Street's fixed commission system on very large block trades particularly those over $500,000.

Securities Acts Amendments of 1975

By 1971 the SEC started to look toward improving overall market structure and started to move in the direction of calling for the creation of a national market system.[30] In 1975 the US Congress passed the Securities Acts Amendments that intended to help pave the way for the creation of a national market system. As required by this act the SEC formed a committee with the goal of creating one centralized stock market for the United States.[31] The committee was tasked to issue a report on how to best create a national market.[32] The SEC had enlisted a former AT&T executive, John Scanlon, to head up the board. Scanlon's telecommunications background was critical to his new role.[33] Goldman Sachs's Gustave Levy would oversee the influential plan put forth by the Securities Industry Association.[34] Congress had also given the SEC new powers to curb anticompetitive rules on the traditional exchanges.[35] It had recognized that the securities markets were a vital institution for the American economy and sought to streamline

American equity markets. The vision of a truly national securities market may not have been achieved for decades to come, but significant advances were made. New equipment was deployed to consolidate price data from multiple markets and to display it in real time, while major clearinghouses were consolidated into the National Securities Clearing Corp.[36] This merger initially faced serious opposition from the antitrust division of justice arguing the creation of a monopoly was not necessary.[37] However, the strengthened linkage between the exchanges actually bolstered competition.[38] The traditional exchanges were beginning to build out the infrastructure of a national market as called for by the SEC mandate.[39]

Rule 390

In 1979, the SEC issued Proposed Rule 19c-3 that would allow exchange members to make markets over the counter for exchange-listed stocks. This was an effort by the SEC to push the NYSE to rescind its Exchange Rule 390, originally named Rule 394, that prevented members from trading NYSE-listed stock off exchange. However, by limiting its applicability to newly issued listings, this proposed rule had a more limited effect than the other proposed versions. However, over the next 20 years it gradually led to half of New York Stock Exchange listings to be traded by NYSE members on the Nasdaq. In response to this proposed rule, the NASD created a subsidiary NASD market services and invested 2 million dollars into it. In 1980 the rule was formally adopted by the SEC, allowing for trade in exchange-listed stocks on the Nasdaq. It was not until 2000 that the New York Stock Exchange completely rescinded Exchange Rule 390. The ability of NYSE members to trade newly listed stocks through Nasdaq and the Third Market overall further weakened the dominance of the New York Stock Exchange.

The Intermarket Trading System

The Intermarket Trading System (ITS) was launched in 1978 originally linking the New York Stock Exchange, the American Stock Exchange, the Nasdaq, the Boston Stock Exchange, the Cincinnati Stock Exchange, the Philadelphia Stock Exchange, and the Chicago Stock Exchange. Finally, at the end of 1999, the SEC rescinded a rule that disallowed the use of the Nasdaq to trade stocks floated before 1979 via the ITS. The ITS would continue to be used into the early 2000s. The main impetus for a national market system was the Securities Acts Amendments of 1975. Another key element in beginning to build a national market system was the implementation of the Consolidated Tape that combined stock trading data from the NYSE, regional exchanges, and the Nasdaq. In 1975 Congress passed the 1975 Amendments to the Securities Exchange Act of 1934 in part intending to create a "national market system." It empowered the SEC to take firm action to link the markets and encourage competition. At the prodding of the SEC the New York Stock Exchange created the Intermarket Trading System (ITS) to link to the American Stock Exchange as well as seven regional exchanges.[40] The ITS functioned as a radically different alternative to a composite limit order book (CLOB) system for creating a national market system that was tried first at the Cincinnati Stock Exchange. The system was built in 1978 by the Securities Industry Automation Corporation, which was jointly owned by the New York Stock Exchange and the American Stock Exchange.,[41][42] However, the NYSE managed to successfully keep the NASD and its recently created Nasdaq system off this new data link for the first few years. In 1978 the Consolidated Quotation System was also launched making available bid and ask data for the exchanges nationwide. The organization that runs both the Consolidated Tape and the Consolidated Quotation System today is known as the Consolidated Tape Association.

May Day

The Justice Department had begun pressuring the New York Stock Exchange to end its century-old practice of fixed commission rates back in 1967. The rapid rise in block trades for institutional buyers brought in rich commissions under the fixed commission system that were increasingly hard to justify. On November 17, 1970, at his speech to the Economic Club in NYC, the NYSE president, Robert Haack, blindsided the Board of Governors who had appointed him by publicly calling for an end to fixed commissions.[43] Big brokerage firms like Merrill Lynch and Salomon Brothers backed Haack, because they knew they needed lower commissions to be able to better compete against the Third Market and other rising players. Haack had become increasingly convinced that fixed commissions were part of obsolete traditions that maintained a private club atmosphere that coddled brokerage firms with inept management.[44] At first in 1971 the NYSE only allowed negotiated commissions for orders over $500,000. Ultimately, the SEC ordered the New York Stock

Exchange to end all fixed commissions on May 1, 1975, a day that came to be known as May Day. The result was the failure of weaker firms, a consolidation and strengthening of the stronger players, and the rise of discount brokers like Charles Schwab. May Day made the NYSE even more dominant by restoring its competitive position in stock trading while favoring the strongest NYSE member firms.

The Cincinnati Stock Exchange

The Third Market was the trading of exchange-listed stocks over the counter. However, the NYSE's Exchange Rule 394 prevented its members from taking part in such trades. The strongest player in the Third Market was Don Weeden and his firm Weeden & Co. In Cincinnati, a novel experiment was launched: the composite limit order book (CLOB). One of the strongest backers of this new system was Donald Weeden, a major investor in Instinet. His family firm, Weeden Holding Corporation, was responsible for handling about 40% of Third Market trades. The proposed system, if implemented nationwide, posed a threat to the income of traditional exchange specialists. Unsurprisingly, the established exchanges fiercely opposed such a move. Under the plan, the other regional exchanges would link to Cincinnati in what became known alternately as the Regional Market System or the Weeden Holding Automated Market.

Although Merrill Lynch conducted significant trading on the Cincinnati Exchange, Weeden was clearly the driving force behind the CLOB initiative. The electronic system may have been ahead of its time, but opposition from the NYSE and the overall securities industry helped keep its role marginal. The effort to fully automate the exchange was headed by Richard Niehoff.[45] Two distinctive features of the computerized system in Cincinnati were that remote access was available at the offices of broker dealers and execution of orders was automatic. No doubt the leadership of the Cincinnati Stock Exchange really was the one who had fulfilled the vision spelled out by Congress in the 1975 Securities Act Amendments, but sadly they were just too small to overcome the NYSE and the entrenched interests.[46] Merrill Lynch pulling out from its sponsorship of computerized trading on the Cincinnati Stock Exchange ended Cincinnati's bid to offer a serious alternative to the NYSE and the Nasdaq. The Cincinnati Stock Exchange moved to Chicago in 1991 and would change its name to the National Stock Exchange in 2003.

Bernie Madoff

The later disgraced Bernie Madoff also played a pivotal role in transforming the Cincinnati Stock Exchange into the first completely electronic exchange in the United States. At one point, Bernie Madoff even served as president of the Cincinnati Exchange. Bernard Madoff was one of the biggest traders on the Third Market.[47] Madoff utilized the market's connection to the New York Stock Exchange through ITS to help build his brokerage into one of the largest stock market makers in the United States. As a member of the NASD, he was originally cut off from the ITS but found a way around that limitation through his seat on the Cincinnati Stock Exchange. Paradoxically, Rule 394 that appears designed to stifle competition to NYSE members gave Madoff an edge by allowing him to trade over the counter NYSE listings, since he was not a member. Madoff was able to transform the Cincinnati Stock Exchange by personally funding its transformation into the first fully computerized exchange. He also applied the custom of paying for order flow utilized for over-the-counter stocks to exchange-listed stocks.[48] Madoff's role as a leader and an innovator for the Nasdaq, the Cincinnati Stock Exchange, and the Third Market made the later discovery of his colossal pyramid scheme even more incomprehensible to the financial community.

Money Market Mutual Funds and Cash Accounts

The first money market fund, the Reserve Fund, was launched in 1970 by Bruce R. Bent and Henry B.R. Brown. Depression-era Regulation Q still limited savings accounts to 5% interest which was inadequate with the 1970s era hyperinflation and CDs were less liquid. Under Regulation Q, checking accounts were not allowed to pay any interest at all. At the time of hyperinflation, the high returns, simplicity, and seeming security of money market funds appeared to be a godsend. However, the 2008 Great Financial Crisis would later highlight the potential risk of money market funds not being Federal Deposit Insurance Corporation (FDIC) insured. In 1977, Merrill Lynch introduced the cash management accounts (CMAs). It combined automatic investments into a money market fund with check writing as well as a credit card. By doing so Merrill pioneered a way for broker dealers to directly compete with traditional commercial banks. The Merrill Lynch CEO Donald Regan's goal was to create a financial supermarket. While the CMAs would come to define major stock brokerages today, Merrill's move into real estate brokerage would prove to be far less successful, ending in the unit being sold to Prudential in 1989. Other major brokerages from Shearson to Fidelity to Charles Schwab would ultimately match Merrill's CMAs. Money market funds would face an aggressive state by state campaign by banks and savings and loans to restrict or even ban them, but it would ultimately end up being a losing effort. Today, money market funds constitute the default investment and money management tool for the modern brokerage account. In 1978 Fidelity started its Fidelity Brokerage Services to offer discount services comparable to Schwab. The growing competition from the mutual fund and brokerage industry for core savings forced Congress to repeal to Regulation Q limits on interest for savings accounts with the Depository Institutions Deregulation and Monetary Control Act of 1980.

Conclusion

By the end of the 1970s, the key pieces that constitute today's modern market structure and industry were in place. The United States had successfully created one centralized clearinghouse for all stocks. The world's first listed stock options exchange was created in Chicago and was soon joined with options trading at major exchanges like Philadelphia and the AMEX. Merrill Lynch's cash management accounts introduced the American consumer new ways to interact with their broker and transformed brokerage accounts into a product more competitive to a bank account. The launch of the Nasdaq began the process of transforming the Wild West of the OTC markets into a worthy rival to the Big Board. Finally, the 1975 Securities Amendments Act firmly established the goal of creating a national market system for stocks the law of the land.

Notes

1. United States. Securities Exchange Commission. Report of Special Study of Securities Markets of the Securities and Exchange Commission. Buffalo, N.Y.]: [W.S. Hein], 1982. Print. House Document (United States. Congress. (88th, 1st Session : 1963). House) ; 88th Congress, No. 95.
2. By WILLIAM D. SMITH. (1966). WALL ST. SPURS COMPUTER USUAGE: Data Chiefs at 2 Exchanges Lead Automation Drive Wall Street Is Increasing Its Use of Computers. *The New York Times*, 127.

3. Kennedy, D. (2017). The machine in the market: Computers and the infrastructure of price at the New York Stock Exchange, 1965–1975. *Social Studies of Science*, 47(6), 888–917.
4. Bradford, P. G., & Miranti, P. J. (2014). Technology and learning: Automating Odd-lot Trading at the New York Stock Exchange, 1958-1976. *Technology and Culture*, 55(4), 850-879.
5. United States. Securities and Exchange Commission. (1963). *Report of special study of securities markets of the Securities and Exchange Commission* (Vol. 2). US Government Printing Office.
6. Bruchey, S. (2011). *The Modernization of the American Stock Exchange 1971-1989* (1st ed.). Routledge.
7. Morris, Edward. *Wall Streeters : The Creators and Corruptors of American Finance*, Columbia University Press, 2015.
8. Robards, Terry. (1969, Mar 06). Private Network is Established for Trading Institutional Stock. *New York Times.*
9. Robards, Terry. (1969, Jun 22). Big-block Matching Spreads. *New York Times*
10. Special to The New,York Times. (1969, Aug 06). S.E.C. Plans Move On Data Systems. *New York Times.*
11. Proposed regulation seeks to regulate proprietary trading systems as stock exchanges. (1993). *Tax Management Financial Planning Journal*, 9(7), 254.
12. Robards, Terry. (1969, Sep 24). Big Board Seeks Change by S.E.C. *New York Times.*
13. Maynard, T. H. (1992). What is an "exchange?" - proprietary electronic securities trading systems and the statutory definition of an exchange. *Washington and Lee Law Review*, 49(3), 833.
14. Robbards, Terry. (1970, Jan 07). Trading Reported for 98 Subscribers by Autex Service. *New York Times.*
15. R. M. (1971, Mar 19). Market place: A 4th Market Now Emerges. *New York Times*
16. Jones, Stacy. (1971, Apr 10). Network Lets Investors Bypass Brokers. *New York Times*
17. By, A. L. (1971, Apr 26). Broadened Role Urged for N.A.S.D. *New York Times.*
18. Big Board is Cool to 'Nasdaq' Plan. (1971, Apr 06). *New York Times.*
19. By, A. L. (1971, Sep 16). Nasdaq's Volume Exceeds AMEX's. *New York Times* (1923-Current File)
20. (1971, Jul 10). N.A.S.D. Keeping Eye On Market Makers. *New York Times.*
21. Martin-Marietta Corp. Acquires Computer Unit: Buys Division of Thompson Ramo for $30 Million New Concern to Be Formed for Systems Design. (1964). *The New York Times*, 37.

22. (1968, Feb 19). N.A.S.D. Outlines Automation Plan. *New York Times*
23. Cohen, M. F. (1964). Cooperative Regulation. Commission Speeches and Public Statements Archive.
24. Armour, L. A. (1972, Feb 28). Central Marketplace. *Barron's National Business and Financial Weekly*
25. Joel Seligman, *Payment For Order Flow And the Great Missed Opportunity*, 18 UC Law Business Journal UC Law SF Bus. L.J. 3 (2021).
26. By Kenneth H Bacon. (1973, Jan 26). Purchase of Nasdaq from Bunker Ramo Sought by NASD in Bid to Expand System. *Wall Street Journal.*
27. By Richard E Rustin. (1973, Oct 24). NASD Weighs Requiring Market Makers to Handle Each Stock for 3 Months or So. *Wall Street Journal.*
28. Rosenberg, John (1980, Jun 15). Computers: A Booming Industry in Fairfield County. *New York Times.*
29. (1975, Jul 17). Bunker Ramo to Sell Nasdaq Unit to NASD for about $10 Million. *Wall Street Journal.*
30. Walter Werner. "The Sec as a Market Regulator." *Virginia Law Review*, 70 (1984): 755-1657.
31. (1975). A Future Central Securities Market System. *Atlanta Economic Review*, 25(1), 28.
32. People and Business. (1976, May 07). *New York Times*
33. Former AT&T Officer to Head an SEC Board. (1976, Mar 05). *Wall Street Journal.*
34. Goldman Sachs's Levy Heads Panel Drafting Central-Market Plan. (1976, Jan 09). *Wall Street Journal.*
35. (1976, Dec 28). Big Board Lifts Rule Concerning Dealing in 'Third Market'. *New York Times.*
36. Du Bois, P.,C. (1977, Feb 14). Tomorrow's Trading. *Barron's National Business and Financial Weekly.*
37. (1976, Nov 23). Clearinghouse Merger at Major Exchanges Again Opposed by U.S. *Wall Street Journal.*
38. Rustin, R. E. (1978, May 12). Intermarket Trading System Pilot Phase is said to Increase Exchange Competition. *Wall Street Journal.*
39. NASD Takes Initial Steps to Link OTC, Proposed National Stock Market System. (1978, Mar 13). *Wall Street Journal.*
40. AMEX TO HELP FORM ELECTRONIC MARKET: EXCHANGE TO JOIN OTHERS PLANNING NEW SYSTEM FOR TRADING. (1977/11/16/, 1977 Nov 16). *New York Times (1923-)*
41. Chapman, P. (2000/08/01/). NYSE's Plan To Dump The ITS - Traders Want Changes in Controversial System. *Traders Magazine*, , 1.
42. Seligman, J. (2002/02//). Rethinking securities markets: The SEC Advisory Committee on market information and the future of the National Market System. *The Business Lawyer, 57*(2), 637-680.

43. Janice Traflet, & Michael Coyne. (2007). ENDING A NYSE TRADITION: THE 1975 UNRAVELING OF BROKERS' FIXED COMMISSIONS AND ITS LONG TERM IMPACT ON FINANCIAL ADVERTISING. Essays in Economic and Business History, 25(1), 131–142.
44. Janice Traflet, and Michael Coyne. "Ending A Nyse Tradition: The 1975 Unraveling Of Brokers' Fixed Commissions And Its Long Term Impact On Financial Advertising Ending A Nyse Tradition: The 1975 Unraveling Of Brokers' Fixed Commissions And Its Long Term Impact On Financial Advertising." *Essays in Economic and Business History*, vol. 25, no. 1, 2007.
45. Andy Hemmer Courier, S. R. (1997). Niehoff back, forming new stock system Nick Niehoff, who pioneered the Cincinnati Stock Exchange's electronic-trading system, is creating an Internet system. *Business Courier*, *14*(24), 3.
46. United States. Congress. House. Committee on Interstate and Foreign Commerce. Subcommittee on Consumer Protection and Finance. (1979). Progress toward the development of a national market system : joint hearings before the Subcommittee on Oversight and Investigations and the Subcommittee on Consumer Protection and Finance of the Committee on Interstate and Foreign Commerce, House of Representatives, Ninety-sixth Congress, first session ... September 21, 24, and 25, 1979. U.S. Govt. Print. Off.
47. Kregel, J. A. (1992). The Organisation of Trading in the Third and Fourth Markets in the USA.
48. Arvedlund, E. (2010). Too Good to Be True: The Rise and Fall of Bernie Madoff. United Kingdom: Penguin Publishing Group.

CHAPTER 6

The Rise of Nasdaq

The Expansion of the Nasdaq in the 1980s

Come the 1980s National Association of Securities Dealers Automated Quotations (Nasdaq) was still not considered an actual stock exchange even though it effectively filled that role. Prominent companies like Apple Computer Inc., the Pabst Brewing Company, Tampax Inc., and Tandem Computers Inc. helped bolster the respectability of the Nasdaq that arose out of the sometimes hazardous jungle of the over-the-counter (OTC) market.[1] From women's hygiene products to novel personal computers that would one day help spawn the revolutionary Macintosh Computer and iPhone, Nasdaq really helped finance many of the companies that would create the future. The forgotten story of Tandem Computers very much reflects the dynamics of the Nasdaq. Tandem was founded by employees from Hewlett-Packard (HP), who sought to build a "fault-tolerant" computer that would never go down as a result of having no single point of failure in the design. This was accomplished through all kinds of means of redundancies including even multiple central processing units (CPUs). Its main product, Nonstop, would become very popular with various financial firms and institutions. In fact, Tandem became a major supplier for both the Nasdaq and the New York Stock Exchange (NYSE). Tandem would later be acquired by Compaq, which itself would go on to merge with HP, in a way returning Tandem back to the HP fold.

M. J. Szanto, *A Century of North American Stock Markets*,
https://doi.org/10.1007/978-3-032-22419-4_6

Hewlett-Packard itself had its original initial public offering (IPO) back in 1957 and has been listed on the NYSE since 1961.

A still strong early leader on the Nasdaq was Apple Computers. This iconic American company was famously started by Steve Jobs and Steve Wozniak in their garage. They sought to make the personal computer a mainstream product for Americans. Jobs himself was also inspired to a large extent by HP. He liked to recount how as a kid he had phoned the CEO of HP for help with a project, and the leading American executive happily helped. HP also built its first product in a garage back in 1939. It was with their Apple 2 that Jobs and Wozniak achieved a breakout hit. A pivotal point for the Nasdaq market occurred at the end of 1980 when the Massachusetts regulators rejected the offering from Apple Computer's IPO. Residents in Alabama, Illinois, Michigan, Oklahoma, Texas, and Wisconsin were similarly barred from taking part in the launch in trading of Apple stock. Still, the IPO succeeded in raising more money than any IPO since the launch of Ford stock in 1956 and created 300 new millionaires. The fervor in the purchase of Apple Stock was fueled by the excitement of the Apple 2 Computer. Apple has traded under the symbol AAPL with Nasdaq ever since its IPO on December 12, 1980, and its rise to today's over 2-trillion-dollar market valuation has paralleled the rise of the Nasdaq, more than any other company.

Perhaps, reflecting the mercurial nature of some brilliant founders and entrepreneurs, Jobs would manage in a few years to get himself fired from the company he had created. However, in the years Steve Jobs spent away from Apple, he managed to transform the computer-generated imagery (CGI) software firm George Lucas had discarded into one of the leading players at the box office, Pixar. Shortly after Pixar had released its blockbuster hit *Toy Story*, it would also have its IPO on the Nasdaq rapidly transforming Jobs into a billionaire. Before *Toy Story*, Jobs's Pixar was an early innovator in medical imaging computers used in conjunction with computed tomography (CT) scans but failed to transform its medical imaging technology into a profitable sustainable business. Apple would go on to help finance the creation of technology powerhouses like Adobe and ARM. As Steve Jobs might have put it, Nasdaq had succeeded by the 1980s of creating the ultimate investment ecosystem for both technology and the future.

Another one of Nasdaq's early successes was having the primary listing for Microwave Communications, Inc. (MCI), but in MCI's early years it struggled to meet even the Nasdaq's lax listing requirements. MCI was the famous upstart that would dare to challenge the telecommunication establishment and prevail. By 1979 MCI's various lawsuits against AT&T, the American state-protected telecommunications behemoth, had gone to the Supreme Court three times. MCI was fighting to have the opportunity to offer its ExecuNet service built on top of a national network of microwave towers and compete as a rival to AT&T's monopolistic long-distance service. In order to accomplish this, MCI needed access to the telephone exchanges controlled by the Bell Telephone System.[2] MCI's fight with AT&T was long and drawn out, but it eventually won out and emerged as one of America's major long-distance companies. However, the journey was not an easy one for the common shareholder and definitely not for the faint of heart. Like many start-ups, investors in the MCI common shares faced dilution from the issuance of warrants, preferred stock, as well as subsequent offerings of common stock.[3] MCI would not only go on to become the major telecommunications provider for Nasdaq but also to become one of America's most valuable companies. Sadly, MCI would get caught up in the WorldCom fraud of the late 1990s that would completely bankrupt and ruin the whole company.

The Small Order Execution System (SOES) was developed in 1984 to serve as an automatic system to quickly route retail orders. The main purpose of SOES was to enable brokers to rapidly execute small orders for their retail clients. The trouble was that a new form of entrepreneur, the SOES bandit, would later realize they could make rapid arbitrage profits, when Nasdaq market makers did not update their listed quotations fast enough. The SOES bandits were some of the first day traders. Even this early automated trading system was not able to help contend with hiding Nasdaq market makers on Black Monday in 1987. Not only did they refuse to pick up their phones, they also refused to list quotes on SOES, lest they be forced to handle money losing trades. The NASD would later have to implement strong rules forcing NASD market makers to honor their posted prices on their respective stock listings.

The Nasdaq was rapidly growing into the vanguard of stock exchanges though it had not yet received the respect it deserved. On some days, the volume of trading would already exceed the New York Stock Exchange. While still described as the OTC market, critical changes were being implemented by the NASD with the encouragement of the Securities and Exchange Commission (SEC) that continued to upgrade the Nasdaq's ability to confront the Big Board head on. In 1982 the NASD enacted a rule requiring traders to disclose data on their recent trades for the 60 most traded issues.[4] Later that year, NASD would include 25 more stocks. In subsequent years the exchange would be able to automatically capture this data, though this system had been ostensibly set up initially as just a quotation system. Increasing transparency reduced the profits of the market makers while benefiting investors with more efficient markets. The risk would have been a withdrawal of market makers leading to loss of liquidity that in the end would undermine efficiency. This did not happen because the listed firms themselves preferred the greater exposure created by the increased disclosure while enjoying being freed from the constraints of the traditional exchanges.

By 1983 the NASD was lobbying the SEC to allow the creation of options for over-the-counter stocks. In 1985 the SEC approved plans by four US stock exchanges as well as the Chicago Board of Options Exchange to trade options on Nasdaq-listed stocks. The four exchanges to lead the way on options for Nasdaq stocks were the American, New York, Pacific, and Philadelphia stock exchanges. The agency also approved a more limited trial program for the Nasdaq to trade options on six of its own listings in "side by side trading." The original six listings were options on Apple, Intel, Tandem, Digital, MCI, and Convergent Technologies. Apple Computers was an early leader in traded Nasdaq options in the United States. The American Stock Exchange (AMEX) took an early lead in Nasdaq options gaining two thirds of the business. Surprisingly, the New York Stock Exchange would also beat the CBOE early on in options trading. The CBOE's early difficulties in competing for Nasdaq options compounded already competitive losses to the NYSE and AMEX in options on stocks listed on traditional exchanges. The CBOE having been founded by the historically agricultural Chicago Board of Trade had a structure that attracted suspicion and distrust among more traditional Wall Street players. Fortunately for the CBOE, the Chicago options institution would go on to build the world's largest market for options on Nasdaq-listed stocks. The CBOE would even later initially list on the Nasdaq as part of its 2010 IPO. For the AMEX, it saw a booming options market as a way to compensate for its own declining stock listings. The NASD was concerned that it was not allowed initially to conduct its own options trading on most Nasdaq stocks. In the market for futures on Nasdaq-based indexes, a battle ensued between the Chicago Board of Trade, the Chicago Mercantile Exchange, and the Philadelphia Exchange.

Progress was also fueled by the desire of the SEC leadership for the eventual creation of a national market system for equities. Congress had passed legislation in 1975 calling for such a system, but only the advancement of the Nasdaq had made it really imaginable. Before the Nasdaq, members of the NASD would have to call around the country in order to complete stock trades on issues not listed on the traditional exchanges. The New York Stock Exchange had been close to being a monopoly in the 1970s until faced with serious competition from the Nasdaq and the fully computerized fourth market led by Instinet. But the motivation behind the push for a national market system was to prevent market fragmentation and preserve high quality markets while still ensuring competition. The Nasdaq also introduced a rival model for price discovery and market making. Whereas the New York Stock Exchange would rely on a single specialist to create markets for a stock, many issues on the Nasdaq might have 20 or more market makers. Trading on the NYSE traditionally revolved around a dedicated specialist, while Nasdaq was said to be a dealer-based market.

The sky was the limit for America's first electronic stock market. The Nasdaq Market List was the group of stocks meeting the highest trading, liquidity, and operating standards. It rapidly grew to rival the scope of Big Board listings. In general Nasdaq had become the favorite venue for new listings. Microwave Communications Corporation of America (MCA) even chose to list its Class A shares on the Nasdaq in addition to its Class B shares.[5] The Nasdaq would continue to be referred to as the over-the-counter market for the rest of the decade, but by all relevant measures it was already a fully functioning stock market and a serious rival to the New York Stock Exchange. Yet how did this come to pass? Why would the National Association of Securities Dealers form a market that could effectively undermine its members' main source of profits? One possible answer would be that they anticipated the eventual value that the Nasdaq would one day achieve. While the New York Stock Exchange was a mutual not for profit organization, the New York Stock Exchange at this time could be valued based on the market value of the seats that gave one membership. The rapid growth of trading volume certainly did a lot to expand potential business for Nasdaq market makers.

The New York Stock Exchange and the AMEX started to experiment with expanded trading hours to contend with the new competition. The American Stock Exchange also actively advocated for new SEC rules to curb the rapid growth of the Nasdaq and correctly pointed out that the use of names like National Market System (NMS) misleadingly implied that Nasdaq was the single market Congress had called for. One advantage

Nasdaq had was it could host trading of exchange listed stocks, while the "over-the-counter" stocks could not be traded on the traditional exchanges. This was undoubtedly unfair, because Nasdaq was already effectively its own exchange but just was not yet recognized as such by the law. For example, today's over-the-counter stocks do not at all have this level of liquidity or institutional trading volume. It now consists of the OTC Bulletin Board administered until 2019 by the Financial Industry Regulatory Authority (FINRA), the successor to NASD, and the private OTC Link, LLC owned by OTC Markets Group, Inc. Some of the concerns raised by AMEX in 1984 had very real validity, though the New York Stock Exchange, still appearing to have near monopoly power, stayed out of the war of words between AMEX and Nasdaq.[6] Listing on the New York Stock Exchange continued to offer firms unrivaled respectability. In some cases, like the insurance firm American International Group (AIG), Nasdaq was little more than a stepping stone toward listing on the Big Board. Yet in other cases the NYSE quickly found itself at a competitive disadvantage due to its stringent listing requirements such as not allowing different classes of shares to have unequal voting rights.[7]

By the mid-decade of the 1980s the Nasdaq had high-flying stocks like Apple and MCI propelling it easily to the ranks of a peer competitor to the New York Stock Exchange. Georgia became the first state to exempt Nasdaq-listed stocks from its Blue-Sky Laws, easing their trade within the state. Gaining that state exemption would end up becoming a battle waged in every state. On one side was the NASD, and on the other was the AMEX and typically the local state securities administrator who did not want to give up its regulatory power. Chicago's Midwest Stock Exchange began the first traditional exchange to offer trading in Nasdaq listings beginning the process of leveling out the playing field.[8] In 1991 the Chicago market would be joined by the Philadelphia Stock Exchange in competing with Nasdaq for trading issues listed on the electronic market.[9] The New York Stock Exchange moved to follow the Nasdaq's lead toward ending its one share one vote standard, even with Canada's leading newspaper warning it "could provoke a brouhaha over the erosion of shareholder rights."[10] But the Nasdaq could not be stopped, with what was still referred to as the over-the-counter market continuing to attract top corporate listings like Citizens Financial Group.[11]

Nasdaq became more international with the addition of a newly installed trading link with the London Stock Exchange. This linkage delivered by means of satellite represented the first intercontinental linkage between securities markets. At the same time the London Stock Exchange (LSE) would also install a computerized trading system modeled after Nasdaq, the Stock Exchange Automated Quotations (SEAQ).[12] The huge regulatory reform of the city's financial sector under Margaret Thatcher known as the Big Bang would convert the venerable LSE into a purely electronic marketplace.[13] The Singapore Stock Exchange soon also established a direct connection with the Nasdaq.[14] Amazingly, only the Tokyo Stock Exchange and New York Stock Exchange beat the Nasdaq in terms of dollar volume in 1985.[15] Nasdaq expanded its trading to London, effectively opening up a new front in its quest to lead the world's exchanges. Nasdaq offered trading in listings found on the New York Stock Exchange and the London Stock Exchange. This was the beginning of the Nasdaq's goal in creating a 24/7 global exchange.[16] This move was followed with the creation of link to Europe's $2.6 trillion Eurobond market, as that market also prepared to computerize.[17] 1986 was the year of Britain's major deregulation known as the Big Bang, where the London Stock Exchange privatized and went private. The challenge they faced in London was British traders were used to lower trade disclosure requirements. The significantly lighter trading volume found in London of US issues could also test the level of transparency requirements the US SEC typically demanded of Nasdaq. Nasdaq built two dedicated transatlantic lines and installed a computer node in London to compete with the LSE's electronic SEAQ International market. Nasdaq's ultimate goal was to create a completely global electronic market that would run 24/7, a vision fueled by the telecommunications revolution.[18]

Even as Nasdaq exploded on the global stage, the NASD as a quasi-governmental self-regulatory organization was still responsible for policing the pink sheets whose price information was compiled by the private National Quotation Bureau long owned by Chicago-based Commerce Clearing Corporation now known as the OTC Markets Group. The NASD also continued to operate its own venue for small stocks in the form of OTC Bulletin Board (OTCBB) stocks, which it had formally established in 1990 at the invitation of the SEC.[19] The OTCBB was partly closed as a result of fraudulent enterprises exploiting the organization's historic link to the NASD to falsely imply some sort of Nasdaq listing or affiliation. The value of the pink sheets listings drastically fell as Nasdaq grew into a major exchange. Yet the NASD was a major force in automating the pink sheets market. The fact that the NASD was the primary regulator of the pink sheets even while continuing to operate its own bulletin board for microcap listings created one of many conflicts of interest which would fall upon the SEC to help mitigate.[20] The NASD got around to fully automating the OTCBB in 2003 but by then had been beaten by alternative trading system Winter Park-based GlobeNet Capital, which in 2002 would be purchased by Archipelago.[21]

The value of the pink sheets drastically fell with the expansion of the Nasdaq into a major exchange. Yet the NASD continued to be a major force in automating the remaining over-the-counter market.[22] NASD successor FINRA continued to operate the OTCBB until it was closed on November 8, 2021.[23] The closure of the OTCBB by FINRA left the OTC Markets Group as the only remaining market for the over-the-counter stocks. Legally the OTC Markets Group runs its markets a registered broker subsidiary, OTC Link, LLC, which runs three Alternative Trading System (ATSs) allowing other brokers to buy and sell OTC stocks on behalf of their customers. The OTC Markets Group affords the ability of firms to register at three tiers of standards and potentially creates for the United States a publicly traded venture market albeit one fraught with risk and uncertainty.

NASD's Small Order Execution System (SOES) was originally launched to expedite orders for retail customers but had to be enhanced to protect investors from locked markets. The SOES was created back in 1983, but new rules were implemented requiring all market makers to participate and even more importantly stand with the system. When SOES was launched in 1984, Apple Computer Inc., Intel Corp., People Express Airlines, and Lotus Development Corp were some of the first listings handled by the system.[24] Like every other system the expanded SOES would come with its own pitfalls. Professional traders would game the system created for retail investors to exploit market makers who did not update their prices fast enough. They came to be known as the SOES bandits. By the early 1990s new day traders further strained the system by learning how to rapidly influence the stock price by overwhelming the system intended for small retail investors. However, by the end of the 1990s efforts were made by the NASD to curtail the activities of the SOES bandits.

The refusal of state regulators to offer Nasdaq-listed stocks the same exemption granted to those listed on traditional exchanges continued to confound the electronic marketplace. The state of Massachusetts effectively blocked its residents from taking part in the Apple IPO. State regulators like those of Canadian provinces discussed in the next chapter wanted to protect their turf but also faced lobbying from the New York

Stock Exchange and AMEX. As this state-by-state fight continued, one of the most defining moments in Nasdaq history occurred, the IPO of Microsoft on March 13, 1986. It started trading with an offer price of $25 but ended the day above $35. Microsoft started its life as a public company with extraordinary strength having the standard operating system for IBM PCs and their clones as well as later Microsoft Word and Excel. Microsoft also had racked up many years of consistent profits, had money in the bank, and absolutely no debt. The pricing on Microsoft's initial offering was quite a bargain by today's standards especially when one factored in its already steady record of earnings growth. The closing price for the day gave the firm a market valuation of over $700 million. By the peak of the dot-com bubble it reached a market valuation of over $600 billion. Today Microsoft has a market cap of over $2 trillion, in large part due to the efforts of current CEO Satya Nadella to give Microsoft a powerful second act with cloud computing. Microsoft stock has been further boosted as of 2023 by its strong leadership position in artificial intelligence.

Black Monday 1987

On Monday, October 19, 1987, the Nasdaq would face its ultimate challenge as global markets took their worst plunge in history. And it faced it quite poorly. Most Nasdaq market makers responded to the unprecedented market volatility by fleeing their roles in providing liquidity greatly aggravating the drop in Nasdaq stocks. Brokers and market makers stopped answering their phones and often took every conceivable action to avoid having to take on any trades. Fortunately, the Nasdaq market was ultimately rescued by the almost inevitable bargain hunters. The initial chaos of the first 2 days of the plunge of the Nasdaq was reminiscent of the much later flash crash that afflicted the Nasdaq and the New York Stock Exchange in 2009. However, what locked up the Nasdaq was not a technological glitch or some cleverly plotted market manipulation gone awry. Nasdaq as an institution was still very new unlike the centuries-old venerable New York Stock Exchange and operated quite a bit differently than any other major stock exchange. When panic hit the New York Stock Exchange, the Nasdaq was beset by an institutional crisis—the financial world's equivalent of a constitutional crisis. Using Watergate as a metaphor, we can conjecture that an institution under such legitimacy pressures will either collapse or emerge ever stronger. The Nasdaq did the latter, and its impressive growth quickly resumed. Chicago would not get off so easily;

the mayhem at the Midwestern derivatives exchanges were far worse. The Chicago Board of Options Exchange was in fact slightly younger than Nasdaq, though the other major derivatives exchanges had both been founded in the nineteenth century. The market turmoil almost caused the collapse of the Options Clearing Corporation requiring a bailout organized by the Federal Reserve to prevent a global crisis. The survival of all three Chicago derivatives exchanges can be partly understood by their institutional strength. The Chicago Board of Trade predates the US Civil War. Still, most market watchers believe that the 1987 NYSE crash began with programmed trading in the Chicago markets going amok. This may help explain why Warren Buffett would later describe derivatives as "weapons of mass destruction." One of the key mechanisms behind the Chicago futures markets crashing the markets were portfolio insurance strategies that depended on the ability to sell futures to hedge risk. The trouble was the Chicago futures markets lacked the liquidity to support exceedingly large sell orders during an escalating panic.

As a result of the devastating stock market crash in 1987, President Reagan appointed former New Jersey Senator Nicholas Brady to head a commission to study the causes of the plunge and learn how to prevent or at least mitigate any repeat episodes in the future. While some critics felt the Brady Commission excessively blamed S&P 500 futures traded on the Chicago Mercantile Exchange, the federal task force did come up with numerous useful guidelines for the Nasdaq moving forward. Undeniably the futures traded on the floors of the Chicago Mercantile Exchange and the Chicago Board of Options Exchange by this time played a huge role in the dynamics of both the New York Stock Exchange and the Nasdaq. The Brady commission as well as many outside observers placed particular blame on portfolio insurance strategies. Portfolio insurance was intended to lead to rapid selling of stock or futures in the event of major declines in prices. However, the blind and automatic nature of these strategies would quickly overwhelm both the stock and the futures markets. A key recommendation of the Brady report was to enact circuit breakers, a series of progressive trading halts designed to slow and accelerate decline in equities. These circuit breakers are still a very important tool for the American stock exchanges to contain market crashes. The rapid recovery in prices for most listings on the New York Stock Exchange and the Nasdaq restored public confidence in the markets and helped fuel the buy-the-dip mentality that has prevailed ever since among American equity investors.

In the aftermath of the 1987 crash, Nasdaq had to still contend with defections to the established marketplaces, primarily the AMEX and the NYSE. The competition was based on two different models for running a stock exchange, with Nasdaq being the potential disrupter. The NYSE primarily relied on an auction centered market, whereas the Nasdaq is built on a dealer-driven market. The NASD responded in part by launching a television advertising campaign which began to build what would ultimately become a powerful brand. One of the most prominent Nasdaq advertisements featured Intel for its production of the leading CPU for IBM compatibles. Nasdaq had begun to form an identity separate from the wider over-the-counter market. The perception of the Nasdaq of just being a newer form of the over-the-counter market made it rife with defections. Compounding its problem were the strict rules preventing a firm from easily delisting from the NYSE or AMEX as epitomized by the NYSE's Rule 500. The Nasdaq tightened the standards for listing with the market and finalized plans for an alternative electronic market called the OTC Bulletin Board, providing a high-tech alternative to the pink sheets. One of the most prominent firms to be listed on this far less stringent, laxly regulated market was Nintendo, the leading video game system manufacturer of the era.

Security concerns grew over the networks that linked Nasdaq traders given its greater dependence on national computer networks that transmitted stock transactions. In 1991 Nasdaq hired MCI to create a backup for Nasdaq's Trumbull Center in Rockville and to build a truly secure national network. MCI also replaced the original network built by AT&T and assumed total responsibility of the whole market backbone which was previously controlled by NASD who had leased lines from several providers. MCI was such a major part of building Nasdaq into what it is today, that the MCI CEO William McGowan was even on the Nasdaq Board of Governors. It was only natural for the same man who successfully took on the nearly total monopoly of AT&T in long distance would also play a big part in leading Nasdaq's challenge to the dominance of the Big Board. Major system malfunctions in July 1994 highlighted the key importance of building as robust of a structure for trading as possible. Nasdaq resiliency was undermined by the occasional ill-fated run in with rogue squirrels with a penchant for chewing power cords.[25] The NASD also replaced its main Unisys 1100 mainframe with the more powerful Unisys 2200 mainframe in 1993. By the mid 1990s the Nasdaq was the world's largest intranet, and the marketplace was already working on expanding its system to exploit the growing popularity and availability of the internet. In 1997, Nasdaq signed a $600 million deal for MCI to upgrade the network allowing for a more than quadrupling of trading capacity paving the way for the Nasdaq to function in the twenty-first century.[26]

SelectNet was established by the NASD in 1988 as an automated network for the market makers to trade larger lots among each other to help maintain liquidity after the 1987 stock crash. While executions had to still be executed offline, SelectNet became the preferred manner for Nasdaq market makers to trade among themselves. The opening up of SelectNet to institutional clients by the end of the 1990s helped lead to greater automation and efficiency of Nasdaq trading. Innovation allowed for greater opportunities for all market participants but also created the potential for problematic conflicts of interest. While intended to facilitate trading and lessen the Nasdaq's dependence on telephones, SelectNet also resulted in increasing market complexity. Further, it gave brokers a way to actually trade against their own customers by potentially using the private network to get better prices. Another potential conflict came out of brokers selling "order flow." This refers to financial compensation for routing the orders from retail customers to particular markets. What is important to understand is even before the launch of the Nasdaq system in 1971, the dealer-based OTC market required market makers to be able to attract order flow. While buying order flow often sounds corrupt (and at times it can be), it was and perhaps still is often the only way for market makers to attract the liquidity needed to create a functioning liquid market.

Nasdaq Growing Pains

Professional traders can at times exploit the lower level of information held by the general public. One of the largest consumers of this order flow in the 1980s and the 1990s was Bernard Madoff, whose brother was the vice chairman of the NASD. Over the past three decades increased competition and regulatory scrutiny have allowed payment for order flow to evolve into a mechanism to provide commission-free rapid trading to retail traders, without significantly worsening the price they get. Another opportunistic if not exploitative strategy was preferencing where a market maker compensates a broker so it can automatically take the other side of the clients' trades if algorithms suggest it would be profitable for the dealer.[27] Despite the virtues of payment for order flow, Nasdaq appeared to be vulnerable to insidious methods of collusion and manipulation by inside players. Major brokers often merged with or owned Nasdaq dealers. Charles Schwab, the pioneering discount retail broker, owned Nasdaq market maker Mayer & Schweitzer Inc., while Paine Webber and Merrill Lynch were themselves market makers. This disincentivized them from seeking the best prices for their customers.

The infamous odd eights scandal led to aggressive investigations by both the Justice Department and SEC. A prominent paper published by two academics demonstrated that Nasdaq market makers diligently avoided posting any share prices involving odd eighths. American equities being quoted in eighths traces back to trading in the 1700s, when the Spanish dollar was the main currency of exchange. The Spanish Dollar had been denominated in eighths. The subsequent investigations by both the Justice Department and the SEC were able to document rife instances of deliberate collusion and coercion. This scheme helped artificially inflate the spread that Nasdaq market makers profited off. Most Nasdaq market makers responded with the argument that as dealers in various issues rather than the auctioneering role of the specialists on the NYSE, they needed a wider spread to stay in business. Surprisingly, it was the later infamous leading third market dealer Bernie Madoff who would be the first to break the even-eighths collusion scheme allowing for lower spreads for retail customers.

The fact that the Nasdaq had fairly lax rules should not be a surprise for a relatively upstart market with innovative technology and procedures. In order to succeed the NASD had to not only attract and retain top listings but also maintain liquidity. Liquidity comes from a constant flow of trades particularly from institutional and professional sources. As the expression goes, nothing comes for free. In order to attract liquidity, the Nasdaq had to provide traders sufficient profit, particularly given that holding positions on the Nasdaq or any market for that market lead to exposure to significant risk. Additionally, while Nasdaq's high-tech nature offered the potential to be more efficient and even fairer than the NYSE's traditional floor setup, its incredible complexity would inevitably be gamed until all the vulnerabilities were addressed. By 1994 Nasdaq was unquestionably a leading global market and now needed to address these concerns and problems in order to preserve its position. Special protections had to be created for small retail investors.

In 1995 the NASD enlisted former Senator Warren Rudman to lead a committee of all-star Wall Street experts to review the operations of the Nasdaq with the hope of finding ways to address the problems and to create a fairer market.[28] The NASD Select Committee on Structure and Governance known as the Rudman Committee was formed. Leading the campaign for a fairer Nasdaq was SEC Chairman Arthur Levitt Jr.[29] The NASD proposed replacing the SOES with a system named N-Prove system, but the exchange ended up sticking with SOES for the time being.[30] In 1995 the Rudman Committee found major flaws in the organization of the Nasdaq Stock Market and the governance of its overseer the National Association of Securities Dealers. In retrospect how could this be a surprise? The NASD was both owner and primary regulator of the Nasdaq. Clearly, the Nasdaq would have to be restructured. The Nasdaq would have to be separated from the NASD market regulation arm, and the board of the NASD had to be more representative of various market stakeholders.[31] The NASD was split into two parts: the Nasdaq Stock Market Inc. and NASD Regulation. Both would still have the NASD as parent organization, and all three organizations have the majority of their board seats filled with people independent of the securities industry. The resulting reforms pushed by the SEC represented the most aggressive efforts by the SEC to break the "Broker's Club."[32] Fears were raised that the diminished profits would reduce liquidity. That never came to pass, because advances in technology and the rapidly growing US economy ensured continual growth in investor demand for Nasdaq listings. With the radical restructuring came the first talk of transforming the exchange into a publicly traded firm.[33]

The Evolving Market Structure in the 1990s

A series of other changes were implemented in the 1990s by the US Congress and the SEC that began to alter the structure of the US Security Markets. One of the most important acts by Congress in promoting federalization of securities is the 1996 National Securities Markets Improvement Act (NSMIA.) This Act completely preempted all state regulations on securities listed on national exchanges (chiefly the New York Stock Exchange and Nasdaq) with the exception of state fraud laws. NSMIA did not preempt state fraud fighting jurisdiction even for federally covered securities as later exemplified by New York Attorney General Spitzer's later sweeping use of New York's Martin Law. Outside of the carve out for alleged fraud, the NSMIA protected major companies from worrying about coping with diverse state jurisdictions. The National Market Improvement Act of 1996 was a major advancement of Federal

Regulation of Securities. For the first time all stocks listed on national stock markets were now exempt from state regulation. The stocks whose regulation was preempted by this Act were named "covered securities." Never again would US states be able to restrict their residents from investing in any stock listed at the Nasdaq or the NYSE. Up until this point the US Congress had not outright preempted state securities laws. This move toward federal preemption does not apply to state fraud laws. The North American Securities Administrators Association (NASAA) agreed with the passage of this act as a way to facilitate a better division of labor between federal and state regulators, while it continued its own work at greater harmonization of state security laws. State laws were no longer applicable for covered securities except in cases of outright fraud. A potential shortcoming in the NSMIA legislation is small businesses are still not exempt from state registration requirements and are still forced to register in every state its equity offerings are sold.[34]

In the 1990s, Nasdaq continued to carve out a role for itself in gaining the listings of many of the hottest and most innovative IPOs of the day. At the same time the Nasdaq was increasingly viewed as a marketplace on par with the New York Stock Exchange, as opposed to just a steppingstone on the way to a listing on the Big Board. On January 1991, Roadway Services became the first Nasdaq-listed stock to get included in the Dow Transportation Index replacing bankrupt Pam Am. However, the New York Stock Exchange retained a near monopoly on blue chip stocks. The launch of the Automated Confirmation Transaction service helped reduce mismatched trades that still continue to plague the Nasdaq.[35] American Express Co., Conner Peripherals Inc., Liz Claiborne Inc., and Nike Inc. were examples of firms that would "graduate" from the Nasdaq and list on the New York Stock Exchange. Back when American Express had left the Nasdaq in 1977, it was considered an oddity to have listings from firms with market capitalization more than a billion dollars on Nasdaq. Tech giants Microsoft, Intel, and MCI would be among the first to break the mold and remain on the Nasdaq with Microsoft and Intel still listed on Nasdaq to this day.[36] Today all the firms valued at more than a trillion dollars trade on Nasdaq.[37]

In 1994 Congress passed the Unlisted Trading Privileges Act (UTP) as an amendment to the Securities and Exchange Act.[38] The UTP was partly a response to the 1993 EU Investment Services Directive, which not only allowed European securities firms to operate throughout the EU but also facilitated and encouraged off exchange trading. It aimed to enhance the liquidity and transparency of stock trading but also helped expand the

Nasdaq's role in the off-exchange trading of NYSE-listed stocks.[39] In 2005, the SEC expanded upon this act by issuing Regulation NMS, with the goal of expanding and improving access to the country's stock markets. These rules and regulations issued by both Congress and the SEC were the culmination of the Congressional National Market System mandate back in 1975. However, the 2013 3-hour outage of Nasdaq stemming from the crash of the Nasdaq's Unlisted Trading Privileges Securities Information Processor (UTP SIP) demonstrated how expanded connectivity increases the potential vulnerability to computer failures and even possibly malevolent actors.[40] Today in a bit of a twist, the Nasdaq is seeking to offer the thinnest trading issues the opportunity to opt out of unlisted trading in order to consolidate their trading and avoid excessive market fragmentation. Nasdaq's argument is for the most thinly traded securities, market fragmentation does more harm than good.

NSMIA also gave far greater exemptive power in implementing and enforcing the Securities Acts of 1933 and 1934 to the SEC.[41] This allowed the SEC to finally issue formal regulations and rules to manage alternative trading systems. The SEC's goal was to figure out how to best integrate alternative trading systems like Instinet into the National Market System.[42] In 1998 the SEC-issued Regulation ATS required all alternative trading systems to register as either a broker dealer or as an exchange, but all of them had to be covered by a self-regulatory organization. They also had to be linked to an exchange and allow members of that exchange to be able to trade on their publicly displayed orders.[43] Under this new regulation, the ATS could form its own self-regulatory organization if it chose to register as an exchange, but it would face substantial expense as a result. Alternatively, it could register with an existing self-regulatory organization which would have been either part of a traditional exchange like the New York Stock Exchange or the NASD which owned Nasdaq—both competitive rivals. The new order disclosure requirements, intended to preserve the National Market System, also could reduce the appeal of the electronic communications networks (ECN)trading venue for institutional clients who needed to hide their trade moves from opportunistic traders.[44] Archipelago filed in 1998 to become registered as an exchange under the new SEC rule in order to compete with the New York Stock Exchange on order flow for NYSE-listed stocks.[45] Island, the second largest ATS, joined Archipelago by also registering as an exchange in 1999.[46] In 1998 the Nasdaq merged with the American Stock Exchange bringing together the world's first electronic exchange with one of the major floor trading markets.[47] The deal represented the industry realization that the days of the floor traders were now very limited. This move also escalated the competition between the Nasdaq and the NYSE with Europe appearing to be the new battlefield. Despite all the seeming promise, the marriage between the AMEX and the Nasdaq was doomed from the beginning.

Nasdaq as a Publicly Traded Company in the 2000s

SuperSOES was an attempt by the NASD in 2001 to greatly expand the SOES system until the SuperMontage system could be fully established. Competing electronic exchanges led by Instinet and Archipelago opposed the SEC's approval of the new system. Consumer advocate groups also worried that the new system may once again disadvantage retail investors by boosting Nasdaq market makers margins at their expenses. Most importantly by creating an automated system now for all trading, this new system transformed Nasdaq from just a pricing data system into a true stock market. Over the subsequent 20 years fears that this system would stifle competitive rivals to the Nasdaq proved misplaced, and the spreads for the retail investors continued to come down. SuperMontage replaced both SelectNet and SuperSOES in 2002. Its implementation completed the process of creating a completely electronic trading exchange. It dynamically and rapidly processes the largest trades through the exchange computers while completely preserving the anonymity of the traders. Very ironically, the culmination of 30 years of Nasdaq evolution occurred at the absolute bottom of the dot-com crash.

By the close of the twentieth century, the NASD prepared the Nasdaq to become a publicly traded firm. The purpose was to monetize its success at creating one of the world's greatest stock markets and to allow the market the flexibility it needed to expand and adapt to the changing conditions of the twenty-first century. Publicly traded shares offered currency to potentially acquire other exchanges as well as facilitate other important strategic transactions. Being a listed firm would also allow for greater access to global capital markets to raise additional funds for infrastructure and technical enhancements when necessary. Nasdaq would have a more flexible ownership and would be disciplined by market forces rather than controlled by a structure largely created by an obscure 1938 law. Nasdaq would also find itself at the end of the twentieth century faced with mounting competitive pressure from the super high-tech electronic communications networks which were moving toward registering legally as stock exchanges. The process of spinning off the Nasdaq from the NASD began with private placements selling the bulk of the ownership to major market participants and finally applying to register the market with the SEC as an official exchange.[48] Its IPO would be delayed by the worst crash in Nasdaq history, and the shares that were already trading floundered on the bulletin board.[49] The Nasdaq would not be listed on the Nasdaq National Market until February 9, 2005, ending its early years as publicly traded firm trading on the bulletin board. The SEC would not approve the Nasdaq as a registered exchange until 2006.

Notes

1. Sloane, L. (1982, Jun 02). Nasdaq Starts its New Quote System. *New York Times.*
2. (1979, Jul 18). MCI v. Bell: From Court into the Marketplace. *New York Times.*
3. CI Communications Warrants. (1979, Jun 27). *Wall Street Journal.*
4. (1982, Oct 27). NASD's Disclosure Rule is 6 Months Old, and Traders Still Find Light Too Bright. *Wall Street Journal.*
5. (1983, Mar 28). Eight New OTC Issues Due This Week, None on Big Board or AMEX. *Wall Street Journal.*
6. Scott Mcmurray. (1984, Feb 10). Amex, NASD Officials Exchange Salvos as Rivalry for Listing of Stocks Heats Up. *Wall Street Journal.*
7. Mcmurray, Scott and Pamela Sebastian. (1984, Jul 10). BigBoard places to review the restrictions it places on listed companies, sources say. *Wall Street Journal.*
8. Cohen, L. (1986, Oct 21). Midwest Exchange Sets January for Start-Up Of Otc Stock Trading. *Chicago Tribune.*
9. Exchange Plans Trade in Nasdaq Stocks. (1991, Dec 12). *Asian Wall Street Journal.*
10. NYSE is Moving Closer to Repealing Standard. (1986, May 06). *The Globe and Mail.*
11. Bill Loving Journal-Bulletin, B. W. (1986, Apr 13). OTC Market Comes of Age as Alternate Stock Exchange Citizens Selected it over NYSE, AMEX. *Providence Journal.*
12. Hinden, S. (1986, Sep 29). Taking Growth in Stride NASD a Well-Kept Secret. *Chicago Sun–Times.*
13. Keyes, J. (1992). The NASD Makes a Move on the Big Board. *Wall Street & Technology*, 10(2), 44.
14. Priscilla, A. S. (1987, May 06). NASD will Exchange Price Quotations with Singapore on 50 Big OTC Stocks. *Wall Street Journal.*

15. Dodds, L. S. (1986, Sep 16). Nasdaq: On a roll. *Financial World*, 155, 84.
16. By Stan Hinden Washington Post,Staff Writer. (1986, Mar 23). Nasdaq to Link With London Market: 24-Hour-a-Day Securities Trading Moves Closer to Reality. *The Washington Post*.
17. Stan Hinden Washington Post Staff Writer. (1986). Nasdaq, Eurobond Market Set Link. The Washington Post (1974-), G3.
18. Michaels, J. (1992). NASD's Global Fumble. Wall Street & Technology, 9(11), 57.
19. News Roundup. (1963, Oct 25). Chicago Firm Agrees to Acquire Publisher Of Stock 'Pink Sheets'. *Wall Street Journal*.
20. Power, W. (1988, Sep 01). NASD Puts off Quoting Stocks in Pink Sheets. *Wall Street Journal*.
21. Chapman, P. (2000/01/01/). Trading & Technology: New ATS for the Little Known Stocks - Ex-NASD Staffers Join Florida Firm's Web Gambit. *Traders Magazine*.
22. Priscilla, A. S. (1987, Jun 05). NASD is Planning Automated System for 'Pink Sheets'. *Wall Street Journal*.
23. Chapman, P. (2010/02//). Market Data: FINRA Proposal Riles OTC Market. *Traders Magazine*, *23*(305), 16.
24. Apple Computer Inc., Intel Corp., People Express Airlines and Lotus Development Corp.
25. S. H. (1994, Aug 03). Bugs and Squirrels Gnaw Away Nasdaq's Image: Bugs and Squirrels Are Gnawing Away at Nasdaq's Image. New York Times.
26. MCI, Nasdaq Ink Deal to Boost Capacity: [Home Edition]. (1997, Nov 21). Los Angeles Times.
27. Torres, C. (1993, Feb 16). Heard On The Street: How Street Turns Your Stock Trades To Gold. *Wall Street Journal*.
28. Getler, W., & Power, W. (1994, Nov 21). Street Insiders Set to Review Nasdaq Market. *Wall Street Journal*.
29. Paltrow, S. J. (1994, Oct 22). Revised System for Small-Lot Trades Decried as Unfair Access: Some Smaller Traders Say The Proposed Change Would Favor Big-Time Dealers. Officials Say It Favors Stability. Series: INSIDE NASDAQ: Questions About America's Busiest Stock Market. Third in a Series. *Los Angeles Times*.
30. Major nasdaq revamping approved. (1994, Nov 22). *Pantagraph*.
31. Power, W., & Vogelstein, F. (1995, Oct 05). Shake-Up at Nasdaq Could Reach Chief. *Wall Street Journal*.
32. Raghavan, A., & Taylor, J. (1996, Aug 09). U.S. Settlement Could Transform Nasdaq By Breaking Dominance Of Brokers `Club'. *Wall Street Journal*.
33. Lohse, D. (1996, Apr 15). Leery About Nasdaq Regulating Itself? Former Aide Thinks It Should Go Public. *Wall Street Journal*.

34. Rutheford B Campbell, Jr. (2000). The Insidious Remnants Of State Rules Respecting Capital Formation. *Washington University Law Quarterly, 78*, 407–1583.
35. Smith, Craig. (1990, Mar 01). New System Offers Quick Verification Of Nasdaq Trades. *Wall Street Journal.*
36. Big Board, Nasdaq Square off over Larger Exchange's Control. (1993, Oct 12). Asian *Wall Street Journal.*
37. By, L. S. (1977, Apr 26). Move to Big Board From O-T-C Is Due By American Express: AMERICAN EXPRESS IS LEAVING O-T-C. *New York Times.*
38. *Unlisted trading privileges: hearing, June 22, 1994, on H.R. 4535, a bill to amend the Securities Exchange Act of 1934 with respect to the extension of unlisted trading privileges for corporate securities* (1994///0,). Superintendent of Documents.
39. Amihud, Y., & Mendelson, H. (1996). A new approach to the regulation of trading across securities markets. *NYUL Rev., 71*, 1411.
40. Kilburn, F. (2014/01/20/). Nasdaq Quits SIP Operator Role Over Stalemate on UTP Tape Development. *Inside Market Data, 29*(13), 1–13.
41. Chen, Lesley. "The Sec's Forgotten Power of Exemption: How the Sec Can Receive Deference in Favor pf Internal Whistleblowers Even When the Text is Clear." *Emory Law Journal* 67.5 (2018): 1043–1075.
42. SEC to issue new ATS rule by year-end. (1998). *Wall Street Letter*, 30(45), 7.
43. Lynn, S. H. (1998, Dec 03). SEC Adopts 'Landmark'rules For Alternative Trading Systems. *The Bond Buyer.*
44. Oesterle, D. A. (1998, Summer). The SEC's Assault On Electronic Trading. *Regulation*, 21, 17–23.
45. Archipelago registers with the SEC to become a national securities exchange. (1999, Aug 09). *PR Newswire.*
46. Island guns for NYSE volume. (1999). *Wall Street Letter*, 31(2), 4.
47. Anita Raghavan. (1998, Mar 12). Nasdaq's Parent Is In Negotiations To Take Control Of The Amex. *Wall Street Journal.*
48. Bresiger, G. (2001). The nasdaq exchange is a few steps closer: Everyone looks to SEC to make next move. *Traders Magazine*, 1–27.
49. Tarquinio, J. A. (2002, Nov 10). *Investing.* New York Times.

CHAPTER 7

The Canadian Investing Landscape

The Canadian stock markets began on a path in some ways very similar to US markets and yet at the same time in certain ways distinct. To begin with all of Canada's provinces have securities laws modeled after the groundbreaking "blue sky" law of Kansas from 1911. Manitoba was the first Canadian province to pass a securities law in 1912 with the other provinces quickly following. The Manitoba Sale of Shares Act empowered the Public Utility Commission to issue licenses authorizing the sale of securities.[1] However, the key difference would come in the midst of the Great Depression and rest upon the limits of federal power in Canada at least as understood by the Canadian Supreme Court today. Today's Canadians can largely thank the British for the overall division of power between the federal and provincial governments and more specifically what was once known as the British North America Act, 1867. The British had intended to create a strong Canadian Federal Government in order to prevent a devastating civil war like recently seen in the United States as well as fend off any threat of an American invasion. However, in some ways the result was actually a relatively weak Federal Government, because the British could not fully anticipate the nature of future economies of the twentieth century. Section 91 of what is now known as the Constitution Act, 1867, clearly gives the Canadian Federal Government power over banking but was never able to be extended to direct authority over the securities markets. In contrast, in the United States President Franklin

M. J. Szanto, *A Century of North American Stock Markets*,
https://doi.org/10.1007/978-3-032-22419-4_7

Delano Roosevelt was able to coax the US Supreme Court to largely accept his revolutionary New Deal legislation which included the foundational federal securities regulation that would serve as a base for all federal regulation of securities since in the United States.

Canada has 13 securities administrators representing the 10 provinces and 3 territories. At first provincial securities acts were significantly legally contested particularly since many of the corporations actually have federal rather than provincial charters. Surprisingly, as previously noted the United States does not have federally chartered corporations; even corporations created as acts of Congress have to get their charter from either a state or the District of Columbia. While corporate law in the United States is entirely handled by the states, in Canada it is partly a federal competency. Ultimately, provincial securities laws in Canada stood the test of time due to the fact that the Canadian Supreme Court has routinely ruled that federal securities regulation is unconstitutional. The Toronto Stock Exchange grew as the main exchange for trading mining and oil stocks in North America and by the 1950s overtook the Montreal Stock Exchange as the top exchange in Canada.[2] Toronto's ascendance as the epicenter of Canadian finance including equity trading has allowed the Ontario Securities Commission to emerge as the dominant regulator of securities in Canada.

The Securities Act and the Ontario Securities Commission

The Ontario Securities Commission (OSC) is a crown corporation that serves as the primary regulator for the markets in Ontario. Given that Canadian finance is centered today in Toronto, the Toronto Stock Exchange (TSX) is the dominant equity market in Canada, and its parent company the TMX Group is also based in Toronto, the OSC is effectively the main government agency overseeing securities in Canada. The central legislation for securities regulation in Ontario is known as the Securities Act. One historic difference between Canadian securities regulations is they are more principle based rather than rule based like American regulators. However, they both are built on disclosures rather than merit-based registration and regulation. The downside of America's rule-based approach is that it can leave open mammoth loopholes for the unscrupulous while needlessly punishing the meritorious with onerous regulation that may not fit the situation. The original act governing securities law in Ontario was the Securities Fraud Prevention Act of 1928. The Securities Act of 1947 expanded required disclosures and civil accountability. The updated Securities Act of 1966 was a response to the report of the Kimber Committee discussed later in this chapter, which further expanded disclosure, created new restrictions on insider trading, and offered protections in cases of takeover bids.

Investment Dealers Association

The Investment Dealers Association of Canada (IDA) was originally founded in 1916 as the Bond Dealers Section of the Toronto Board of Trade then known as the Bond Dealers Association of Canada (BDAC). The BDAC served a major role to raise money for Canada's military in World War I. In 1924 it took on the name Investment Bankers Association, but restrictions on the use of the word 'bank' by the 1934 Bank Act soon prompted another name change. In 1934 it changed its name to the Investment Dealers Association, which it would keep until 2008. The Ontario Securities Dealers Association was founded in 1941 to represent Ontario over-the-counter brokers. In the 1940s massive fraud from Ontario boiler rooms exploded with scams aimed at unwitting Americans. Ontario securities regulation landscape was shaped as a conflict between angry American politicians, regulators, and law enforcers against an extremely powerful and influential Ontario mining lobby. The outcry from American regulators was so bad at the 1944 National Association of Securities Administrators, the issue could only be dealt with in closed door session as to not to lead to an "international incident."[3] In 1947 the new Ontario Securities Act gave official legal recognition to the self-regulatory powers of the Toronto Stock Exchange, recognized as well as codified the authority of the Investment Dealers Association, and created the brand new Brokers Dealers Association to take over control of the over-the-counter market. The BDA would serve as Canada's equivalent of the NASD but would never take off.

The Canadian Investment Regulatory Organization

In 2002 the self-regulatory functions of the Toronto Stock Exchange and its sister venture exchange were spun off to create the Market Regulation Services (RS). The purpose was to facilitate the necessary independence for a credible securities regulation as the Toronto Stock Exchange prepared for its initial public offering (IPO).[4] By separating it from the Toronto Stock Exchange, it allowed the RS to assume oversight over Canada's venture exchange in the West, the Canadian Venture Exchange (CDNX).[5] This spin-off also enabled the newly created RS to also oversee the growing number of alternative trading systems in Canada. Spun-off market regulators like the RS are able to charge alternative trading systems for the necessary market oversight, preventing them from free riding off a traditional exchange in this regard.[6] In many ways, the RS quickly assumed the role of a national securities regulator, though not necessarily reaching the quasi-governmental status of the National Association of Securities Dealers (NASD) which merged into today's Financial Industry Regulatory Authority (FINRA) in the United States. The rules under which RS regulates by are known as the universal market integrity rules (UMIR).[7] The UMIR continues to govern trading in Canadian equities to this day. Alternative trading systems were represented by a member of the board of RS.

In 2008 the Market Regulation Services merged with the Investment Dealers Association leading to a single self-regulatory organization (SRO) for Canada's securities landscape. The newly unified SRO took on the name the Investment Industry Regulatory Organization of Canada (IIROC).[8] The newly streamlined regulatory landscape in Canada helped facilitate the oversight of newly created alternative trading systems and paralleled the merger in the United States of the NASD and the New York Stock Exchange (NYSE) Member Regulation.[9] In 2022 the IIROC agreed to merge with the Mutual Fund Dealers Association (MFDA) of Canada creating in 2023 the Canadian Investment Regulatory Organization (CIRO). This recent regulatory consolidation partly just reflects the declining role of mutual funds in North America with the rapid ascent of exchange-traded fund (ETFs) in both the United States and Canada. The significance of the role played by the MFDA was on a secular decline.

Porter Report and the Kimber Committee

A major review of Canada's financial system was done by the Royal Commission on Banking and Finance led by Dana Porter. The 1964 Porter Report came out with a recommendation for a federal securities regulator.[10] In October 1966 the attorney general assembled a committee on securities legislation that came to be known as the Kimber Committee, after the man who would chair it. Its work and report would become

Canada's equivalent of the SEC Big Study on the Securities Markets. John Kimber was a graduate of Osgoode Hall Law School and was master of the Supreme Court after years working as an attorney before becoming vice chairman and then chairman of the Ontario Securities Commission.[11] Kimber would go on to become the chairman of the Toronto Stock Exchange in 1967 after completing his work which would lead to a complete restructuring of Ontario securities law. Many of the recommendations from the Kimber Report would be incorporated into the Ontario Securities Act of 1967.

Early Efforts for a Federal Securities Regulator

As early as 1967, the Ontario Securities Commission had proposed a national securities regulator then referred to as Canada Securities Commission (CANSEC) with authority delegated from the provinces.[12] While provincial participation would be completely voluntary, those that joined would benefit from harmonized and streamlined filings. In 1979 the Canadian government finally responded with *the Proposals for a Securities Market Law for Canada*.[13] The proposed law would have also had a cooperative structure with the provincial regulators.[14] In 1994, the Ontario Securities Commission once again put forward a proposal for a national securities regulator, but after a few years of discussions and negotiations nothing had come to pass.[15] The 1994 proposal would have created a national organization named the Canadian Securities Commission.

The Canadian Securities Administrators

The primary umbrella organization for provincial and territorial securities administrators is the Canadian Securities Administrators (CSA). However, until fairly recently this organization has played a rather informal, limited role. Two developments have greatly expanded the role of the CSA. First, in 2003 the CSA established a permanent secretariat in Montreal. Even more significantly, in 2004 the CSA launched the securities passport system to facilitate full reciprocity for the various decisions made by all the local securities regulators. While Ontario did not formally join this new accord refusing to cede local power, its own rules were altered to facilitate working alongside this new national system effectively making Ontario a de facto party to this system. The end result is the key hurdle for registering new securities is getting past the local regulator rather than having to struggle with 13 separate regulators. This is critical for registering national securities offerings in the time one would expect in a modern advanced economy.

Canada's passport system is an example of a multilateral instrument drafted by the CSA but then adopted by multiple provinces and territories. It becomes a national instrument if it is adopted by all provinces and territories. One key multilateral system is the previously mentioned passport system. While technically not adopted by Ontario, the cooperation of Ontario makes the passport effectively a national instrument. Another key example of a national instrument is the System for Electronic Document Analysis and Retrieval (SEDAR). The adoption of the multijurisdictional disclosure system (MJDS) system by all Canadian provinces and territories in coordination with the Securities and Exchange Commission (SEC) also represents a national instrument. Another project of the Canadian Securities Administrators was the universal securities legislation project (USL). It led to a new Uniform Securities Act and a Model Securities Administration Act.

Wise Persons' Committee and the Hockin Panel

Canadian Finance Minister John Manley appointed Harold MacKay to review securities regulation. The results of his work have come to be known as the MacKay Report. MacKay ultimately recommended the creation of the Wise Persons' Committee on which he would serve as the vice chairman.[16] The main recommendations of the Wise Persons' Committee would be the creation of a national securities regulator. In response to the global financial crisis the Canadian government formed the Expert Panel on Securities Regulation also known as the Hockin Panel. The Canadian Finance Minister Jim Flaherty had appointed Tom Hockin to run the panel. Hockin had previously been Minister of State for Finance and then Minister of State for Small Business and Tourism under Prime Minister Mulroney. The key concerns addressed by the Hockin Panel were ways to address the levels of potential systemic risk revealed by the Financial Crisis while also ensuring a competitive Canadian arena for the global capital markets. A key recommendation of the panel was the formation of a federal securities regulation. In response, the Federal Government created the Canadian Transition Office under legislation passed in 2009. The Canadian Transition Office drafted a proposed Canadian Securities Act. This Federal Securities Act would have created a national securities regulation known as the Canadian Securities Commission. This prospect was permanently thwarted by a 2011 decision by the Canadian Supreme Court ruling the proposed act unconstitutional.

The Cooperative Capital Markets Regulatory System

Following the Supreme Court decision against the proposed Canadian Securities Act, most of Canada's provinces joined with the Federal Government to create the Cooperative Capital Markets Regulatory System. On its board served Harold MacKay who had played a key role with the Wise Persons' Committee. The Cooperative System was designed to address the concerns previously expressed by the Supreme Court essentially following the roadmap provided by the court. The underlying concept was the intended delegation of authority by the provinces to the proposed agency. The agency tasked to establishing this system was the Federal Capital Markets Authority Implementation Organization. Ultimately following the COVID pandemic, the political will to follow through on the plan evaporated, and the Federal Government shut down the Federal Capital Markets Authority Implementation Organization (CMAIO) ending all hopes of there being a national securities regulator in Canada.[17]

Impact of Sarbanes-Oxley

Some of the current US rules imposed on publicly traded firms come from the controversial US Sarbanes-Oxley (SOX) legislation. Canadian firms cross listed on American exchanges are already required to comply with SOX giving them all the resulting benefits as well as costs from these expanded rules. The fact that small capitalization Canadian firms can be exempt from those recently applied American rules can distinguish Canadian markets, particularly the Toronto Stock Venture Exchange. Such regulatory diversity can favor a more competitive marketplace. Investors seeking the stricter rules of the SEC and US exchanges can focus in on investing through American exchanges, while those comfortable with more lax rules can also enter the Canadian markets. However, in 2002 Ontario passed certain key clauses related to executive accountability inspired by the groundbreaking American legislation. All of Canada's provinces and territories followed suit except for British Columbia, who stuck to the Canadian tradition of following principle-based regulation.[18]

OSC Reciprocal Orders

Canadian-American securities regulatory cooperation is unique in a number of ways. The United States long lacked formal treaties with Canada related to securities regulation; securities law and procedure were largely left untouched by the North American Free Trade Agreement (NAFTA). Yet the level of cooperation with the US federal regulator, the SEC with the provincial and territorial securities administrators greatly exceeds coordination with the transnational regulatory network of global regulators largely embodied by International Organization of Securities Commissions (IOSCO). Cooperation between the United States and Canada is largely achieved by the signing of memoranda of understanding between the SEC with the provincial authority or with their umbrella organization Canadian Securities Administrators.[19] Critical to the cooperation between the respective countries is the major role administrative rule making plays in defining the law offering the administrative regulators to enact as well as enforce new rules without requiring the intervention or assistance of the legislatures.[20] A prominent example of a SEC penalty being reciprocated by the Ontario Securities Commission was the case of Conrad Black.[21]

OSC reciprocal orders based on SEC actions serve a dual purpose. They ensure that Canada does not serve as a haven for grifters and swindlers who could use the Maple Leaf state as a platform to target neighboring Americans and to protect Canadian locally from individuals identified by the SEC as unscrupulous. Central to the licensing of securities professionals is to ensure their character and ability to act in good faith on the behalf of various types of clients. Before changes in the extradition law, Toronto was a hot bed of boiler room operations targeting Americans that were out of reach of the FBI.[22] The challenge in amending the extradition treaty between Canada and United States was the concept of double or dual criminality. Ordinarily extradition is only allowable if the act is criminal in the location where it was committed and where the suspect is apprehended. Many American securities crimes were not explicitly addressed in Canadian law either on the federal or the provincial level, and there was strong opposition in Canada to making an exception for criminal securities law.[23]

Quasi-Criminal Offenses

One particular area of Canadian law that can be confusing to the American observer is quasi-criminal offenses. In the United States, quasi-criminal offenses often refer to traffic offenses, which generally need to be proven beyond a reasonable doubt like American criminal charges given the threat to one's driving privileges. Contempt of court actions leading to jail time would be another American example of quasi-criminal proceedings. In Canada, quasi-criminal charges play a much bigger role. While criminal law is the exclusive domain of the Canadian Federal Government, provincial regulatory agencies have the authority to prosecute under provincial law quasi-criminal offenses. Provincial prosecutors can ask judges to dole out jail time for quasi-criminal offenses. This means the Ontario Securities Commission does not have to rely on federal prosecutors or the Royal Mounties to put away bad players on Bay Street, though the OSC's cooperation with federal authorities has grown in recent decades. Quasi-criminal securities cases are heard in the Ontario Court of Justice as spelled out by the Ontario Provincial Offenses Act. Similar to the United States, the required burden of proof is beyond a reasonable doubt. Provincial quasi-criminal offenses are complimented by Federal Criminal Code as well as common law criminal offenses primarily related to fraud that can be tried in Federal Courts. In 2003 the Canadian Federal Government created the Integrated Market Enforcement Teams run by both the Royal Canadian Mounted Police and the Canadian Department of Justice.

Canadian Protectionism

Canadian laws have often promoted protectionism and more aimed at protecting the status quo than serving identifiable public welfare objectives. In 1966, the Canadian Parliament acted to amend the Bank Act in order force Citibank to yield its control of Mercantile Bank, which Citibank had purchased in 1963.[24] The influential and wealthy Rockefeller family was able to enlist the help of the US State Department against this appropriation.[25] Notably threats of American retaliation did not stop this act of Canadian protectionism.[26] However, Citibank was allowed a decade to exit the bulk of their stake in Mercantile. Merrill Lynch's acquisition of failing Royal Securities Corporation in 1969 resulted in Merrill gaining an additional seat on both the Montreal and Toronto Stock Exchanges posing a serious threat to the Canadian traders clubs that could not be left unanswered. The Royal Securities Corporation had been the launching pad of the finance career of famous Canadian-British businessman and politician Max Aitken.

Four Pillars of Financial Regulation Canada

Historically there were four pillars of financial regulation in Canada. They were the banks, the securities industry, insurance, and trust companies. These separate pillars were maintained by preserving clear distinctions between the respective industries. In this book we are almost entirely interested in Canada's banking and securities industry with a particular focus in on the securities industry. Securities law is handled on the provincial level, while banking laws are handled on the federal law. Corporate law is handled by both the provincial governments and the Canadian Federal Government. The separation between the securities and banking industries in Canada was greatly lessened by the Little Bang, which will be discussed later in the book. Company founders and managers can decide between incorporating at either the federal level, and similar to the United States, a company incorporated in any province is free to operate in any Canadian province or territory as long as it is properly registered locally. Canada's Little Bang largely ended the divisions that these four pillars represented.

Lack of Jurisdiction in the United States

The authority of Canadian exchanges and their respective regulators is challenged by their very limited jurisdiction for transactions made in the United States. One of the most spectacular incidents of investors using American exchanges to bypass the rules of Canadian exchanges was the hostile takeover of Brascan by the Toronto Bronfmans. Brascan was a Canadian firm owning diverse ventures in Brazil. Brascan's rejection of Edper's buyout offer led Brascan to attempt to purchase Woolworth as a defense against the takeover. While clearly motivated to fend off the Bronfmans, had Brascan succeeded in acquiring Woolworth, it would have been the largest hostile takeover at the time.[27] Woolworth management had fought off the bid claiming that the bid was "grossly inadequate" and accusing Canadian Imperial Bank of Commerce (CIBC) of double dealing by financing the bid, despite its preexisting relationship with Woolworth.[28] CIBC had provided $700 million of financing for the attempted takeover, despite being Woolworth's largest lending creditor.[29] The Woolworth management would better serve their shareholders by accepting the bid from Brascan, because within a few short years they had closed all of their stores in North America, and the company was well on its way into oblivion. In the end the Bronfmans were able to take control by accumulating shares on the American Stock Exchange. Brascan sued arguing that Edper's action was in effect a tender offer which would mean that the Bronfmans had violated the Williams Act of the Securities Exchange Act of 1934 including disclosure requirements. The Court of the Southern District of New York ruled in favor of the Bronfmans that their pickup of stock at a premium did not constitute a tender offer.[30] The more significant issue is that the Bronfmans had violated the rules of the Toronto Stock Exchange by acquiring a firm listed on the Toronto Stock Exchange (TSE) through a foreign exchange.[31] While the acquisition was targeting the firm's cash, Brascan became the Bronfmans' most important investment vehicle evolving into today's Brookfield, one of Canada's largest private equity firms.

The Multijurisdictional Disclosure System

The SEC and the Canadian provincial securities regulators created the multijurisdictional disclosure system (MJDS) in 1991 as a system for Canadian securities to get automatically registered with the United States. The multijurisdictional disclosure system (MJDS) was a system agreed to by the Canadian provincial securities administrators and the US SEC allowing cross-border securities transactions to be conducted following a firm's home disclosure rules. Not only can a Canadian firm largely use Canadian forms to distribute to Americans and filed with the SEC, but there is no separate SEC review. The MJDS established a mechanism for the SEC to routinely defer to the Canadian or provincial regulator and vice versa. This reciprocity was made possible by the extensive American and Canadian securities laws.[32]

One of the reasons MJDS is not utilized as frequently as many might expect is the US Regulation S exempts transactions conducted in foreign marketplaces. Recall that a Regulation S exemption applies when the transaction and the marketing of the security are conducted entirely outside of the United States. This does not preclude a contemporaneous offering within the United States covered under other rules. Another reason that Canadian firms have not had to rely exclusively on MJDS is their preexisting ability to exploit the Rule 144A exemption. As discussed previously Rule 144A exempts sales of securities sold privately to qualified investors with investible assets more than 100 million dollars. Overall, large Canadian companies can fairly readily access American capital markets even without utilizing the benefits offered by MJDS.

Nonvoting Shares

Nonvoting shares are a big feature in the Canadian equity marketplace. They are issued in family-run firms to preserve the control of the founders and are used to comply with protectionist measures in numerous industries that require firms to be controlled by Canadians. Yet they are often a source of concern and not always viewed favorably in terms of corporate governance or even fairness.[33] The case of Canadian Tire was particularly egregious. The founding family dominated control of the firm through their special voting shares despite owning a small minority of the firm. One of the firm's bylaws was created to protect the nonvoting shareholders by converting their shares into voting shares in an event of a takeover bid. Their lawyer Rene Sorell found a loophole around this coattail clause, allowing the Billes family to get a deal to sell their shares at a substantial premium. The Ontario Securities Commission struck down this arrangement on the basis of a total lack of fairness.[34] On the other hand nonvoting shares can insulate managers from the whims of changing shareholders and allow them to focus in on the long game.[35] The Toronto Stock Exchange has required strong coattail protections for nonvoting shareholders following the attempted Canadian Tire heist.

Brookfield

Brookfield's roots began with the creation of Edpar which served as an investment vehicle effectively for the inheritance of Edward Bronfman and Peter Bronfman. Their uncle, Samuel Bronfman, had created the Seagram's Liquor company, which evolved into one of Canada's largest firms. While the portion still remained to be a tidy sum, Samuel's difficult relations with their father led him to cut their holdings, forcing them to sell substantial shares at an unfavorable price and prohibited them from working at Seagram. This forced them to set out on their own. While their lack of experience and youth may have initially led to mixed results, they ultimately built Brascan into one of the most dominant forces on the Toronto

Stock Exchange through an intricate web of holding companies with Edpar at the center.

Edpar was able to gain control of Brascan, a Brazilian power company traded on the Toronto Stock Exchange and controlled by Canadians by buying most of the key shares on the American Exchange and the London Stock Exchange bypassing rules set by the TSE. As previously mentioned the main legal case resulting in the United States had to do with whether they violated the Williams Act by not complying with the rules set for tender offers in the United States. This hinged upon whether their market actions could be properly construed as a tender offer. The Bronfmans were going after Brascan's free cash but then transformed Brascan into one of their main vehicles for private equity styled deals. Brookfield was the name of one of the real estate firms they had purchased. By the early 1990s, the Bronfmans found themselves badly overextended and were forced to retrench. To move beyond the freewheeling days during Bronfman control, Brascan assumed the name Brookfield. Brookfield, however, has assumed the path blazed by the Bronfman Brothers as a leading investor in Canada and around the world.

Today the Brookfield family of firms offers many investment options for equity investors in Canada and the United States. The parent firm Brookfield Asset Management (BAM) is listed on the Toronto Stock Exchange, the New York Stock Exchange, and the Euronext. BAM is a component of the S&P TSX 60. Brookfield Property Partners (BPY) is a subsidiary that is structured as a limited partnership and is traded on the Nasdaq and the Toronto Stock Exchange. The advantages and disadvantages tax wise in Canada and in the United States stem from the income flowing through without paying separate corporate tax. The structure also results in no reported operating income. Brookfield Property REIT (BPR) is structured as a real estate investment trust (REIT) for Americans who would benefit from the tax advantages of owning shares in an REIT. In June 2014 BPY absorbed Brookfield Office Properties, the Brookfield subsidiary focused in on investing in office buildings. Brookfield Renewable Partners is the Brookfield devoted to looking for profitable investments in renewable energy, and Brookfield Infrastructure Partners buys into infrastructure projects around the world. Overall, Brookfield Asset Management is a very broad-based private equity operation that opportunistically looks for good investments in all industries around the world.

As is the case in the United States, Canadian private equity provides a major alternative source of financing to the public markets. Many of the largest investors in private equity are public pension funds including the Canadian Pension Plan Investment Board (CPPIB), the Ontario Teachers' Pension Plan (Teachers), the Ontario Municipal Employees Retirement System (OMERS), and the Caisse de depot et placement du Quebec (Caisse).[36] The two most storied Canadian firms in the world of Canadian Private Equity are Onex and Brookfield. Onex was founded by private equity pioneer Gerald W. Schwartz, a former colleague of American giant Jerome Kohlberg Jr. who went on to cofound American private equity pioneer Kohlberg Kravis Roberts in NYC. Before founding Onex Schwartz cofounded media giant Canwest with Izzy Asper.[37]

The Venture Capital Market

In today's markets a great deal of investing in the capital markets occurs in the private markets. For start-ups and early-stage companies, much of the private funding takes the form of venture capital. The early inspirations for Canadian private equity were major American tech success stories like Apple, Digital Equipment, and Lotus Development.[38] Technology has once again become prominent in the Canadian venture capital realm.[39] Some of the players investing in Canadian venture capital world are established technology firms. The Federal Government has also established the Venture Capital Action Plan which subsidizes major Canadian venture capital funds with matching funds. Overall the Federal Government is the largest investor in venture capital in the country.[40] Meanwhile, in Ontario the provincial government has created the Ontario Venture Capital Fund (OVCF). The OVCF is a partnership of the provincial government and private companies. The Quebec government helps fund federal matching of venture capital funds but has not created a separate government led fund. Montreal actually led Canada for the size of VC deals for the first quarter of 2018.[41] The Alberta government launched Alberta Enterprise in 2008 to support venture capital activity in the province. One recent investment by Alberta Enterprise was in the Panache Fund for $5 million.[42] British Columbia was an early pioneer of generous tax credit for private investments in venture capital. American venture capitalists are also always on the lookout for opportunities up north. For example, innovative Toronto app developer VarageSale received $34 million funding from Sequoia Capital and Lightspeed Venture Partners.[43] VarageSale was founded by a kindergarten teacher, Tami Zuckerman.[44] Sequoia and Lightspeed are both really top California firms who are backed by very deep-pocketed investors and are very adept at successful exits for start-ups either with sales to major large cap companies or IPOs on major US exchanges. Last year Zuckerman sold her startup to VerticalScope, another Toronto tech firm.[45] The challenge facing Canada in terms of American venture capital is that the big players tend to focus in on select areas in the United States, India, China, and Israel.

The venture capital market in Canada is extraordinarily similar to the United States. Certainly, there is not the scale of deals and funding rounds that are seen in places like Seattle, Silicon Valley, or Boston. Generally, the Canadian VC market from Toronto to Montreal to Vancouver would rest heavily in the mid-market category. However, even major North American financial centers like Chicago have also struggled to attract the type of VC activity found in the more innovative parts of the United States or the United Kingdom and Israel. Overall the Canadian market is very well saturated with VC funding, but the scarcity of unicorns, VC companies valued at a billion dollars, demonstrates that Canada is still not a superpower in venture capital investments.[46] The composition of exit strategies between Canadian and American firms varies somewhat with Canadian start-ups less likely to end in an initial public offering (IPO).[47] However given the constantly changing calculus in whether staying private or going public is the better strategy, it is not clear if this is a fundamental weakness of the Canadian venture capital market. The government of Canada has used the Federal Venture Capital Action Plan to fund Northleaf Venture Catalyst Fund, Teralys Capital Innovation Fund, Kensington Venture Fund, and HarbourVest Canada Growth Fund. HarbourVest Partners is a Boston firm making it the only American firm to manage a VC fund backed by Venture Capital Action Plan (VCAP).[48]

One very uniquely Canadian phenomenon is the labor-sponsored venture capital corporations (LSVCCs) which are VC funds sponsored by labor unions. LSVCCs are starting to have a diminished role as the favorable tax treatment is largely being phased out in Canada.[49] Some research indicated that LSVCCs were less efficient than private VC funds.[50] The new government-sponsored funds have the advantage of having private investment capital as well as private firms managing the funds. One of the big focuses of Canadian venture capital is healthcare and biotechnology. Agrisoma Biosciences is one current start-up in Canada that is developing genetic engineering technology for agriculture. Monteris Medical is a start-up developing medical tools for the treatment of brain tumors. Clearwater Clinical develops tools for audiology and endoscopy.

Another big area for Canadian VC funds is cleantech. For example, Hortau has developed an advanced irrigation system for crops. Power Survey is a company that designs tools to make electric grids more efficient. Despite all of the government support for venture capital, Canada is really unable to escape being eclipsed by the United States in general and Silicon Valley specifically. The largest successful Canadian start-up of the past couple decades is Shopify. In 2015 it simultaneously went public on both the Toronto Stock Exchange and the New York Stock Exchange. Shopify is one of the leading firms providing ecommerce services for small businesses.

Private Equity

The two most significant publicly traded private equity firms in Canada are Onex and Brookfield Asset Management. Many of the largest institutional investors in Canada are government-sponsored pension funds including Ontario Municipal Employees Retirement System (OMERS), Ontario Teachers' Pension Plan Board (Teachers), Canada Pension Plan Investment Board (CPPIB), and Caisse de depot et placement du Quebec (CDPQ), and they all run substantial private equity operations in house as well. Three of the top ten largest private equity players in the world are Canadian: the Canada Pension Plan Investment Board, the Ontario Teachers' Pension Plan, and Caisse de depot et placement du Quebec.[51]

The largest Canadian institutional investor is the CPPIB which manages the Canadian Pension Plan for all provinces but Quebec. In 2013 the CPPIB in conjunction with Ares Management purchased Neiman Marcus, but its equity investment would be wiped out during the midst of the COVID pandemic.[52] Another very large pension plan in Canada is Ontario Teachers' Pension Plan. The largest private equity deal in Canadian history would have been the leveraged buyout (LBO) of BCE, the holding company for Bell Canada, by a group of private equity investors led by Ontario Teachers' Pension Plan (OTPP), but the transaction was scuttled by KPMG refusing to pass it on solvency grounds. Ironically solvency tests are rarely required for LBOs, but in this case it was an effort by BCE to immunize itself from lawsuits from bondholders.[53] One other noteworthy acquisition of the OTPP private equity wing, Teacher's Private Capital, was the purchase of GNC in conjunction with Los Angeles-based buyout shop Ares Management.[54] Ontario also has the Ontario Municipal Employees' Retirement System (OMERS). The Caisse de depot et placement du Quebec (CDPQ) oversees pensions for Quebec. In Canada endowments are also very large investors. For example, the University of Toronto Asset Management Corporation (UTAM) was established in 2000 to manage the assets for both the university endowment and employee pensions.[55] As a result the UTAM manages roughly $10 billion.

Another major investor group in the Canadian markets is the insurance companies. Two of the largest Canadian insurance companies by assets are Manulife Financial and Sun Life Financial. Similar to the United States many of Canada's insurance companies were originally established as mutual companies and in recent decades demutualized and went on to become public companies. Manulife underwent the demutualization in 1999.[56] Sun Life Financial followed suit the next year.[57] In both cases the policyholders were rewarded with shares in the newly formed companies as well as cash. Manulife's acquisition of John Hancock in 2004 cemented a very strong American presence for the company. The significance of Canadian insurance companies is twofold. They represent a very large segment of the market valuation of the Toronto Stock Exchange, and they also are some of the biggest investors in equity both private and public.

Onex

Onex really is the private equity giant in Canada other than Brookfield. Onex is the creation of Gerry Schwartz who worked at Bear Stearns under private equity giant, Jerome Kohlberg. He also worked with Henry Kravis and George Roberts who would go on to create with Kohlberg the iconic American private equity group Kohlberg Kravis Roberts & Co (KKR). Schwartz cofounded the Canadian media group Canwest in 1976, which will be discussed in the next chapter, and then went on to found Onex in 1984. Onex has managed to outperform KKR over the long run and amazingly today was Canada's largest employer by virtue of its various portfolio firms until recently overtaken by Canadian grocer, Loblaw.[58] Onex has successfully captured a number of really high-profile deals that have propelled the firm to the top levels of global private equity firms. One of the big deals was picking up in air catering division of American Airlines, Sky Chefs. Later Onex went on to purchase IBM's manufacturing division, Celestica. Early last decade Onex returned to the airliner business in a big way. Scotiabank alumnus Seth Mersky came to Onex loaded with experience, ideas, and contacts. Mersky realized that the major downturn in the air travel business that followed 9/11 had fostered a substantial buying opportunity especially given major pent-up demand in China and India. The opportunity Mersky found was airplane production plants in Kansas and Oklahoma that Boeing was ready to unload. Onex has also been a frequent participant in local Canadian private equity deals.

OMERS

The Ontario Municipal Employees Retirement System (OMERS) was created by a 1962 act of the Ontario legislature to manage all of the pensions for all of the municipal employees in the province. In 2006 Ontario restructured OMERS handing over much of the control to the municipal governments it serves.[59] One of the largest acquisitions for OMERS has been Alexander Mann Solutions, a global recruiting company.[60] Another major acquisition was US liquid transportation services firm, Kenan Advantage Group, from Goldman Sachs and Centerbridge Partners.[61] Back in 2010 OMERS also purchased United States Infrastructure Corporation.[62] OMERS is also a major investor in publicly traded firms including TSX 60 component firm Constellation Software. OMERS' current stake in Constellation stems from private equity investments made many years before its IPO.[63] OMERS has also been a large investor in real estate, represented by large private equity transactions involving Canadian REITs as reflected in its $3.8-billion-dollar acquisition of Oxford Properties Group which had doubled the size of its property portfolio.[64] Oxford Properties currently serves as the investment and management vehicle for all of the real estate holdings held by OMERS. OMERS joined with Alberta Investment Management Corp to take control of European cinema firm.[65] OMERS' purchase in partnership with UK-based Apax Partners of Canadian media firm Thompson's textbook unit helped Thompson fund its purchase Reuters.[66] OMERS and Apax have renamed the textbook firm Cengage. The Chicago Skyway is current owned by OMERS Infrastructure, CPP Investment Board, and Ontario Teachers' Pension Plan.

Canada Pension Plan Investment Board

The Canada Pension Plan Investment Board is one of the world's largest sovereign wealth funds. The Canada Pension Plan serves as the equivalent of America's Social Security. Today its invested assets are rapidly approaching a half of a trillion dollars, and it is led by Goldman Sachs veteran, Mark

Machin.[67] Canada is paying top dollar for the first foreign-born leader of CPPIB that it aggressively recruited for the move north.[68] Machin's predecessor, Mark Wiseman, has assumed control over BlackRock's global active equity.[69] One of the CPPIB's largest investment jointly made with Ares Management was Dallas based Neiman Marcus in 2013[70] A critical expansion of CPPIB was taking over the private equity financing arm of General Electric. To earn the best return for the Canadian taxpayers it is enlisted to serve, the pension fund seeks to invest in the technologies and products of tomorrow.[71] Very noteworthy is its nearly single-minded focus on total returns on a global portfolio means it has a limited effect on Canadian capital markets. The managers are not going to be very motivated to also promote local development concerns given their pay tends to be more correlated to the fund's financial performance.

Ontario Teachers' Pension Plan Board

The Ontario Teachers' Pension Plan Board (Teachers) also ranks very high among Canadian pension funds. Before 1990 the pensions of teachers in Ontario were managed as a provincial agency. The legislature chose to spin it off as an independent private agency jointly sponsored by the provincial government and the Ontario Teachers Federation. For property investments on the west coast of the United States, Teachers has partnered with the Macerich Partnership.[72] Macerich gets its name from the combination of the founders first names: Mace Siegel and Richard Cohen. Macerich became a publicly traded REIT on the New York Stock Exchange in 1994 and is currently a component of the US S&P 500. During summer of 2018 reports surfaced that Teachers was considering possibly taking over Macerich entirely. The private equity division of Teachers is known as Teachers Private Capital.

Notes

1. Gillen, M., & Potter, P. (1998). The Covergence of Securities Laws and Implications for Developing Securities Markets. NCJ Int'lL. & Com. Reg., 24, 83.
2. Michie, R. C. (2006). The global securities market a history. Oxford University Press, 231.

3. Armstrong, C. (2001). Moose pastures and mergers: The ontario securities commission and the regulation of share markets in canada, 1940–1980. University of Toronto Press. Page 46.
4. Theresa Tedesco, C., Business Correspondent. (2003, Mar 03). TSX offshoot taking on role of national market regulator: [National Edition]. National Post.
5. Howes, C. (2002/01/24/, 2002 Jan 24). CDNX likely to benefit from new regulator: Independent body: Market Regulation Services owned by TSE and IDA: [National Edition]. *National Post.*
6. Macey, J. R., & O'Hara, M. (2005/11//). FROM MARKETS TO VENUES: SECURITIES REGULATION IN AN EVOLVING WORLD. *Stanford Law Review, 58*(2), 563–599.
7. "Recent Changes in the Regulation of Financial Markets and Reporting in Canada." *Accounting Perspectives : A Journal of the Canadian Academic Accounting Association = Perspectives Comptables : Revue de l'Association Canadienne Des Professeurs de Comptabilité.*, vol. 6, no. 1, 2007.
8. hecter, B. (2008, Jun 10). New body replaces venerable IDA; IIROC; SRO will oversee the integrity of trading. National Post.
9. Shecter, B. (2008/06/10/, 2008 Jun 10). New body replaces venerable IDA; IIROC; SRO will oversee the integrity of trading. *National Post.*
10. Anisman, Philip. "The Proposals for a Securities Market Law for Canada: Purpose and Process." Osgoode Hall Law Journal 19.3 (1981): 329–367.
11. (1967/03/01/, 1967 Mar 01). Kimber, of Ontario Agency, Chosen: KIMBER TO HEAD TORONTO BOARD. *New York Times.*
12. Anisman, P. (1981). The Proposals for a Securities Market Law for Canada: Purpose and Process. *Osgoode Hall LJ, 19*, 329.
13. Anisman, Philip. "The Proposals for a Securities Market Law for Canada: Purpose and Process." Osgoode Hall Law Journal 19.3 (1981): 329–367.
14. Piane, S. (2013). *Less Talk, More Action: Ending the Futile Debate on a Canadian Securities Regulator to Focus on Resolving the Real Issues* (Order No. 1571151).
15. Spilke, E. (2012). *Why Canada's "Costly" Securities Regulation Regime Ensures Better Decision-making.*
16. Howlett, K. (2003, Feb 19). Ottawa planning to set up 'wise persons' committee. *The Globe and Mail.*
17. Willis, A. (2021/03/31/). *Federal and provincial governments shutting down national securities regulator project, sources say: The federal Finance Department will announce as soon as Thursday it is closing the six-year-old Capital Markets Authority Implementation Organization and laying off its staff.* The Globe and Mail.

18. Pillay, S. (2003). Forcing Canada's Hand The Effect of the Sarbanes-Oxley Act on Canadian Corporate Governance Reform. Manitoba Law Journal 30, 285–314.
19. Friedman, K. B. (2008). Through the Looking Glass: Implication of Canada-United States Transgovernmental Networks for Democratic Theory, International Law, and the Future of North American Governance. Alta. L. Rev., 46, 1081.
20. Atkinson, T., & Price, C. (2014). The ontario securities commission's public interest power: The primacy of principles. Canadian Journal of Administrative Law & Practice, 27(2), 205–217.
21. Mrland, J. (2014/06/16/). *OSC refuses to throw out Conrad Black's misconduct case.* The Globe and Mail.
22. Armstrong, C. (2001). Moose pastures and mergers: The Ontario Securities Commission and the regulation of share markets in Canada, 1940–1980. University of Toronto Press.
23. Timbers, W. H., & Pollack, I. M. (1955). Extradition from Canada to the United States for Securities Fraud: Frustration of the National Policies of Both Countries. Fordham L. Rev., 24, 301.
24. Leyton-Brown, D. (1974). The Multinational Enterprise and Conflict in Canadian-American Relations. International Organization, 28(4), 733–754.
25. Alan Toulin, T. S. (1985, Oct 16). Mercantile's lifespan marked by controversy: [FIN Edition]. Toronto Star
26. Newman, P. C. (1978). The Distemper of Our Times (No. 112). McGill-Queen's Press-MQUP.
27. Thompson, D. N. (1979///Autumn). BRASCAN VS. WOOLWORTH—IT WOULD HAVE BEEN THE LARGEST HOSTILE TAKEOVER IN HISTORY. *Business Quarterly (Pre-1986), 44*(3), 69.
28. Seaton, P. (n.d.). *The Woolworths Museum.* The brass neck of Brascan. https://www.woolworthsmuseum.co.uk/1970s-brascan.html
29. ANDREW H MALCOLM Special to The New,York Times. (1979/04/24/, 1979 Apr 24). Canada's Tight Banking Ties: Intricate Links To Businesses Are Maintained A Necessary Arrangement Canada Banks Maintain Intricate Ties to Business The Role of Bank Boards. *New York Times.*
30. Keany, Sutton, & Sussman, Robert J. (1980). Securities: Commentary: The elusive definition of tender offers. (Second Circuit review: 1979–80 term). Brooklyn Law Review, 46(4), 1045–1069.
31. Best, P., & Shortell, A. (1988). The brass ring: Power, influence and the Brascan empire. Random House Canada.

32. Drummond, A. T. (1991). Securities Law Internationalization of Securities Regulation-Multijurisdictional Disclosure System for Canada and the US. Vill. L. Rev., 36, 775.
33. (March 6, 1987 Friday). The muzzled owners. The Globe and Mail (Canada).
34. Karen Howlett; (January 14, 1987 Wednesday). Canadian Tire ruling to have widespread impact. The Globe and Mail (Canada).
35. Karen Howlett; (January 14, 1987 Wednesday). Canadian Tire ruling to have widespread impact. The Globe and Mail (Canada).
36. Tedesco, T., & Shecter, B. (2016, Oct 15). 'Masters of the Universe'; Inside the Risky Strategies that have Turned Canada's Top Pension Plans into Global Investing Powerhouses. *National Post.*
37. Flavelle, D. (1999, Aug 25). Onex's Gerald Schwartz: A Formidable Dealmaker; Onex Chief Makes Bold Bid to Merge Canada's Competing Airlines Bay Street Financier has Proven Track Record. *Toronto Star.*
38. Best, A., & Mitra, D. (1997). The Venture Capital Industry in Canada. *Journal of Small Business Management,* 35(2), 105–110.
39. Wong, N. (2017). Canadian Tech Venture Capital Funding Reaches 8-Quarter High. *Bloomberg Wire Service,* Oct 26, 2017.
40. Cumming, D., Johan, S., & Macintosh, J. G. (2017). A drop in an empty pond: Canadian public policy towards venture capital. *Economia e Politica Industriale,* 44(1), 103–117.
41. Serebrin, J. (2018, Apr 25). Montreal leads in venture-capital financing: Report. *Montreal Gazette.*
42. Alberta Enterprise Corp. Makes Investment of $5 Million in Panache Ventures. (2018). *Wireless News,* March 15, 2018.
43. Mcgee, Niall. (April 15, 2015 Wednesday). Investment; Venture capital pool is Deep Now But Shows Signs Of Drying Up. *The Globe and Mail.*
44. Tami Zuckerman. (2017). *Toronto Life,* 51(2), 30.
45. Falconer, K. (2017). Venture-backed VarageSale sold to VerticalScope. *PeHUB,* Nov 9, 2017.
46. Shmuel, J. (2016, May 07). On the hunt for northern unicorns; canada's venture capital moment. *National Post.*
47. Cumming, D. & Macintosh, J. (2003). Venture-Capital Exits in Canada and the United States. *The University of Toronto Law Journal,* 53(2), 101–199.
48. Falconer, K. (2016, Apr 05). Harbourvest Canada Growth Fund Nets $375 Mln In Final Close. *PeHUB.*
49. Johan, S., Schweizer, D., & Zhan, F. (2014). The Changing Latitude: Labor-Sponsored Venture Capital Corporations in Canada. Corporate Governance-An *International Review,* 22(2), 145–161.

50. Cumming, D. & Macintosh. (2006). Crowding out Private Equity: Canadian evidence. *Journal of Business Venturing*, 21(5), 569–609.
51. Staff, T. (2017). These Investors Are Dominating Private Equity. *Institutional Investor.*
52. Milstead, D. (2020). Neiman Marcus's bankruptcy filing wipes out Canada Pension Plan's stake in the company: Luxury retailer couldn't handle the debt that CPPIB used to buy the company. The Globe and Mail.
53. Lattman, P. (2008, Dec 11). BCE Leveraged Buyout Deal Collapses. *Wall Street Journal.*
54. 8-K: GNC Holdings, Inc. (2011). EDGAR Online-8-K Glimpse, pp. EDGAR Online-8-K Glimpse, April 12, 2011.
55. Kelly, B. (2000). U. of Toronto Establishing Sub. *Pensions & Investments*, 28(5), 2-2,62.
56. Short Takes: Manulife Plans Shift From Mutual to Stock.(Brief Article). (1999). *American Banker*, 164(99), 9.
57. Canadian Insurance Firm Okays Complete Public Listing April 2000. (1999). *BusinessWorld*, 1.
58. The Year Of Living Dangerously. (2014, 06). *Financial Post Mag*, 32-3537-3941.
59. Daw, J. (2005, Jun 02). Shift in control of OMERS sparks fears of tax increase; employers, workers to run pension fund queen's park moves inflame union rivalry. *Toronto Star.*
60. (May 10, 2018 Thursday). Omers Private Equity Announces Agreement to Purchase Alexander Mann Solutions. *Thomson Reuters ONE.*
61. Kirk Falconer. (June 18, 2015 Thursday). OMERS Private Equity to acquire trucking business Kenan Advantage. *peHUB.*
62. (May 18, 2010 Tuesday). Deal Closes on the Acquisition of United States Infrastructure Corporation by OMERS Private Equity. *Marketwire.*
63. Barry Critchley. (March 09, 2000 Thursday). Constellation closes private financing: Growing software firm doesn't rule out IPO down the road. *National Post* (Canada).
64. Barry Critchley. (March 09, 2000 Thursday). Constellation Closes Private Financing: Growing Software Firm Doesn't Rule Out IPO Down The Road. *National Post* (Canada).
65. Dummett, B., & Cummins, C. (2013, Jun 11). Corporate News: Canadian Funds Take Big Stake in Cinema Chain. *Wall Street Journal.*
66. Singer, J. (2007, May 12). Thomson's Sale of Unit to Aid Pursuit Of Reuters. *Wall Street Journal.*
67. Moose in the market; The Canada Pension Plan Investment Board. (2019, January 19). *The Economist*, 430(9126), 74(US).
68. Nelson, J. (2016, May 20). CPPIB's World View: Pension Fund Taps Machin. *The Globe and Mail.*

69. Krouse, S. & Dummett, B. (2016, May 19). Canadian Pension Fund Chief to Join Blackrock; Mark Wiseman, Chief Executive of The Canada Pension Plan Investment Board, To Become the Money Manager's Head of Global Active Equity. *Wall Street Journal.*
70. Spector, Mike & Cimilluca, Dana. (2013, Sept 9). Investors are poised to pay $6 billion for Neiman.(Ares Management LLC, Canada Pension Plan Investment Board and Neiman Marcus Inc.) (Business). *The Wall Street Journal Eastern Edition.*
71. Shecter, B. (2018, Nov 21). CPPIB eyeing disruptors. *Sudbury Star.*
72. Macerich And Ontario Teachers' Pension Plan Board Expand Their Joint Venture With $535 Million Transaction. (1999, Nov 02). *PR Newswire.*

CHAPTER 8

The Consolidation and Evolution of Canadian Exchanges and Trading Networks

On March 15, 1999, all the major Canadian exchanges signed a specialization agreement giving each marketplace its own particular role. Montreal would become Canada's exclusive derivatives marketplace. Montreal's senior stock listings were supposed to be shifted over to Toronto. All of the junior listing exchanges in the West were combined into the newly formed Canadian Venture Exchange (CDNX). This served to maintain Toronto as the major center for Canadian equity trading and Montreal for exchange traded derivatives. Quebecois feared the loss of equity trading in the province, but there were also concerns in Ontario that the derivatives market assigned to Montreal or the junior listings assigned to the CDNX would prove more lucrative than the senior equity listings. Some even thought a Canadian junior exchange could one day evolve into another Nasdaq.[1] Canada's traditional exchanges all gave money to Montreal to build out its derivatives markets, and the Toronto Stock Exchange (TSE) transferred its existing options market to Montreal as well. Toronto also handed over its own junior market, the Canadian Dealer Network, to the newly formed CDNX. Montreal took over sole ownership and control of the Canadian Derivatives Clearing Corporation. The specialization agreement came with a 10-year expiration, which would later serve as one impetus for the TSX to merge with Montreal.

Both the Montreal Exchange (ME) and the Toronto Stock Exchange underwent demutualization in 2000 as part of a broader global

M. J. Szanto, *A Century of North American Stock Markets*,
https://doi.org/10.1007/978-3-032-22419-4_8

movement. From the mid-1990s to the end of the 2000s virtually all the world's major exchanges became for-profit firms. Demutualization involves converting a not-for-profit mutual firm into a for-profit company owned by the shareholders. Initial shares were granted to the exchange's seat owners and were restricted from being sold for a couple years. The TSX Group finally went public through an initial public offering (IPO) in November 2002. Converting into a publicly traded firm for the most part tends to transform exchanges from private for members-only clubs into public, dynamic, and rapidly evolving private enterprises.

The Canadian Venture Exchange

The two main exchanges that were merged to become the Canadian Venture Exchange (CDNX) were the Vancouver Stock Exchange (VSE) and the Alberta Stock Exchange (ASE). Both had very checkered histories. Forbes had once infamously labeled the VSE the "scam capital of the world." The city has often been the center of many highly speculative issues if not outright frauds. The ASE was most known for the infamous BRE-X $6 billion gold fraud. Clearly the CDNX did not come from the most auspicious origins. The Winnipeg Stock Exchange was also folded into the CDNX as well as the junior listings from the Canadian Dealer Network in Toronto and from the Montreal Stock Exchange completely consolidating the most speculative small cap listings. The absorption of the relatively tiny Winnipeg market also gave the residents of Manitoba a stake in the newly merged Canadian junior market.[2] The creation of a single national publicly traded venture market may prove to be a very ambitious and far-sighted plan on the part of Canada's stock trading establishment at least in the long run. The ambition was to create a leading incubator perhaps even for the whole world.

Unfortunately, the merger did not immediately lead to the hoped for improvements in liquidity. The dot-com crash followed by the global market downturn conspired to crush any hopes the merger offered at rapidly reviving Canada's junior equities markets. Firms like WorldCom and Enron had introduced a great deal of cynicism on the part of investors about speculative bets, and Vancouver and Alberta were always notorious for fraud and other abuses. An additional flaw of the market is it lacked the market makers or specialists found in markets like the New York Stock Exchange that can help ensure liquidity. Fortunately, part of the specialization agreement involved close collaboration between the Canadian

Depository for Securities, a wholly owned subsidiary of the Toronto Stock Exchange, and the CDNX. The CDNX also sought to expand its business by opening an office in Toronto, which required a lengthy approval process by the Ontario Securities Commission (OSC). A presence in Toronto was badly needed because much of the CDNX's business still came from western Canada, since it was the amalgamation of markets from British Columbia and Alberta. It had been hoped that recruiting the chairman of the Alberta Securities Commission, Bill Hess, as president of the CDNX would offer the revamped junior listings markets renewed credibility. Instead, Hess lasted only 2 years at the helm.[3]

At a time when the TSX's senior listings were dominated by tech high-fliers like Nortel, Blackberry, and even Bell Canada, it was only natural for the CDNX to also be heavily concentrated in technology issues. Sadly, in issues related to finance like in politics, timing can be everything. The CDNX having loaded up tech firms on the eve of the dot-com crash would lead to inevitable consequences. Continued price manipulation and fraud also helped doom the market at least in this incarnation. One example of that, Golf North Properties Inc., may have succeeded on its own merit over the long run, but its meteoric rise turned out to be fueled by boiler room-styled tactics that ripped off unaware buyers.[4] In this case the malfeasance appears to have not been the work of the company itself but the small securities firms it hired to promote its stock.[5] Blackberry board chair Jim Balsillie was able to line up the money to buy out the minority investors and take the company private, ending its misadventure with the CDNX. Golf North has managed to thrive to this day, and Balsillie is the sole owner.

Nasdaq Canada

Once again, the government of Quebec acted to foil Ontario's dominance in finance. The provincial regulators authorized Nasdaq to open a Canadian branch in Montreal likely violating the spirit of the specialization agreement. This was not an accident; Quebec Finance Minister Bernard Landry actively refused to allow the Montreal Exchange to transfer its small caps to the CDNX as already agreed upon.[6] Ultimately the listings had to be transferred, regardless of the feelings of Quebec nationalists. Montreal just lacked the depth or breadth of a market for equity listings.[7] If they were not moved as promised, the companies were ready to take matters into their own hands and jump ship.[8] Once the deal was officially announced, it was revealed that Quebec had been secretly negotiating with Nasdaq for a Montreal affiliate even before the specialization agreement was signed, which raised doubt about whether Quebec even acted in good faith.[9] The domestic political angle was an effort to please the Quebec nationalists; the hope was to upend Toronto's growing financial dominance. Nasdaq Canada ended up becoming another casualty of the dot-com crash. Nasdaq's growing financial losses forced it to give up on its ambitious plans for a truly global marketplace.[10]

Derivatives Trading in Montreal

Opposition to the shift of derivatives trading to Montreal also occurred in Toronto. The first talk of having all large cap stock trading done in Toronto and the derivatives exclusively traded in Montreal had first occurred in 1986.[11] Yet opposition still existed after the deal had been concluded in 1999. Toronto-based independent futures traders were some of the early vocal critics of the deal.[12] The Montreal Stock Exchange's original motivation was to carve itself out the role of being the "Chicago" of Canada by controlling the increasingly lucrative derivatives market, which would make up for the fact that Montreal's equity market was already in irreversible decline.[13] The strongest opposition in Quebec to the specialization agreement came from the powerful Caisse de dépôt that represented the largest pension fund in Quebec. The bet on derivatives turned out to be a very smart bet, except it would later turn out to be a moot point due to the subsequent 2008 merger between the Toronto Stock Exchange and the Montreal Stock Exchange.

Ultimately the Toronto Stock Exchange decided to outright acquire the CDNX by purchasing the members' seats and integrating its operations into those of the TSX. This illustrates how an exchange can transform from a mutual company through a sale to an already demutualized exchange. The government of Quebec may not have been pleased with this change, but the traditional rival stock markets were no longer viable. The shift of the listed equities business to Toronto was an irreversible process. The CDNX was rebranded the TSX Venture, and the combination allowed unified marketing and trading functions. While the venture market has not exactly been smooth, at least the TSV is now fully backed by one of the world's largest exchanges. The total consolidation of equity trading by the Toronto Stock Exchange also meant the Ontario Securities

Commission is more than ever the primary regulator for stock trading in Canada.

TSX Venture Exchange

The TSX Venture Exchange considers itself the world's only public trading venture exchange. Raising capital through this market is considerably cheaper for start-up management teams and founders than the traditional private venture capital (VC) market. On the other hand, absent from this setup is the guidance and help from experienced VC firms. The listing requirements for the CDNX are looser than the London Stock Exchange Alternative Investment Market and without the adult supervision provided by the Nominated Advisors (Nomads) approved by the London Stock Exchange regulators. The CDNX certainly is a Laissez-faire buyer-beware environment. The benefit provided by having this market is providing an easy outlet for firms to have a publicly traded exchange for shares that can be used as currency for mergers and to incentivize employees. By listing on a major exchange, shareholders are provided with a secondary market as well as liquidity. The ultimate goal would be for listings on the TSX Venture Exchange to graduate to the regular Toronto Stock Exchange. The percentage of graduations from the TSX Venture Exchange have been impressive, but the performance of the broader venture market leaves a lot to be desired. Most of the trading should be relegated to insiders with a special interest in the firms as well as in highly sophisticated traders and investors. While decades ago, the Securities and Exchange Commission (SEC) worked desperately to track down boiler rooms on Bay Street in Toronto imploring their Canadian colleagues to act, the TSX Venture Exchange remains a place a little bit too friendly for today's Jordan Belfort. As recently as in 2011 the US Securities and Exchange Commission had to file fraud charges against Bozidar (Bob) Vukovich previously investigated by the Vancouver police for unrelated stock manipulation and fraud. The TSX Group purchased the CDNX in 2001.

Demutualization and Consolidation

At the turn of the millennium, the Toronto Stock Exchange was beset by challenges. Technical glitches were all too common with what was already an entirely electronic exchange. Liquidity was threatened by the captive investment dealers owned by the big banks as a result of the Little Bang handling the trading in house. Competition for liquidity and order flow had already become a problem with the emergence of alternative trading systems (ATS).[14]

Most of today's stock exchanges globally had begun their existence as essentially private trading clubs. Max Weber was one of the earliest to study the sociology of financial exchanges including stock markets:

> *The oldest of the exchanges were gatherings on an open, occasionally enclosed, plaza. Later most, and now probably all, of these gatherings take place in great closed halls. From early on, it was naturally necessary that there be a body or instrument that could exercise a "policing" over the market. It is just the same now, for everywhere there are "commissioners" appointed who uphold the basic order of the place. In addition, however, the older market- and exchange-organizations also had a member—and the overwhelming majority of exchanges, including the German ones, still have it—whose special purpose it was to facilitate the absolutely most expeditious conclusion of business: the "broker."*[15]

The Montreal Stock Exchange and the Toronto Stock Exchange had retained this clubby atmosphere through the end of the 1990s, though the market for the "seats" that earned membership into the exchange had by then become a hot commodity. The very first equity bourse to demutualize was the Stockholm Stock Exchange in 1993. By the turn of the century, Amsterdam, the Australian Exchange, Helsinki, Hong Kong, London, Montreal, and Toronto had all demutualized.[16] This began a nearly 20-year process of the vast majority of major exchanges around the world transforming from not-for-profit mutual firms into a for-profit company owned by the shareholders. Initial shares in the Toronto Stock Exchange were granted to the exchange's seat owners and were restricted from being sold for a couple years. Subsequently, the TSX Group finally went public through an IPO in November 2002. The Montreal Exchange did not have to raise any money through its listing. Between its lucrative monopoly on Canadian derivatives trading and its sizable stake in the Boston Options Exchange (BOX), the ME was just rolling in dough.[17] The purchase of the Boston Stock Exchange by the Nasdaq allowed the Montreal Exchange to consolidate its ownership of the Boston Options Exchange due to Nasdaq's planned divestiture of the options exchange.[18] The BOX became the first foreignly owned financial exchange in the United States. Converting into a publicly traded firm for the most part tends to transform exchanges from private for members only clubs into public, dynamic, and rapidly evolving private enterprises. At the end of 2007, the TSX and the Montreal Exchange entered into an agreement to merge. All approvals were gained, and the process was completed in 2009. Canada ended the last decade with one absolutely dominant exchange.

Canadian Securities Exchange

However, the TMX Group would not be left without any rival. The Canadian Securities Exchange (CSE) was formed in 2003 to compete with the TSX for equity listings and trading making it the first new stock exchange in Canada in 70 years. It was originally known as the Canadian Trading and Quotation System Inc.[19] The parent company of the CSE is the CNSX. The CSE has served an important trading venue for American cannabis companies. While the TMX Group allows for Canadian cannabis firms to trade on both its senior and junior markets, it currently prohibits American cannabis firms, as a result of not wanting to run afoul of American federal law.[20] The largest shareholder in this upstart exchange was the Urbana Corporation.[21] In 2013 the CSE obtained further financing from the Dundee Corp with Dundee CEO Ned Goodman becoming Deputy Chairman of the exchange.[22] Ned Goodman has parlayed a background in geology combined with business as well as work in various mining ventures into a multibillion-dollar investment empire. The strong mining presence in the Canadian Securities Exchange made him a natural investor and partner. Goodman had worked with Edper, then founded Beutel Goodman with Austin Beutel, and then moved on to found his Dundee Corporation.[23] In 2016, the exchange created the CSE Composite Index which includes the 73 largest firms listed on the exchange.[24] In 2017 the exchange launched the subset CSE25 Index representing the 25 companies with the largest market capitalizations.[25]

While the CSE share of market trading and listed companies is absolutely tiny compared to the dominant TMX Group, it offers needed competition in the Canadian equity landscape.[26] It can be hard to find companies listed on the CSE not in some way related to the cannabis industry. At first look Glance Technologies is a somewhat novel payment system. With a little bit more study it becomes clear this is yet another marijuana-related firm. One of Glance Technologies' main partners is Cannapay Financial Inc. However, Glance has also expanded its payment applications to one that targets Chinese consumers visiting North America.[27] In 2016, the exchange created the CSE Composite Index which includes the 73 largest firms listed on the exchange.[28] Also CNSX markets launched Pure Trading as one of Canada's alternative trading systems for trading issues listed on the TSX and the TSX-V. In 2013, this off exchange trading was incorporated into the main CSE platform allowing for one system for all equity trading.[29] The CNSX partnered with Nasdaq to provide software both for the CSE and for Pure Trading.[30] Pure Trading is a lit market, meaning that its trades are visible to the public. As discussed elsewhere in the book, institutional investors often need to put through their orders in dark markets, to prevent others from unfairly profiting from their trades at the expense of big institutions including mutual funds and pension funds.

The Alpha Group

The Alpha Trading Systems was created in 2007 by Canadian banks to serve as an alternative trading platform to the TMX Group. Ironically, it was the CEO of the TMX Group, Tom Kloet, who would criticize Alpha's ownership by Canadian banks as returning "back to the days when trading venues and exchanges were owned by select participants with conflicted interests and an ability to work in concert."[31] Kloet would ultimately find himself signing off on a merger with Alpha Group and a takeover of the whole TMX Group by a bank-led consortium. With the Alpha Group, TMX would gain access to Canada's most powerful dark pool for trading. Dark pool markets allow institutional investors to make large trades without publicly revealing their identity or size of orders preventing traders from exploiting that information at the institution's expense. The Alpha Group had competed with the TMX Group for trading on stocks listed on the TSX Venture Exchange as well as the senior listings on the Toronto Stock Exchange.[32] While the newly reconstituted Alpha Exchange remained as an alternative trading exchange within the TMX Group, the CEO of the TMX, Tom Kloet, quickly shut down the TSX Alpha Exchange as an alternative venue for actual listings. Efficiency was gained by consolidating the IT operations of both the TMX Group and the TSX Alpha Exchange.[33]

Chi-X Canada

One of the earliest alternative trading systems in Canada was Chi-X Canada. Instinet created Chi-X Canada in 2008. Japan's Nomura had purchased Instinet back in 2006.[34] Instinet chose to use the global brand Chi-X for its Canadian ATS building utilizing systems it had built around the world.[35] The original Chi-X Europe platform was launched by Instinet in 2007. Its name reflected chi being the 22nd letter in the Greek alphabet representing the crossing of trades through buyers and sellers. Major institutional investment players including Goldman Sachs, Morgan Stanley, Lehman Brothers, UBS, and Citadel joined as minority investors in Europe Chi-X.[36] Chi-X Japan was launched in 2010.[37] Chi-X Australia launched in Australia in 2011 with Bank of America, Morgan Stanley, and Goldman Sachs all quickly taking minority stakes in the ATS.[38] In 2016 J.C. Flowers acquired Chi-X Australia and Chi-X Japan. In 2016 Nasdaq acquired Chi-X Canada. This gave Nasdaq control of the Chi-X and CX2 platforms and access to roughly one fifth of equity trading in Canada.[39] Tal Cohen, the former CEO of Chi-X Global Holdings, became senior vice president and head of North American Markets at Nasdaq.

Proposed TMX Merger with London Stock Exchange

Following the global phenomenon of securities exchanges undergoing demutualization, there was a wave of transnational mergers. In the last decade newly privatized exchanges started to look toward mergers as a way to gain synergies and grow. It was felt that the global nature of the markets required strong international connections. One of the biggest transnational stock exchange mergers was the combination of the New York Stock Exchange with Euronext. In order to seal the deal, Euronext had to outbid a rival bid by Deutsche Börse. In the same year as the NYSE joined up with Euronext, the Nasdaq combined with Nordic-based OMX Group. While the Nasdaq is largely an American exchange, the OMX runs exchanges in Sweden, Denmark, Finland, Iceland, and the Baltic states. Nasdaq hoped for cost savings from realized synergies and to gain a foothold in Europe particularly in the Nordic and Baltic region as well as in Eastern Europe.

The TMX Group was almost drawn into this groundswell with what was billed as a merger of equals with the London Stock Exchange Group. However, local Canadian financial institutions were able to defeat this plan with a rival bid with their consortium which they named the Maple Group. The Maple Group was successful in taking over the TMX Group and joining it with Canada's clearing firm for stock trading, the Canadian Depository for Securities, as well the main rival exchange, the Alpha Trading systems. The Canadian Depository was originally created in 1970 as a central clearinghouse for Canadian securities trading and has greatly expanded and evolved ever since.

The rise of cross border exchange mergers would naturally lead to a move for the Toronto Stock Exchange to tie up with another exchange internationally. After two very large transformational transatlantic exchange mergers involving the New York Stock Exchange and the Nasdaq, the London Stock Exchange and the TMX Group seemed a very natural fit. The merger with the London Stock Exchange Group (LSEG) would have been a merger of equals. A very similar merger attempt was made around the same time between the Australian Stock Exchange (ASX) and the Singapore Exchange (SGX). The deal was announced on October 24, 2010. While ultimately it also failed, it helps shed light on the overall global environment affecting the attempted merger between the LSEG and TMX. In both cases economic nationalism may have played a key role in thwarting the deal. The SGX deal was ultimately rejected by Australian Treasurer Wayne Swan on April 8, 2011.

The Maple Group

The Maple Group Acquisition Corp was formed by local Canadian financial institutions to thwart the effort by the London Stock Exchange to take over the TSX. It represented four of Canada's largest banks: CIBC, NBF, Scotiabank, and TD Bank. The Bank of Montreal and Royal Bank of Canada were unable to join because they were already advising for the London Stock Exchange deal.[40] This effort was initially opposed by the exchange because the management felt that being part of a larger more global enterprise would be more beneficial for long-term growth.[41]

The British Columbia Securities Commission (BCSC) sought special assurances that the integrity of the Toronto Venture Exchange would be preserved by maintaining TMX board members with experience in venture capital. Its leverage was ultimately limited by the fact that securities commissions of Quebec and Ontario as well as the federal authorities had already approved the deal. The Maple acquisition of the TMX was combined with a simultaneous merger with the Canadian Depository for

Securities Limited (CDS) and the Alpha Exchange, a rival alternative exchange. The TMX Group had tried to buy CDS previously, but the banks had worried it would give the exchange too much pricing power. Perhaps, the fact that the banks were the sponsors of the takeover vehicle allayed the banks' concerns over potential exchange excesses. Still to this day the CDS clears for all the stock exchanges in Canada including the Canadian Securities Exchange and the Alpha Exchange. It is the second largest central counterparty in the world.

The battle for control and ownership of the TMX Group was vigorously fought between the conglomerate of Canadian financial institutions and the TMX management and their would-be partners at the London Stock Exchange. Pitted against TMX CEO Tom Kloet was former Montreal Stock Exchange CEO Luc Bertrand as head of the Maple Acquisition Group.[42] The London Stock Exchange countered by offering TMX Group and London Stock Exchange shareholders a juicy dividend intended to both financially reward investors while at the same time reassuring them of the future viability and strength of the merged entity.[43] An appreciation of the share price, the main currency of the proposed merger, also acted to sweeten the deal, but in the end it was not enough. Realistically, the London Stock Exchange could not match the financial strength of the vast majority of major financial institutions in Canada put together. One would think combining Canada's dominant stock and options trading group with its largest trading rival would face a steep hurdle from the Canadian Competition Bureau, but it was ultimately approved with little restrictions.[44]

The Maple Group's initial bid was considered hostile, because the TMX Group's management was ostensibly committed to the merger with the London Stock Exchange Group. Given that bid was hostile, the Maple Group had to comply with TSE bylaws requiring that no one investor own more than 10% of the exchange stock. They did this by expanding to include the largest Canadian pension funds: the Caisse de dépôt et placement du Québec, the CPPIB, and the Ontario Teachers' Pension Plan.[45] The London Stock Exchange merger plan was defeated when the required 2/3 vote of shares in support was not forthcoming. The final technical element of the Maple Group deal was that the merger had to be done as a two-part transaction. Since the Maple Group was newly formed in Canada, it was not registered with the US Securities and Exchange Commission. Given the large component of American ownership, American securities laws had to be respected, which prohibited the Maple Group from making a broad securities offering under multijurisdictional disclosure system (MJDS). The share component of the offering to the shareholders of the TMX Group would have to be issued by the TMX Group itself making it a two-step merger. The deal largely left the TMX Group Management unchanged, with CEO Tom Kloet left in charge of presiding over the newly consolidated exchange while bringing in Luc Bertrand as chairman of the board.

The name of the winning bidder for the TMX Group, the Maple Group, strongly suggested economic nationalism as a motive as was the case for the defeat of the SGX's bid for the ASX. In the case of Australia, it was the Australian national regulators that defeated the bid. In fairness, suspicions that the Singapore Exchange was using their own inflated stock to purchase a far larger exchange on the cheap were not without merit. The success of Maple led to the Canadian banks and major financial institutions growing their control and influence over the TMX Group. Further by acquiring the smaller rival Alpha Exchange and the Canadian Depository for Securities in the same transaction, they strengthened the horizontal monopoly represented by the TMX Group while also at the same time creating an element of vertical integration as well.[46] What is noteworthy about the TMX case is the creation of the Maple Group was initiated by Canadian Banks and then expanded to other major domestic financial institutions. These were powerful vested interests that had a strong motive in preserving the status quo. Further their success ensured that they would maintain a dominant role in the control of today's TMX Group and by extension the Canadian securities markets.

NEO Exchange

Canada's newest exchange is the Aequitas NEO Exchange now owned by the Chicago Board Options Exchange (CBOE). Aequitas is derived from the Latin word for fairness, and neo is the Greek word for rebirth. The major shareholders of this new exchange are Barclays, BCE (Bell Canada), CI Investments, IGM Financial, OMERS, and RBC Dominion Securities.[47] The Neo Exchange is built on the software platform MillenniumIT owned by the London Stock Exchange Group.[48] MillenniumIT was a Sri Lankan firm that the LSEG had acquired back in 2009.[49] The NEO Exchange uses its own proprietary methods to foil the abuses of high-frequency trading by creating speed bumps and has implemented a designated market maker program to provide listed companies guaranteed liquidity. The goal is to level the playing field between investors and predatory high-frequency traders.[50] The TMX Group has responded with its own plan for implementing speed bumps, but the Aequitas NEO Exchange claims that the changes being enacted at the TMX actually favor the high-frequency traders at everyone else's expense.[51] By being registered as a securities exchange NEO was able to quickly gain the listings for a number of major exchange-traded funds. NEO's first dual listed stock was Nobilis Health Corp. Nobilis had previously delisted from the TSX and was traded exclusively on the NYSE. Now it is traded on both the TSX and the NYSE, allowing Canadian investors the opportunity to buy shares of the firm on a local market. Like the CSE, the NEO Exchange is also very open to American cannabis companies despite the current ambiguity with American law.

Taking on the TMX Group's near monopoly of exchange-based trading can be an uphill struggle in some ways reminiscent of Nasdaq's early struggle with the AMEX and the NYSE, but without the backing of the powerful regulators found in the United States. Aequitas had filed a complaint with Canada's Competition Bureau over the onerous terms for receiving TMX trading data.[52] Canada lacks the national market system that Congress and the SEC worked to build allowing all exchanges to operate on a level playing field.[53] The Canadian Securities Administrators has responded by issuing rules to promote greater fairness in the distribution of exchange data and is based on the principles of the American National Market System as created by Congress and implemented by the SEC.[54] The cofounder of Aequitas, Jos Schmitt, was also the founder of the Alpha Exchange, which was absorbed by the Maple Group and is now wholly owned and controlled by the TMX Group under the name, the TSX Alpha Exchange. RBC, one of the only major Canadian financial institutions not to back the Maple Group acquisition of the TMX Group, had enlisted Schmitt to create the Aequitas Neo Group.[55] In 2018, the Neo Exchange became the first Canadian exchange with a bitcoin fund, First Block Capital Bitcoin Trust, though only for accredited investors.

While the restructured TMX Group is more than ever the dominant player in securities trading in Canada, the two still independent Canadian stock exchanges, the Canadian Securities Exchange and the Neo Exchange, offer the potential for additional competition and innovation. Moreover, a great deal of the trading volume is handled by alternative trading systems within Canada, outside of traditional exchanges. Today Canada retains a very vibrant dynamic equity trading market. In some ways no other country offers the opportunities for very small companies to list. Numerous

American companies have listed on the TMX TSX Venture market in Vancouver, because their only alternative would be to trade on the over-the-counter market in the United States. Jos Schmitt has formed the Aequitas NEO Exchange which has not only gained traction for trading but also won business for actual stock listings.[56] The NEO Exchange uses proprietary methods to foil the more abusive practices of a high-frequency trading, which may be of benefit in American markets as well.[57] In 2022 the Chicago Board of Options Exchange purchased NEO, which owned NEO Exchange and NEO Connect. The following year, the CBOE brought both NEO and its MATCHNow trading platform together under its subsidiary CBOE Canada. MATCHNow had originally been formed in 2008 and was purchased by the CBOE in 2020. MATCHNow had been formed to provide a dark pool for institutional investors by Triact, a Canadian subsidiary of Investment Technology Group. Today CBOE Canada has 260 listings primarily Exchange-Traded Fund (ETFs), Canadian depository receipts, and Special Purpose Acquisition Companies (SPACs).

Many Canadian retail customers have special accounts created for investing in American stocks separate from the ones used for domestic listings. These accounts are so common, many Canadians use cross-listed firms as a cheap method for currency conversion by buying the shares on the American exchange in American dollars and selling them on the TSX Group in loonies or vice versa. This is known as Norbert's Gambit.[58] Norbert Schlenker was an investment advisor in British Columbia who founded his own firm, Libra Investment Management. Canadians depend on the larger American equity market to better diversify their investments. Further the integration of North American manufacturing particularly after the Auto Pact means many Canadians can only invest in their own employer by entering the American equity market.

Canada's trading markets have become transformed by alternative trading systems (ATS) and novel ways to handle order flow. There are seven major alternative trading systems in Canada: Bloomberg Tradebook Canada, Chi-X Canada/CX2 Canada, Instinet Canada Cross (ICX), Liquidnet Canada, MATCHNow, Omega ATS, and TMX Select.[59] Chi-X Canada has been acquired by Nasdaq and is being converted to a stand-alone exchange intended to compete head on with the TMX Group.[60] One challenge for Canadian equity markets is the United States allows broker dealers to pay for order flow, while that practice is banned in Canada. This leads to a competitive disadvantage and stock market orders being rerouted through the United States.[61] Gaining regulatory approval for ATS was a long struggle in Canada. When Bloomberg Tradebook and Instinet first arrived, they were only allowed to be used for transactions on foreign securities. Instinet was blocked from buying a seat on the Toronto Stock Exchange. Now that the TSE has gone entirely electronic, the distinction between exchanges and alternative trading systems has really gotten blurred.[62] The Canadian Securities Administrators led by the OSC sought to bring competition to the marketplace by allowing alternative trading systems.[63] The entrance of alternative trading systems in Canada has also grown concerns about market fragmentation.[64] The existence of dark alternative trading systems also reduces overall market transparency.[65] There are concerns alternative trading systems would skim the least informed orders increasing the costs of trades on the exchanges, but some research actually suggests this is not the case.[66]

Instinet, previously discussed in the book, finally announced its plan to offer trading in Canadian securities in 2006.[67] The launch of Instinet Chi-X Canada opened up the Canadian market to electronic trading networks just as Instinet had done for the United States in 1968.[68] Instinet Senior Vice President Tal Cohen oversaw the launch of this alternative trading market in Canada.[69] In 2008 the parent firm of the Canadian Securities Exchange beat Chi-X Canada by creating Pure Trading, the first ATS with a fully continuous auction market.[70] Chi-X Canada, however, quickly captured large shares of the trading in major TSX listings.[71] In 2016 Nasdaq acquired Chi-X Canada.[72] This purchase gave Nasdaq significant access to a large chunk of Canadian equity order flow.[73] Nasdaq went on to hire Tal Cohen to run its North American equities business.

Notes

1. November 26, 1999 Friday). Toronto The Loser: TSE at Risk from Exchange Restructuring, Brokers Say. *National Post (Canada).*
2. Adam Killick. (May 03, 2000 Wednesday). Bill Clears Way for Winnipeg to Join CDNX: Asset Transfer. *National Post* (Canada).
3. Brent Jang. (November 30, 2001 Friday). Hess Faced an Untenable Task as First CDNX President. *The Globe and Mail* (Canada).
4. McNish, J. (2002, Apr 15). Golf North delisting another bogey for CDNX. The Globe and Mail.
5. Richard Blackwell. (February 13, 2001 Tuesday). Montreal Exchange To Shift Equities; Will Transfer Rump Of 130 Stocks To CDNX; Upon Approval By Quebec Regulators. *The Globe and Mail* (Canada).

6. Peter Kennedy British Columbia Bureau. (November 18, 1999 Thursday). CDNX To Take Cue From Investors And Diversify BROAD BASE President William Hess Says The Canadian Venture Exchange Plans To Prosper By Acting As An Incubator For Oil And Mining Juniors, As Well As Emerging Information Technology And Biotechnology Firms. *The Globe and Mail* (Canada).
7. Shearmur, R. (2001). Financial Flows and Places: The Case of Montreal. Canadian Public Policy / *Analyse De Politiques*, 27(2), 219–233.
8. Gibbens, Robert with files from John Schreiner and Ian McKinnon. (1999, Nov 12). Quebec's small-cap exchange faces problems, warns industry liquidity issue; ASE president says 'we'll have to live with it'. *National Post*.
9. Séguin, Rhéal. (April 28, 2000 Friday). How Quebec played the markets and won; Minister describes Montreal Nasdaq coup. *The Globe and Mail* (Canada).
10. Marotte, Bertrand. (September 20, 2003 Saturday). Nasdaq nixes plans for separate Canadian stock exchange; Phase 2 of 'Nasdaq North' cancelled; Quebec-style operation envisaged for B.C. *The Globe and Mail (Canada)*.
11. Montreal Exchange may shift stock trading to Toronto Says it would still deal in bonds, options, futures: [Final Edition]. (1996, Jan 23). *Toronto Star*.
12. Exchange reforms to include Quebec guarantees Efforts to ease fears come as Toronto futures traders push to halt move to Montreal: [National Edition]. *National Post*.
13. Greenwood, J. (1999, Mar 15). ME braces for political firestorm: Modelling after Chicago: Plan is to get out of equities and focus on derivatives: [National Edition 1]. *National Post*.
14. Macklem, Katherine. (May 01, 2000 Monday). Nightmare on Bay Street: Systems break down, customers are fed up, new competitors are clawing at the door and there's a trading horror lurking upstairs. No wonder the Toronto Stock Exchange is going to hell. *National Post* (Canada).
15. Weber, M. (2000). Stock and Commodity Exchanges [Die Börse (1894)]. *Theory and Society*, 29(3), 305–338.
16. Azzam, I. (2010). Stock exchange demutualization and performance. *Global Finance Journal*, 21(2), 211–222.
17. Willis, A. (2006, Dec 02). Montreal exchange walks tightrope to IPO. *The Globe and Mail*.
18. Gibbens, R. (2007, Oct 03). MX plans to boost stake in Boston Options Exchange: [Final Edition]. The Gazette.
19. Critchley, B. (2003, Mar 07). CNQ promises a better market: Cook aims to have new stock system running by summer: [National Edition]. *National Post*.
20. George-Cosh, D. (2017, Sep 14). Banking & finance: Exchange looks at marijuana stocks. *Wall Street Journal*.

21. Marketwire. (2013). Urbana Corporation Acquires Final Tranche of CNSX Markets Inc. Benzinga.com, p. Benzinga.com, March 21, 2013.
22. Press release: Dundee corporation joins urbana corporation in making a strategic investment in CNSX markets inc. (2013, Sep 30). *Dow Jones Institutional News.*
23. Hanley, W. (2005, Apr 23). Nothing but value: Beutel, Goodman has the discipline to stick to its core strategy: [Toronto Edition]. *National Post.*
24. CSE Reports Record Trading Volume, Total Listings as Growth Continues in 2015. (2016, January 13). *Internet Wire.*
25. Canadian securities exchange launches CSE25 index. (2017, Sep 19). *Investorideas.Com Newswire.*
26. Malakian, A. (2011). Canada Rising. *Waters*, 26–30.
27. Glance technologies announces joint venture targeting mobile payment app for chinese tourists. (2017, Apr 26). *Canada NewsWire.*
28. CSE Reports Record Trading Volume, Total Listings as Growth Continues in 2015. (2016, January 13). *Internet Wire.*
29. Kilburn, F. (2013). CNSX, Pure Prep Unified Data-Trading System. *Inside Market Data, 29*(7), 1–13.
30. Malakian, A. (2011, 07). Canada Rising. *Waters*, 26–30.
31. Erman, B. (2010, April 22). Alpha Group aims to win status as full stock exchange. *Globe & Mail* [Toronto, Canada], p. B1.
32. Andrew Willis. (April 19, 2010 Monday). TSX, Alpha exchange fire; Exchanges battle for junior stock trading. Breaking News from *globeandmail.com*
33. Stafford, P. (2012). TMX to close Alpha listings business. *FT.Com*
34. David Turner in Tokyo and Norma Cohen,in London. (2006). FT.com site: Nomura to buy broker Instinet: [1]. *FT.Com*
35. Instinet trading system renamed Chi-X Canada. (2007, Dec 06). *The Globe and Mail.*
36. Cohen, N. (2008, Jan 11). Instinet brings new investors to Chi-X: [LONDON 1ST EDITION]. *Financial Times.*
37. Chi-X Japan Eyes Full Nikkei 225 Rollout. (2010). *Wall Street Letter*, 2.
38. Whipp, L. (2011). Five financial firms invest in Chi-X Global. *FT.Com*
39. Nasdaq to Acquire Chi-X Canada. (2015, Dec 08). *Dow Jones Institutional News.*
40. Cummins, C., Dummett, B., & Caroline, V. H. (2011, May 30). Canadian rivals see round 2 in TMX spat. Wall Street Journal (Online).
41. Dummett, B. (2011, May 21). TMX opposes bid to trump LSE deal. Wall Street Journal.
42. Cummins, C., Dummett, B., & Caroline, V. H. (2011, Jun 01). Canadian Rivals See Round 2 in TMX Spat. *Wall Street Journal.*

43. Simon, B. (2011). LSE and TMX add dividend to boost merger bid. *FT.Com*
44. Gray, J. (2011, Jul 01). High hurdles face Maple bid from competition watchdog. *The Globe and Mail.*
45. King, M., Barnea, A., & Qayyum, F. (2014). The Maple Acquisition of the TMX Group Inc., Richard Ivey School of Business Case Collection.
46. Bolger, R. (2012). Canada TMX Sale Wins Competition Bureau Approval. *International Financial Law Review.*
47. Madhavi Acharya-Tom Yew. (March 21, 2015 Saturday). New Aequitas NEO Exchange poised for start of trading. *thestar.com*
48. United states: Aequitas Neo Exchange Goes Live in Canada Using Full Suite Of Millenniumit Trading Technology. (2015, Apr 21). *Asia News Monitor.*
49. (October 20, 2009 Tuesday). MillenniumIT acquired by London Stock Exchange. *Daily Mirror* (Sri Lanka).
50. D'Antona, J., Jr. (2015). Ontario securities commission approves aequitas neo exchange. *Traders Magazine.*
51. TMX reforms need reform. (2014, Dec 23). *National Post.*
52. Dummett, B., & McNish, J. (2015, Dec 08). Upstart picks regulatory fight with toronto stock exchange operator; aequitas innovations alleges TMX group charges excessive stock-quote data fees. *Wall Street Journal.*
53. Aequitas aims to break the virtual canadian market data monopoly. (2015, Dec 08). *Business Wire.*
54. Ontario Securities Commission. (2016). CSA Notice of Approval-Amendments to National Instrument 23–101 Trading Rules and Companion Policy 23–101CP to National Instrument 23–101. Trading Rules.
55. Castaldo, J. (2015, 04). A Kinder, Gentler Stock Market. *Canadian Business*, 88, 44–49.
56. Trichur, R. (2015, Mar 27). Upstart Canadian Exchange Aims for Market Share of 20% in 4 to 5 Years; Aequitas NEO Exchange Plans to Compete with Toronto Stock Exchange. *Wall Street Journal.*
57. Shecter, B., & Pett, D. (2014, Nov 29). Flash Boys Hit Speed Bump; High-Frequency Traders Meet a Market Match - for now. *National Post.*
58. Bortolotti, Dan. "Norbert's Gambit: A Better Way To Buy U.S. Dollars." *MoneySense* [Toronto] 2011: 10. Web
59. Foley, & Putniņš. (2016). Should we be afraid of the dark? Dark trading and market quality. *Journal of Financial Economics*, 122(3), 456–481.
60. Nasdaq to Acquire Chi-X Canada, Providing Access to Canadian Market. (2015). *M & A Navigator, M & A Navigator*, Dec 14, 2015.

61. Dummett, B., Trichur, R., & Hope, B. (2014). Canada Regulator Looks into Rerouting of Stock-Trade Orders to U.S.; Regulator Concerned About Impact of Loss of Order Flow. *Wall Street Journal* (Online).
62. Aroline, V. H. (1999, Jul 03). Canadian regulators move to allow ATSs. *The Gazette.*
63. Whittington, L. (2001, Aug 17). Alternative trading systems get green light; securities regulators to announce rules for electronic exchanges. *Toronto Star.*
64. Jaworski, A. (2008, March 3). Canada Stepping Out of U.S. Shadow New ATSs likely to bring market fragmentation, opportunities. *Securities Industry News.*
65. Kwan, Masulis, & Mcinish. (2015). Trading rules, competition for order flow and market fragmentation. *Journal of Financial Economics*, 115(2), 330–348.
66. Barclay, M., Hendershott, T., & McCormick, D. (2003). Competition among Trading Venues: Information and Trading on Electronic Communications Networks. *Journal of Finance*, 58(6), 2637–2665.
67. Canada: Instinet Competes In Canada. (2006, Dec 05). *The Ottawa Citizen.*
68. TSX Faces Competition As Instinet Plans Launch. (2007, Jun 11). *The Gazette.*
69. Elizabeth. (2007). Northern Exposure: Canadian Exchanges Dabble In The US And Gear Up For Competition On Every Front. *The Investment Dealers' Digest: IDD.*
70. Pure Trading: Pure Trading Enhances Offering With Connection To TNS. (2008, Feb 14). *M2 Presswire.*
71. Hi-X Canada ATS Limited; Chi-X Canada Surpasses Five Million Shares In Trading Volume. (2008, Oct 02). *Computer Technology Journal.*
72. Nasdaq To Acquire Chi-X Canada. (2015, Dec 08). *Nasdaq OMX's News Release Distribution Channel.*
73. Steele, A. (2015, Dec 09). Global Finance: Nasdaq Agrees To Buy Chi-X's Canada Unit. *Wall Street Journal.*

CHAPTER 9

A Survey of Representative Canadian Companies

Despite Canada's relatively small size, its capital markets are incredibly dynamic and robust. There are many venture capital firms in Canada, though none of them are particularly large. There are rarely big hits or unicorns, start-ups valued more than a billion dollars, but overall Canada is not a superpower in venture capital. The two largest Canadian technology firms have not left investors with very happy endings. Nortel was never funded by venture capital but rather was a creation of the North American Bell System created in the nineteenth century. Canadian law did not allow foreigners to own patents forcing Bell Canada to create Northern Electric as an alternative hardware provider to Western Electric, AT&T's main supplier.[1] Due to Canada's immense size, Northern Electric became a world leader in fiber optics technology. Nortel Networks was created as a result of a transformative merger with California-based Bay Networks.[2] The tech bubble at the end of the 1990s led to Nortel getting terribly overextended and then crashing hard. An accounting scandal last decade ultimately was the final blow to Nortel, though some argue the total flight of investors and creditors may have been more the result of guilt by association with major cases of fraud like WorldCom and Enron.[3] Blackberry's demise ultimately came as a result of Apple's revolutionary iPhone. In an effort to boost the outlook for domestic startups, Canada has numerous government programs on the federal and provincial level to subsidize and support the venture capital industry.

M. J. Szanto, *A Century of North American Stock Markets*,
https://doi.org/10.1007/978-3-032-22419-4_9

The S&P/TSX 60 is the most widely used index of Canadian large cap companies. Generally, its components are the firms with the largest market valuations though adjustments are made to keep the industries balanced. Another reason it does not always include all of Canada's largest companies is inclusion is based on free float rather than just total market valuation. Canadian equity markets compete with American markets for both listings and order flow. Trades for various issues that originate in Canada can often be routed across the border to American exchanges and alternative trading systems. Very famously brothers Peter and Edward Bronfman were able to take control of Canadian-Brazilian power company Brascan in large part by purchasing shares on the American Stock Exchange flouting the rules of the Toronto Stock Exchange.[4] The TMX Group also aggressively competes with American exchanges for listings. Many major firms like Cameco and Bombardier are cross listed on the Toronto Stock Exchange (TSX) and the New York Stock Exchange (NYSE) or the Nasdaq. Recently, IMAX and Lululemon chose to delist from the Toronto Stock Exchange believing that being listed on a major American exchange was sufficient for their funding and liquidity needs.[5] The Toronto Stock Exchange has also established itself as one of the largest marketplaces for mining and commodity issues and aggressively competes with the Australian Stock Exchange in this sector. Additionally, the Toronto Stock Exchange has sought to become an alternative North American destination for technology firms from countries like China and Israel, and the TMX Group has opened up a special office in Israel as a result.[6]

Crown corporations created by the Federal Parliament or the provincial legislatures play a large role in the Canadian economy. Canada's largest railroad company, Canadian National (CN), and its largest airline, Air Canada, were both originally federal crown companies before they were privatized. Bombardier's world leading regional jet division, Canadair, was also a crown company it purchased. The world's largest uranium mining firm, Cameco, was formed through the merger of two crown corporations that were also privatized. Canada's world leading reactor technology, known as Canada Deuterium Uranium (CANDU), was also developed by federally owned companies. SNC-Lavalin Inc. purchased this technology from Atomic Energy of Canada Limited (AECL). The world's oldest operational reactor outside of the United States at Chalk River is still owned by AECL. As historically the only supplier of vital medical radioisotopes for North America, its planned shutdown has posed a huge challenge to clinics and hospitals throughout the United States and Canada.

Mining and Energy

Canada's largest component of its economy is resource based including mining and energy. The Toronto Stock Exchange vies with the Australian Stock Exchange as the world's primary place to list mining and energy issues from all over the world. The largest mining firms are Teck Resources, Rio Tinto Alcan, Vale Canada, First Quantum Minerals, and Cameco.[7] Rio Tinto is the largest aluminum mining company in the world, but it is now fully owned by British Australian giant Rio Tinto which is only traded in London, New York, and Australia. Canada is often best known for its hydrocarbons and petrochemicals. In 2023 Teck Resources fought off a hostile takeover from Switzerland's Glencore but in 2025 chose to merge with Anglo American. The prospects of the merged company look grand given the massive global electrification drive. Tech Anglo will be based in Canada, but the primary listing is planned to be at the London Stock Exchange (LSE). Institutional investors have been lobbying to keep Tech Anglo in the S&P/TSX 60. Like its economy Canadian stock exchanges tend to be heavily focused on commodities, mining, and energy. Agnico is listed on both the New York Stock Exchange and Toronto Stock Exchange. It is a major producer of silver, nickel, cobalt, as well as gold. Its name is the combination of the symbols representing the chemical elements of silver, nickel, and cobalt. Nutrien was another Canadian firm listed on both the NYSE and the TSX. Nutrien is the largest potash producer in the world and was formed by the merger of Potash Corporation and Agrium in 2018. Potash was originally a crown corporation established by the government of Saskatchewan in 1975 in an effort that led to the effective nationalization of the industry by the provincial government. It was listed on the Toronto Stock Exchange in 1989 as part of a government led privatization. Nutrien is also second in nitrogen fertilizers.

Alimentation Couche-Tard

The largest Canadian company by market cap is Alimentation Couche-Tard, a colossal international operator of convenience stores. Amazingly, the company is relatively new and began as a single convenience store in Laval, Quebec, in 1980. Alimentation is one of the greatest Canadian rags to riches stories.[8] The company founder, Alain Bouchard, had lived in a mobile home as a child after his father's company had gone bankrupt. He expanded Alimentation in 1985 by purchasing eleven existing

Couche-Tard stores. The company is listed on the Toronto Stock Exchange having previously been listed on the Montreal Stock Exchange before Montreal was converted into a purely derivative exchange. Notably, this company is not cross listed on any non-Canadian exchange. The share structure of the firm remains controversial because Bouchard and his four sons effectively control this company through a special class of shares with greater voting rights. However, many other family-founded firms long kept this power from Disney to Ford to the Bancroft's Dow Jones before they sold to News Corp.

Alimentation Couche-Tard's presence in America began with the purchase of Circle K in 2003 for $804 million. Alimentation Couche-Tard Inc's largest American purchase of San Antonio-based CST Brands was completed in 2017 for $4.4 billion. CST Brands was the retail operations of Valero Energy Corporation. The CST stores have been rebranded as Circle K. This acquisition made the company the largest owner of convenience stores in North America. Circle K convenience stores are still smaller in number than the leader in the United States, but Couche-Tard leads in North America overall. Couche-Tard stores in English Canada have been rebranded as Circle K. In 2024 Couche-Tard made a failed attempt to acquire the Japanese owner of 7 Eleven convenience stores. Today Couche-Tard's official brand name outside of Quebec is Circle K.

Cameco is the largest publicly traded uranium producer. The largest investor in Cameco is Toronto-based investment manager Beutel, Goodman & Company Ltd. The second largest holder of Cameco stock is Quebec public pension manager Caisse de depot et placement du Quebec. Cameco was the result of the merger of two crown corporations, Saskatchewan Mining Development Corporation and Eldorado Nuclear Limited, in 1988. Cameco had its initial public offering (IPO) on the Toronto Stock Exchange in 1991 and is now also listed on the New York Stock Exchange. Cameco has uranium mines in Kintyre and Yeelirrie, Australia. The Kintyre uranium deposit was originally discovered by a mining company now owned by Rio Tinto. It was bought by a joint venture between Cameco and Mitsubishi. Cameco acquired the Yeelirrie uranium project from BHP Billiton in 2012. Due to a 6-year slump in uranium prices, Cameco considered closing its mines in the United States which are rather small. However, Russia's invasion of Ukraine in 2022 helped revive the uranium and nuclear markets globally. In 2022 Cameco purchased Westinghouse Electric Company in conjunction with Brookfield Renewable Partners. Today Westinghouse boasts nearly half of the nuclear reactors around the world utilize Westinghouse designs, and the company is playing a leading role in the world's nuclear renaissance.

Other than Cameco, the other major publicly traded firm involved in Canada's nuclear industry is SNC-Lavalin which bought CANDU from the crown corporation Atomic Energy of Canada Limited (AECL). CANDU reactors, a uniquely Canadian technology, are specially supported by Cameco. CANDU reactors generally operate on unenriched uranium unlike most reactors that require low enriched uranium, but the design allows for many alternative fuels including plutonium and thorium due to its use of heavy water. CANDU reactors are particularly resilient to meltdowns, but their production of plutonium and tritium necessary for advanced thermonuclear warheads also raises weapons proliferation concerns. Canada may no longer lead the world in nuclear technology generally, but it is still the world's largest producer of uranium which powers the entire nuclear industry. China is a major customer of Canadian built reactors.[9] In 2023 SNC-Lavalin changed its name to AtkinsRéalis. Atkins was the name of a storied British engineering and construction firm SNC acquired in 2017, and Réalis is intended to honor the firm's Quebecois roots. Atkins continues to be exclusively listed on the Toronto Stock Exchange, though it also trades on the over-the-counter (OTC) pink market in the United States.

Despite never having developed nuclear weapons, Canada is a power in terms of nuclear technology due to being a leading designer and manufacturer of nuclear reactors. The first nuclear reactor built outside of the United States was built in Chalk River, Ontario, in 1945. The Chalk River Laboratories was started in 1944 partly in support of joint Anglo-American efforts with the Manhattan Project. Today the largest producer of radioisotopes in North America is Ontario Power Generation, a crown corporation entirely owned by the provincial government. Hopefully, that will one day be the only type of nuclear power anyone needs to be concerned with. The military significance of Canada's uranium reserves is mixed, because Canadian law prohibits its sale for military use leaving the US military potentially reliant on existing military stockpiles. The US military relies on domestic stockpiles of highly enriched uranium built up decades ago to build nuclear warheads and power nuclear-fueled warships. While Canada is a vital supplier of uranium for the United States, domestic American politics has challenged the previously close relationship. The US Commerce Department has opened up an investigation of US uranium imports threatening to expand the Trump Administration's trade war to uranium.[10]

Canadian companies are very commonly cross listed particularly on American exchanges. There are numerous advantages to cross listing for Canadian firms. Firms listed on American exchanges gain access to greater liquidity and a far wider group of investors. Exchanges like the New York Stock Exchange provide greater credibility but also exposure. Trading on major American exchanges can actually build branding with Americans for Canadian firms that either have significant business in the United States or at least may want to expand south at some point in the future. This poses certain challenges and threats to the TMX Group. As previously stated, listings in the United States can allow alternative trading systems to engage in trading or routing practices prohibited in Canada by the exchange, CIRO, or the provincial securities administrator. Potentially more seriously the TMX Group could lose substantial liquidity if trading heavily shifts to a major American exchange. Occasionally, Canadian firms may also be listed on the London Stock Exchange and the Australian Exchange. This reflects Canada's position in the Anglosphere and the Australian Stock Exchange's position as a major competitor to the TMX Group in mining and energy firms. Canada's close cultural, linguistic, and economic ties to the United States are both a blessing and a curse for the TMX Group. The Toronto Stock Exchange basically teeters between existing as merely a regional exchange and functioning as a major global exchange. In the past there may have been the potential for the TMX Group to one day even become a peer competitor with the New York Stock Exchange and the Nasdaq, but now its exchanges have been largely relegated to function as a regional exchange or at best serve small niches not well served by truly global exchanges.

Shopify

The most successful tech start-up in Canada since Nortel and Research in Motion, now unfortunately both defunct, is Shopify. Shopify was founded by German immigrant Tobias Lütke. Lütke combined his lifelong passions for computers and snowboarding to found his first company, Snowdevil, an e-commerce sites for snowboards. He and his partners used the platform created for Snowdevil to launch Shopify in 2006, a commercial e-commerce platform now used even by large companies like Whole Foods and Tesla. In 2022, Lütke joined the board of lead crypto site Coinbase and is one of the richest people in Canada.

Banking Stocks

Canadian banks Toronto Dominion, Royal Bank of Canada (RBC), and Bank of Montreal (BMO) are cross listed on the TMX and the NYSE. While Toronto Dominion (TD) was formed by the merger of two nineteenth-century Canadian banks in 1955, it did not get listed on the NYSE until 1996. That same year, TD bought American discount broker Waterhouse, beginning what would become a major American presence. BMO had been the first Canadian bank to list on the NYSE in 1994. RBC was the first Canadian bank to be allowed to conduct corporate underwriting in 1991 and in 1995 was listed on the NYSE. Over the past 30 years TD and BMO in particular have greatly expanded their US footprint. In 2006 TD acquired American discount broker Ameritrade but then sold it to Schwab in 2020. Today TD bank still has over 6 million banking customers in the United States.

Railroads

Both of Canada's largest railroad companies are cross listed on both the Toronto Stock Exchange and New York Stock Exchange. While Canadian National was a crown corporation until it was privatized, Canadian Pacific (CP) was granted a private corporate charter shortly after the British North America Act created the modern state of Canada. Canadian National also played a major role along with Bell Canada and Canadian Pacific in building out Canada's telecommunications infrastructure. While both Canadian National and Canadian Pacific are today important components of the S&P TSX 60, they have taken on a very North American character through mergers and acquisitions. The core to the current business of both Canadian National and Canadian Pacific is intermodal terminals that fully exploit the container revolution. These combine continental railroad networks with both major trucking and shipping lines.[11] Like other North American railroad companies, both heavily utilized telegraphs to maintain business operations. Between the vital role telegraphs played in operations and the useful placement of railroad track, CN and CP became major players in the telegraph industry. They jointly formed Canadian National-Canadian Pacific Telecommunications (CNCP Telecommunications) which became one of Canada's largest long distance telephone companies.

Canadian National

Canadian National (CN) is Canada's largest railroad and was a crown corporation that was privatized in 1995. Canadian National was originally formed after World War I after the federal government salvaged the company from the lines of a series of bankrupt companies. The move to take it public came in large part as a response to railroad deregulation in the United States. In 1999 a proposed merger with the Burlington Northern Santa Fe Corp. was thwarted by the US Surface Transportation Board. No subsequent major merger between US and Canadian railroads had occurred until Canadian Pacific joined with Kansas City Southern in 2023. Vancouver is Canada's busiest container port. Vancouver relies heavily on Canadian National to deliver cargo to the rest of Canada as well as major US cities like Chicago. Consequently, much of the federal government's investment in the port infrastructure is geared toward improvement in track facilities in partnership with Canadian National and Canadian Pacific.[12]

CN's largest investor had been Microsoft's founder Bill Gates through his Cascade Investments vehicle. Bill Gates' stake in CN had approached Canada's limit of 15% for foreign stakes in domestic railroad companies, but in 2018 the Canadian Parliament raised the limit to 25%.[13] Gates has been reducing his holdings in CN in recent years. In 1997 Canadian National Railroad augmented its American presence by replacing its Chicago intermodal terminal with a far larger one.[14] CN's subsequent purchase of Illinois Central in 1998 greatly expanded the firm's reach into the United States.[15] The Illinois Central Railroad traced its history to the first US federal land grant for a railroad completed back in the 1850s. In 2001 CN made another major Midwestern purchase, the Wisconsin Central Limited, a railroad previously spun off from Canadian Pacific.

By 2007 Canadian National faced an increasing traffic jam in Chicago, its largest transportation hub in the United States.[16] To bypass the Chicago metropolitan area CN purchased the railway subsidiary of US Steel, whose lines ring the urban area.[17] CN had previously tried to reroute some of its freight over lines owned by Omaha-based Union Pacific.[18] Some of this traffic started to interfere with traffic in Chicago suburbs including Franklin Park.[19] Canadian National's new routes in Chicago's northwestern suburbs posed challenges for municipal regional transit authority Metra, resulting in the agency raising its concerns with the Federal Surface Transportation Board.[20] CN's history in Chicago dated back to 1924 when it launched passenger service.[21] By 1927 the Canadian government was already purchasing stock in Midwestern railroad firms to ensure access to the strategically located region.[22]

Via Rail Canada was created as the passenger subsidiary of Canadian National and then spun off as its own crown corporation. Canadian Pacific's passenger lines were also transferred over to be owned by Via Rail in 1978.[23] Canada's major airline Air Canada was also still a crown corporation. One avenue for privatizing crown corporations was the Canada Development Corp. which precludes share ownership by foreigners.[24] By 1985 the federal government sought to privatize both Air Canada and Canadian National. Brian Mulroney had come into office inspired by Margaret Thatcher and Ronald Reagan to privatize the Canadian government's sprawling investments represented by crown corporations as well as equity investments in major firms through the Canadian Development Corporation.[25]

Canadian Pacific

Unlike CN, Canadian Pacific was privately incorporated shortly after Canadian Confederation. It was awarded a corporate charter by the Canadian Parliament in 1880. The construction of the railroad was a key condition by British Columbia for joining the Canadian Confederation. It was a venture heavily subsidized by the federal government intended to help link Canada with the newly admitted province of British Columbia. The company was intended to help thwart Yankee incursions into Canada's Pacific region. Ironically, Canadian Pacific has in recent years sought mergers with major American railroad companies. An aggressive investment by Bill Ackman's Pershing Square Capital Management in 2011 is widely credited as the impetus for a major restructuring of the firm that drastically boosted efficiency and profitability of the firm.[26] Bill Ackman's investment turned out to be one of Pershing Square's most profitable investments. In 2022 Pershing Square once again invested in Canadian Pacific Kansas City (now merged with a US railroad.). While Canadian National and Canadian Pacific are two of the most important listings on the Toronto Stock Exchange, today they are both very much North American transportation giants.

Bausch Health

One of the most prominent firms in Canada is Bausch Health. Bausch was actually founded as International Chemical and Nuclear Corporation in California by a Yugoslavian immigrant, Milan Panic. Panic was a champion Yugoslavian cyclist who defected to the United States in 1956. Its blockbuster drug was hepatitis treatment, Ribavirin. In July 1992 Panic became prime minister of Serbia.[27] The firm's financial transactions always appeared enigmatic, and the firm would be caught up in Balkan politics. ICN struggled to regain a plant in Serbia that had been seized by forces under the control of Serbian strongman, Milosevic. Galenika Pharmaceuticals, formerly a Yugoslavian state-owned business, had always been an acquisition made under very unusual if not suspect means.[28] After getting elected as prime minister of Serbia, Galenika got hit by US sanctions aimed at Serbian President Milosevic. Sexual harassment scandals in 2002 played a role in ending his leadership of ICN Pharmaceuticals. In one case, not only did he engage in a pattern of sexually harassing the firm's director of employee relations, Debra Levy, he fired her only after fathering her child. He settled that case for $3.5 million.[29] With mounting accusations from numerous women, serious concerns from the SEC about financial and reporting irregularities, and a floundering share price, it should be no surprise shareholders were beginning to panic.[30]

After the founder of the company was ousted, it was renamed Valeant Pharmaceuticals. A merger with Canadian pharmaceutical firm Biovail allowed Valeant to gain the more favorable tax structure up north.[31] The merger created a large Canadian pharmaceutical giant while leaving Valeant CEO Michael Pearson in place to head the amalgamation.[32] Biovail came with its own baggage having been subject to many regulatory actions and investigations by the Ontario Securities Commission and the US Securities and Exchange Commission.[33] Biovail's founder, Eugene Melnyk, was a Ukrainian immigrant who lives a flashy lifestyle quite reminiscent of Milan Panic. Melnyk owns the National Hockey League team Ottawa Senators and waged a campaign to block Blackberry co-CEO Jim Balsillie's efforts to obtain his own National Hockey League (NHL) franchise in Canada.[34] In 2007 Melnyk stepped down from leadership of the firm and reached a settlement with the Ontario Securities Commission.[35] Melnyk later had to pay over a million dollars' worth of fines to the US Securities and Exchange Commission for what effectively amounted to fraud and faced 5-year bans from senior leadership positions in publicly traded firms imposed by both the Ontario Securities and Exchange Commission and the SEC.[36] Biovail was also targeted by a false information campaign led by Stephen Cohen's S.A.C. Capital in order to manipulate the stock in favor of the fund's short positions.[37] Biovail had been the largest publicly traded pharmaceutical company in Canada.

The firm took a new name, Bausch, after one of its most successful American pharma acquisitions. The name Valeant was dropped after scandals over abusive and exploitative price rises. Bausch had been taken private by Warburg Pincus in 2007. Valeant's nearly $9 billion dollar highly leveraged deal to take over Bausch + Lomb was fueled by historically low interest rates.[38] Bausch + Lomb is very famous for its leading contact lenses lines, but its acquisitions of Advanced Medical Optics (AMO) had made it a leader in refractive and cataract surgery. AMO's acquisition of VISX and IntraLase brought the market leaders for excimer and femtosecond lasers into the AMO fold. Bausch Health conducted an IPO for its Bausch + Lomb eye health subsidiary in 2022 but still retains a controlling ownership interest.

Magna

Canada's largest manufacturer, Magna International, is also cross listed on both the Toronto Stock Exchange and the New York Stock Exchange. Austrian immigrant Frank Stronach established Multimatic in 1957 as a tool and die company. A contract with General Motors in 1960 gave the firm its start in the auto industry. The United States Canada Auto Pact of 1965 opened up the US car industry to Canadian manufacturers, and in 1969 the firm merged with publicly traded Magna. A 1977 capital restructuring introduced two classes of shares cementing a dominant voting control for Stranach.[39] In 1981 Magna focused its operations on car production. Magna is part of an auto manufacturing ecosystem that we find in Ontario as a result of the North American Auto Pact to a far greater extent than the telecommunications hardware center that revolved around Nortel at its height.

Today Magna has four divisions: body exteriors and structures, power and vision, seating systems, and complete vehicles. With his purchase of Steyr, Stronach had gone back to his Austrian roots in order to expand into building entire cars.[40] Magna often places its car parts plants adjacent to factories where the cars are assembled by Magna customers. Magna's complete vehicles division will actually produce an entire car in house. Already the Magna Steyr division in Austria is the world's largest contract auto manufacturer. It continues to produce key models for Mercedes, BMW, and Toyota. With a view to the future Magna has partnered with Beijing Automotive Industry Holding Co to create a new electric car joint venture.[41]

Oleg Deripaska

In 2007 the now notorious Russian oligarch Oleg Deripaska took a controlling stake in Magna in a transaction known as Project Pearl.[42] Deripaska was able to gain control using Stronach's super voting shares. Stronach's collusion with Deripaska's ambitious goal of becoming a dominant force in the global auto market was intended to allow the eccentric founder to better monetize his control of the firm.[43] This illustrates the danger with this capital structure popular in Canada. If you do not want Oleg Deripaska or worse Putin himself taking over your country's major firms, encouraging good corporate governance practices might be a good idea. That year Magna unsuccessfully launched a bid backed by Toronto-based private equity firm Onex Corp., and New York-based Blackstone Group to take over Chrysler. Deripaska hoped to use Magna's technology to create a world-class Russian car giant. However, the financial crisis led to Oleg Deripaska having to surrender his stake in the firm back to founder Stronach. Oleg Deripaska has recently become famous in the United States as convicted felon Paul Manafort's main financial backer. As Magna rapidly expanded during the past couple decades, the firm's corporate governance was viewed very unfavorably by investors since Stronach's special shares retained all control of the firm for him for which he richly exploited. In 2010 it ultimately cost $870 million to buy out Stronach's controlling stake in Magna.[44]

Bombardier

Another major cross listed Canadian manufacturer is Bombardier. Bombardier reflects the truly global challenges faced both by Canadian manufacturing and by Canadian equity markets. Historically Bombardier was a snowmobile manufacturer, but its purchase of government-owned airplane manufacturer Canadair in 1986 left it also a major player in aerospace. Bombardier's regional jet segment in particular is a powerful example of how a Canadian crown corporation can be privatized and become a global leader. Bombardier was able to transform the Canadian government's money-losing investment in regional jets into a global leader in the segment.[45] Stiff competition from Brazil's Embraer has resulted in an effective duopoly in regional jets represented by Bombardier's CRJs and Embraer's ERJs. The C Series was the most ambitious project for Bombardier, but it quickly ran into financial trouble. The Canadian government ended up bailing out the endeavor after a billion-dollar investment from Quebec proved inadequate to keep the company afloat. Ultimately it would be Airbus that saved the C Series by funding the plane as a new joint venture with Airbus the majority owner. The marriage between Airbus and Bombardier was cemented by the threat of trade tariffs on the part of the United States. Embraer responded by forming a new partnership with Boeing, but the deal was thwarted by the COVID pandemic and Boeing's financial problems stemming from flaws in the 737 Max. Over the past 20 years Bombardier has also heavily invested in the production of modern trains resulting in the company becoming a major supplier to rapid transit systems around the world. The C Series which directly challenged the domination of the jumbo jet category by Boeing and Airbus was a step too far even with bailouts by Quebec and the Canadian federal government. Today the C Series is nearly entirely owned by Airbus and sold as the A220. Mitsubishi purchased the CRJ program which had only been rivaled by competitor Embraer in the 1990s and early 2000s for regional jets.

Restaurant Brands

Restaurant Brands is the result of the merger of iconic Canadian donut and coffee chain Tim Hortons with Miami-based Burger King. Back in 2001 UK Liquor giant Diageo picked up Burger King. Diageo's investment went bad resulting in it having to offload BK to a group of private equity groups led by Texas Pacific Group.[46] Once the fast-food chain and the markets recovered, the buyout group was able to recoup much of their money through a successful IPO in 2006. Burger King was picked up by Brazilian American private equity firm 3G Capital, in a deal that became one of the most successful leveraged buyouts (LBO) in recent years.[47] The majority shareholder 3G Capital is the private equity firm that originally purchased Burger King in an LBO transaction. Warren Buffet's Berkshire Hathaway helped finance the merger and also maintains a significant stake in the combined company. Critics described this deal as a tax inversion intended to save paying money owed on capital gains in the United States by fleeing to more favorable tax laws in Canada.[48] The deal brought together an American fast-food giant with an iconic Canadian brand.[49] The power of the combination and the tax advantage is reflected by Buffett previously passing up on acquiring Burger King.[50] Canada's Onex had already bought BK's distribution service division back in 1992.[51]

Recently some Canadian firms have bypassed Canadian exchanges to list only on an American bourse demonstrating that the TMX will have to fight to keep its position in Canadian listings while at the same time trying to boost international issues as well. One such company women's yoga apparel chain, Lululemon, chose to delist from the TSX in 2013 leaving Nasdaq as its exclusive trading venue. Lululemon was founded in Vancouver 1998 as a yoga apparel brand fortuitously at a time that yoga was beginning to explode. Lululemon is considered to be the firm that if not pioneered athleisure, it at least revolutionized the category. The COVID shutdowns really boosted the entire athleisure category, which for a while rocketed Lululemon stock into a leading performer. To a large extent Lululemon's action appeared to be aimed at reducing costs with the firm claiming that the TMX Group offered insufficient liquidity to make its Toronto listing worthwhile, when it was also listed on the Nasdaq.[52] Lululemon was viewed by many to be outside of the TMX Group's perceived strengths in banking, mining, and energy. At the same time, the firm also announced that its CEO Christine Day was also leaving, leaving the firm at a time of turmoil that clouds any analysis of its decision to abandon the TSX market or its immediate effects.[53] The TMX Group has a scarcity of financial listings due to the highly concentrated nature of Canadian banking and finance, while the media and telecom sector is a surprisingly large component of the TSX exchange business in terms of market valuation and trading volume.

Imax

Even more recently, in 2015 Imax also chose to delist from the Toronto Stock Exchange and rely solely on its listing on the New York Stock Exchange.[54] This was a symbolic blow the TSX, given the iconic role in Canadian cinema that Imax has played. Imax is an absolutely iconic Canadian firm. *Tiger Child*, the first Imax film, was shown at Expo'70 in Osaka, Japan. The producer of *Tiger Child*, Roman Kroitor, is also considered one of the founders of Imax. The first permanent Imax theater was installed in Ontario Place in Toronto in 1971. Today this cinema company uses the digital light processing technology from Texas Instruments. In

1994 a somewhat struggling Imax was taken over in an LBO transaction orchestrated by Wechsler, Gelfond, and investment banking firm Wasserstein Perella & Co. for only $80 million.[55] Three months later Imax had its IPO on Nasdaq and Toronto Stock Exchange. Imax celebrated its tenth anniversary on the Nasdaq on June 10, 2004.[56] Seven years later Imax moved its American listing to the New York Stock Exchange demonstrating the very competitive nature of American stock listings.[57] Imax is currently the 31st largest industrial firm on the New York Stock Exchange by valuation.[58] The loss of the Lululemon and Imax listings was a tough blow for the Toronto Stock Exchange.[59] Two factors may deter Canadian firms from abandoning the local markets: a domestic listing can be viewed as a matter of patriotism, and the requirements and hurdles to obtain a listing on a major America exchange are typically going to be even more stringent than the Toronto Stock Exchange. Many firms are not going to find the additional costs of a domestic listing that burdensome.

The TMX Group has not obtained the type of global status that once seemed possible. Thwarting the merger with the London Stock Exchange left the TMX without strong ties overseas, and US stock exchanges have only grown in global dominance. US federal laws against cannabis left many American cannabis firms only with the option of listing in Canada, and both the main TSX exchange and the TSX Venture Exchange have had some traction in attracting listings from places like Israel and Asia. However, Canada still has a strong and large economy and can offer an attractive alternative for capital formation in the future. Listing in Canada offers a hedge against regulatory, currency, and even immigration uncertainty in the United States. Canada's independence from both the United States could conceivably offer advantages for stock listings and trading comparable to how many Caribbean islands are favorable places for establishing trusts and even bank accounts. Knowledge and familiarity with Canadian exchanges and their listings offer North American investors and traders the opportunity to look beyond just the NYSE and Nasdaq for profit-making opportunities.

Notes

1. Rens, J. G. (2001). Invisible Empire: A History of the Telecommunications Industry in Canada, 1846-1956. McGill-Queen's Press-MQUP.
2. Morrison, S. (1999, Apr 07). Nortel Strategy Convinces The Doubters: Its Move Into Data Networking Appears To Be Paying Off, Writes Scott Morrison: Financial Times.

3. Bagnall, J. (2012, May 10). How Review was Done Remains a Riddle; And the Trial May be Unable to Solve It. The Ottawa Citizen.
4. Davidson, J. (1979, May 01). Edper buys 3,276,400 Brascan on Amex. The Globe and Mail.
5. Kiladze, T. (2015, Mar 03). Can We Call a Truce in the Trader-TMX war? The Globe and Mail.
6. Q3 2017 TMX Group Ltd Earnings Call - Final. (2017, Nov 10). Fair Disclosure Wire.
7. Robertson, G., Dixon, G., Jang, B., Avery, S., & al, e. (2013, 06). Rankings By Industry. Report on Business Magazine, 76.
8. McCann, J. (2002, Jan 01). Sucking Up Profits: How Did Alain Bouchard Take The Lowly Convenience Store And Turn It Into A Retail Juggernaut That Pulled In Almost $2 Billion Last Year? Hint: By Realizing That Blue Ice Can Bring In A Lot Of Cold Cash. National Post.
9. SNC-Lavalin Signs An Agreement In Principle For A Joint Venture With China National Nuclear Corporation & Shanghai Electric Company. (2016, Sep 22). Canada NewsWire.
10. Swanson, A., & Plumer, B. (2018, Jul 19). U.S. Inquiry into Uranium Imports May Signal New Front in Trade War. New York Times.
11. Putzger, I. (2000). Intermodal Innovation: Canada's Railways Are Investing Big In Short-Haul Intermodal Technologies. Canadian Transportation Logistics, 103(1), 34.
12. Canada: The Government of Canada invests in transportation infrastructure for the Port of Vancouver in British Columbia. (2018, May 18). Mena Report.
13. Wingrove, J., & Tomesco, F. (2017, May 16). Canada hikes ownership limit for bill gates-backed CN rail. Bloomberg Wire Service.
14. CN Inaugurates New Gateway Intermodal Terminal at Harvey, Illinois - The "Hub Within The Hub". (1997). Business Wire, p. 5161127.
15. Burke, J. (1998, February 16). CN Takes IC. Traffic World, 253(7), 17.
16. Deveau, S. (2007, May 24). Canadian National Railway has Chicago Hangups; Rail Congestion. National Post.
17. Miller, J. P. (2007, Sep 27). Canadian National To Buy EJ&E; $300 Million Deal Eases Urban Routes. Chicago Tribune.
18. Schmeltzer, J. (2004, Nov 27). Diverting Rail Freight Around City May Be Just The 1st Move. Chicago Tribune.
19. Lan To Unsnarl Chicago Rail Hits Snag In Suburbs (2008). Washington, D.C.: NPR.
20. Wronski, R. (2008, Mar 24). Metra Spars With Railroad Over Line Use. Chicago Tribune.
21. C. & N. W. Canada Through Service. (1924, Feb 29). Wall Street Journal.
22. (1927, Aug 25). Canadian National Acquires Stock. Wall Street Journal.

23. Romain, K. (1978, Sep 30). Via Rail Takes Over Passenger Services. The Globe and Mail.
24. Anderson, R. (1979, Nov 21). Government May Have Way to Sell Corporations. The Globe and Mail.
25. MacDonald, L. I. (1985, Aug 14). Petro-Can Fuels Crown Company Policy. The Gazette.
26. Owram, K. (2016, Aug 05). CP an Ackman Win, No Matter How You Keep Track. National Post.
27. Gomez, J. M. (1992, Jul 03). Founder's Leap To Politics Could Benefit ICN Pharmaceuticals: Milan Panic's Departure Could Calm Waves He Made With Financial Community. And His Flamboyant Style Could Serve Him Well As A Yugoslavia Peacemaker, Opening More Doors For The Firm. Los Angeles Time.
28. ICN Seeking To Reclaim Yugoslavia Plant; Pharmaceuticals: Firm Reportedly Will Invest up to $50 Million in Factory Taken Over by Milosevic. (2000, Oct 10). Los Angeles Times.
29. White, R. D. (2002, Jun 13). ICN Chief Milan Panic Resigns. Los Angeles Times.
30. Lublin, Joann S. and Rhonda L. (2000, Apr 06). The In Crowd: ICN CEO Milan Panic Does Quite Nicely When It Comes to Pay; Critics Say a Look at the Company's Board Explains Why. Wall Street Journal.
31. Norman, J. (2010, Sep 29). Valeant Closes Merger Move To Canada. Orange County Register.
32. Prashant. (June 23, 2010 Wednesday). United States: Drugmaker Biovail to Buy Valeant in $3.3 Billion Deal. TendersInfo.
33. Biovail Reports Significant Improvements in Corporate Governance. (2005, May 05). Business Wire.
34. Warren, K. (2009, Aug 21). Senators Owner Melnyk Fires Back At Balsillie; RIM Chief 'Willing To Say Anything To Buy Franchise'. National Post.
35. May 18, 2007 Settlement Agreement Between Mr. Eugene Melnyk and The Ontario Securities Commission. (2007, Jun 22). Canada NewsWire.
36. Shecter, B. (2011, May 06). Melnyk Banned From Boardroom For Five Years; Deal On Sanctions. National Post.
37. Lampf, lipkind, prupis & petigrow announces $4 billion class-action lawsuit by biovail shareholders filed against SAC capital, steven A. cohen, gradient analytics, banc of america securities and B of A analyst david maris. (2006, Mar 24). Business Wire.
38. WSJ Blog: Valeant's Bausch & Lomb Buy Another Debt-Fueled Deal. (2013, May 27). Dow Jones Institutional News.
39. Lilley, W. (2006). Magna cum laude : how Frank Stronach became Canada's best-paid man. McClelland & Stewart.

40. Magna steyr debuts to automotive community. (2001, Mar 05). PR Newswire.
41. Magna's parts: The magna empire comprises seven units, each run by a company veteran. (2002, 09). National Post Business,46.
42. Nicolas, V. P. (2007, Jul 31). Some Magna Shareholders Wary of Deal; Voting on Aug. 28; Russian Billionaire To Share Control With Stronach. National Post.
43. Keenan, G., & McNish, J. (2007, May 11). How An Oligarch Got A Grip On Magna. The Globe and Mail.
44. Gray, J., & Keenan, G. (2010, Aug 18). Ontario court approves magna's controversial stronach buyout. The Globe and Mail.
45. Sheila McGovern of, The Gazette. (1989, Apr 01). New jet means 3,000 jobs: Bombardier. The Gazette.
46. Adamy, J. (2006, May 19). Burger King IPO Climbs 2.9%, Lacking Sizzle of Rivals' Debuts. Wall Street Journal.
47. Schaefer, S. (2015, Nov 02). M&A Flashback: 3G Capital's Whopper of a Buyout. Forbes.
48. Ferdman, R. A. (2014). Burger King Could Save A Whopping Amount of Money by Moving to Canada. The Washington Post.
49. Erman, B. & Strauss, M. (2014, Sep 17). The Path to a Sweeter Deal. The Globe and Mail.
50. Buffett Scotches Burger King Idea. (2002, Nov 27). Financial Times.
51. Noble, K. (1992, Apr 14). Canada's LBO King Bites into Burger King Onex Buys Arm of U.S. Fast-Food Chain. The Globe and Mail.
52. WSJ Blog: For Lululemon, TSX Delisting is a Bottom-Line Move. (2013). Dow Jones Institutional News, Jun 11, 2013.
53. Shaw, H. (2013, Jun 11). Lululemon Begins Search for New CEO; Company Will Delist from TSX, Stay On Nasdaq. National Post.
54. IMAX Corporation Announces Voluntary Delisting from Toronto Stock Exchange. (2015, Jan 12). Canada NewsWire.
55. (October 2002). Gelfond Richard And Bradley Wechsler Of Imax Corp.: A Really Big Show. Institutional Investor.
56. IMAX Corporation Celebrates 10th Anniversary Of Nasdaq Listing; Opens Nasdaq Stock Market. (2004, Jun 10). Canada NewsWire.
57. PRESS RELEASE: IMAX Corporation To List Shares on the New York Stock Exchange. (2011, Jan 31). Dow Jones Institutional News.
58. Stock review: Imax Shares Post Best Month in Five Months. (2019). Melbourne: News Bites Pty Ltd.
59. Kiladze, T. (2015, Mar 03). Can We Call a Truce in the Trader-TMX War? The Globe and Mail.

CHAPTER 10

Telecommunications and the Media in Canada

One of the most dynamic sectors on the Toronto Stock Exchange (TSX) has been telecommunications. Canada's telecom sector is entirely dominated by four giants: BCE (Bell Canada), Telus, Rogers Communications, and Shaw Communications. Currently Canada's media world is also heavily concentrated among three leaders: Bell Media, Rogers Media, and Corus Entertainment (spun off from Shaw Communications but still controlled by Shaw family). I also spend some time discussing key firms that helped shape these media giants. The bulk of the stations and programming for today's Corus Entertainment comes from media assets built up by Israel Asper's Canfield. I trace the roots of the three major private broadcast networks in Canada: CTV (Bell Media), CityTV (Rogers Media), and GlobalTV (Rogers). I also discuss the history of Chum Limited due to its role in the launch of the CityTV Network and most of Bell Media's cable specialty channels. Chum Limited is also significant in launching the careers of many of the key figures in Canada's telecom and media world like Moses Znaimer. The founder of Cantel went on to create Sirius Satellite radio in the United States after selling to Rogers. I also segue into how America's satellite radio wars last decade played out in Canada.

Canada's telecommunication infrastructure has always been world leading and pioneering. The inventor of the telephone Alexander Graham himself lived most of his life in Canada. As one of the largest countries in

M. J. Szanto, *A Century of North American Stock Markets*,
https://doi.org/10.1007/978-3-032-22419-4_10

the world, but also sparsely populated, Canada was one of the big adopters of microwave towers to link the nation's telephone, radio, and television networks together.[1] This revolutionary technology transmitted audio, video, and data nearly instantaneously.[2] Canada's microwave links were the longest ever created due to Canada's immense size and the vast distances separating her Pacific cities from her Eastern and Central cities. These 1950s highways of data and information were every bit as critical to the unity of the Canadian nation state as the buildup of nineteenth-century railroads.[3] The greatest innovation in telephony in Canada since was the development of the cellular networks, largely built over the 1990s and 2000s. These networks were fully built up by three very large and wealthy telecom giants: BCE (Bell Canada), Telus, and Rogers Communications. Telesat Canada was chartered as a crown corporation by the Canadian parliament in 1969 creating one of the world's largest fleets of communications satellites.

Canada's media and telecommunications landscape is very much the product of historical circumstances and very powerful personalities. A lot of it probably would seem incomprehensible from an American standpoint without historical context. Its rich history and strongly expressed path dependence almost demand to be told in any discussion or analysis of these sectors. Throughout the entire world, we are living in a time of great change in telecommunications that Canada is not immune from. Nonetheless, I have no doubt that Canada's media marketplace as it is today is worth studying. We can never escape path dependence. For example, in the United States, despite the power of social networking, CNN, Fox News, and MSNBC—which is built upon the news division of one of the original big three American TV networks—continue to serve as a powerful force in American society. Even if Canadian media is ultimately eclipsed by their neighbors to the South, we can learn a great deal from this historical example that will help shed light on future media developments in the Internet age.

BCE

Bell Canada had almost effectively become Canada's only telephone company. While Alexander Bell, the primary inventor of the telephone, had been born in Scotland, he largely lived in Canada. Consequently, it should be no surprise that Bell Canada was one of the original members of the Bell Network led by AT&T. Despite its early lead, Bell Canada's dominance in the Canadian telephone market was solidified by the pure ruthlessness of its president, Charles Fleetford Sise. Due to import restrictions, Northern Electronic was founded to make the equipment for Bell Canada. Antitrust cases in the United States would ultimately force AT&T to divest from Bell Canada and Northern Electric. However, at the turn of the twentieth century it was actually local Canadian municipalities who led the fight against Bell Canada and the overall North American Bell system.[4]

The BCE holding company was created by Bell Canada in 1983 in order to allow for its diversification strategy. As a telephone company Bell faced substantial regulation; having a holding company would allow unrelated divisions not be affected by these restrictions. At the time of the restructuring Bell still owned a majority stake in Northern Telecom, which was the second largest telephone equipment manufacturer in North America.[5] The mid-1980s were a time of many very aggressive acquisitions by BCE as well as some dramatic bidding wars with the Reichmans. Bell Canada took a major stake in natural gas company TransCanada as well as taking over Canada's largest real estate firm, Daon Development. Daon Development was renamed BCE Development Corp and was effectively transformed into a subsidiary of BCE.[6] Subsequently BCE Development purchased the substantial American real estate holdings of Canadian firm Oxford Development Group.[7] The assets purchased from Oxford included office and real estate properties in Minneapolis, Chicago, Denver, St. Paul, and Phoenix doubling the size of BCE Development Corp.[8]

By 1990 BCE had stepped away from its moves toward becoming a large conglomerate leading to sales of big stakes in TransCanada and Encor.[9] By the beginning of 1990 BCE's real estate endeavor had turned bad. Peter and Edward Bronfman's Carena Development Corp assumed control over the portfolio.[10] This was the foundation of today's Brookfield Properties, one of the largest real estate firms in North America. As previously discussed Carena was part of the Bronfmans' intricate web of interlocking corporations that at one point controlled a huge part of the Canadian economy. Brookfield Properties' parent firm, Brookfield Asset Management, is the direct successor to the old Bronfman Private Equity Empire. The current structure and business model of BCE basically took form since the late 1990s. The CEO of BCE in 1998, Jean Monty, understood the potential synergies of content and delivery. However, his acquisition of Teleglobe proved problematic, and BCE was forced to spin it off a couple years later.

Michael Sabia took over BCE in 2002 with the mission of consolidating and refocusing BCE's core telecommunications assets. Under Sabia's leadership he repurchased Ameritech's share of Bell Canada.[11] One of his first divestitures of noncore assets was the sale of the directory business to Kohlberg Kravis Roberts & Co. and the Ontario Teachers' Pension Plan.[12] In 2006, BCE completed last decade's round of divestitures of stakes in Bell Globemedia including the CTV network it acquired in 2000 to The Woodbridge Company Limited, Ontario Teachers' Pension Plan, and Torstar Corporation.[13] Woodbridge is the holding firm of the Thomson family, and Torstar is the publisher of the Toronto Star. Torstar gained a stake in its rival newspaper, the Globe and Mail, as well as a position in television broadcasting.[14] This sale also resulted in Woodbridge raising its stake in Bell Globemedia to 40%. The Thomson Family had maintained a smaller stake when they had sold the Globe and the Mail to Bell in 2000. Sabia also moved to transform Bell Canada into an income trust, but changes to the Canadian tax code ended the favorable status of income trusts.

In 2008 a buyout group led by the Ontario Teachers' Pension Plan reached a deal with the BCE management to take BCE private for $35 Billion in what would have been the largest private equity transaction in history. Teachers had won an aggressive bidding war for Bell Canada fought against a group consisting of Canada Pension Plan Investment Board (CPPIB), Caisse de dépôt et placement du Québec, and Kohlberg Kravis Roberts & Co.[15] In addition to Teachers, equity financing was also provided by Providence Equity Partners, Madison Dearborn Partners, and Merrill Lynch Global Private Equity.[16] In many ways the deal was really the brainchild of Providence Equity Partners founder, Jonathan Nelson, but of course Canadian law required the majority stake to be held by Canadian owners necessitating his partnership with Teachers.[17] The financing was provided by Citigroup Inc., Deutsche Bank, Royal Bank of Scotland, and Toronto-Dominion Bank.[18] Once a deal had been achieved, members of the winning syndicate boasted of the relatively small portion of the deal financed by debt. US buyout firm Kohlberg Kravis Roberts & Co and Texas Pacific Group had just completed a significantly more leveraged takeover of TXU Corp. Due to the fact that Teachers' takeover of BCE ultimately failed, the TXU buyout remains the largest in history. Despite the lower level of leverage, Fitch responded to the deal's announcement by downgrading BCE's debt based on concerns about the adequacy of the firm's cash flow to support the debt.[19] What ultimately killed what almost turned out to be the largest private equity deal in history was the condition placed into the agreement that the accounting firm KPMG would have to grant the deal a positive solvency report. Bell Canada hired Price Waterhouse Coopers to issue its own solvency report in a last ditch effort to save the deal.[20] Ironically solvency tests are rarely required for leveraged buyouts, but in this case it was an effort by BCE to immunize itself from lawsuits from bondholders.[21] Usually it would be the buyers who seek such an opinion. Central to the collapse of the deal was the escalating global financial meltdown. Bell Canada hoped to use the rival PWC opinion to persuade KPMG to change its ruling. Of course, the acquiring consortium that had agreed to acquire BCE could have certainly accepted a change in terms and accepted the PWC opinion over the KPMG ruling, but the growing financial crisis had given the buyers cold feet as well. At this point it was difficult to look past concerns about BCE's pension gap. Teachers had achieved a number of objectives as an existing major shareholder in BCE including successfully changing the company management without the deal's completion.[22] A lawsuit filed by the bondholders was heard by the Canadian Supreme Court attempting to kill the deal. While the deal fell apart anyway, the unanimous decision of the court rejecting the right of bondholders to unilaterally torpedo takeovers set a vital precedent for Canadian Corporate Law.[23] The excellent financial track record of BCE profits and positive BCE stock appreciation strongly suggest this would have ended up by far the most lucrative LBO deal in history.

Nortel Networks

Northern Electric was originally founded to work around Canadian patent laws and import restrictions. It became Bell Canada's equivalent to AT&T's Western Electric. Northern Electric's products also included televisions but by the early 1970s began to focus on telephone infrastructure. In 1971 Northern Electric and Bell Canada merged their research labs to create Bell-Northern Research as a local version of Bell Laboratories in the United States.[24] In 1976 the firm changed its name to Northern Telecom.[25] Fortunately, AT&T continued to promote Northern Telecom's equipment to affiliated Bell operating companies.[26] To understand how devastating Northern Telecom's ultimate collapse and failure would be to Canada's high-tech scene, one would only need to read the lead sentence in a 1985 article in the Globe and the Mail about the firm's tripartite corporate structure and future competition with AT&T and other firms: "the big question about Canada's only world-class technology company has been whether it had the marketing savvy to match its technical prowess."[27] Canada's only other firm to ever become a major technology giant in high tech was Blackberry. Northern Telecom's cousin in the United States, Western Electric, faced its own challenges as the US courts broke up the North American Bell System Colossus ruled by AT&T. Northern Telecom would aggressively market its digital and cellular telecommunications infrastructure equipment to American companies in the 1980s including making key inroads into Southern Florida. Washington Post's Florida Cellular Telephone Co. became one of the first firms to use technology from Northern Telecom in Florida back in 1985. Cellular One's early network of microwave towers connected to Bell South's network through a Northern Telecom digital switch in Fort Lauderdale.[28]

It would be no exaggeration to say that the Bell System monopoly vaguely resembled a communist country's corporate structures given its heavily centrally planned nature.[29] Yet Bell Laboratories in the United States and the entire Bell System including Bell Canada were continuously the source of a great deal of innovation and advancement. As previously mentioned Bell Canada took part in the building of the microwave towers that linked Canada's telephone, radio, and television networks nationwide. In the United States Bell Laboratories developed the transistor to replace the vacuum tubes in telephone switching equipment. Today the transistor is the building block of all modern electronics. Canada was a major source of innovation also because of its huge size and difficult geography. While microwaves were used to link Canadian Broadcasting Corporation stations in the 1930s, the first microwave relay for telephones in the world was used to link Prince Edward Island with Nova Scotia in 1948. The microwave radio network created by the Trans-Canada Telephone System in 1958 was the longest in the world.[30] By the early 1980s Northern Telecom was one of the leaders in regard to fiber optics and digital switching equipment. The result was Ottawa briefly became a mini Silicon Valley, spawning many smaller high-tech companies like Mitel which had its initial public offering (IPO) on the New York Stock Exchange in 1981. All of these smaller tech firms fed off the tech ecosystem created by Bell Northern Research.[31] Mitel's ultimate decline came from its inability to develop products as lucrative as its old PBX which was based on increasingly obsolete technologies in our digital world. Mitel has taken on a lot of different forms and incarnations since its heydays in the mid-1980s including a disastrous IPO on the Nasdaq in 2010.[32] Nortel beating out

AT&T for a joint venture in China for telecom equipment in 1995 helped establish Nortel as an international player.[33] Still Nortel ended the 1980s well behind the recently privatized former French state-owned firm Alcatel and former corporate aunt AT&T.[34] In the formerly incestuous relationships of the old North American Bell System, it is hard to know whether aunt, grandmother, or mother is the best analogy for the past AT&T relationship to Nortel (formerly Northern Electric and Northern-Bell Labs).

Corning and Siemens purchased some of Northern Telecom's optical network manufacturing assets in 1994.[35] This deal allowed Corning to capture the Canadian market for fiber optics while at the same time bolstering its production capacity worldwide.[36] But Northern Electric was far from done as a major networking infrastructure firm. In 1998 in an all-stock deal of nearly $18 billion Northern Electric bought Bay Networks, a major Silicon Valley area rival to networking giant Cisco.[37] This came at a time of a number of similar mergers worldwide and reflected an understanding of the growing convergence of telephony and Internet technologies. The Northern Telecom merger with Bay Networks represented a major turning point for telephone infrastructure firms that still shapes our world today.[38] Following this blockbuster tech merger, the firm assumed the new name Nortel to convey its broadened focus in networking.[39] A couple years later Nortel picked up Internet hardware firm Alteon in another all-stock deal almost as large.[40] Nortel CEO John Roth saw the key to Nortel's future as significant acquisitions similar to those that helped grow rival Cisco.[41] In doing so he had launched a take-no-prisoner war with Cisco and Lucent (formerly Bell Laboratories and Western Electric).

In many ways the dot-com bubble mirrored the subprime housing bubble of the next decade. Increasingly speculative deals were being made with accelerating zeal based on little more than faith that the good times were never going to end. It brings to mind that Kansas Blue Sky law that inspired all of the securities acts in Canada and the United States was based on the fear that some scams were built on nothing but thin air. Nortel aggressively marketed its stocks to vulnerable employees as well as the public, even as it entered into highly dilutive deals buying firms of questionable long-term value.[42] Nortel extended vendor financing to many shaky bets exposing itself to substantial credit risk once the tech bubble burst.[43] One of the mistakes made by Nortel was aggressive acquisitions sacrificing the great potential of cheaper organic growth from what had already been one of North America's most innovative firms.[44] Amazingly the management had effectively dismantled Bell-Northern

Research.[45] The possibly more fateful mistake was to hire investigators from American law firm WilmerHale in 2004, who quickly accused Nortel of accounting fraud. Rather than exposing malfeasance on the part of Nortel executives, many see WilmerHale as effectively killing the storied firm with false accusations. To this day they have not been able to back up allegations leveled at the firm at a critical point.[46] In the midst of the Great Recession Nortel declared bankruptcy and had its assets liquidated. Nortel's upstart American rival, Ciena, won the auction for its core unit.[47] Buying Nortel contributed no small measure to Ciena's stellar performance last year.[48]

At its heyday Nortel led the world in the vital fiber-optic networking market that links today's world. The dot-com boom lifted Nortel shares to such a lofty level, at its height, Nortel shares represented a full third of the value of the Toronto Stock Exchange. The dot-com bust left Nortel as the largest bankruptcy in Canadian history. Efforts to restructure and revive Nortel as an ongoing concern failed, leaving this storied Canadian tech giant the ignominious fate of being liquidated at rock-bottom prices. The drastic decline of Blackberry, another Canadian dot-com highflier, has left the Canadian high-tech landscape rather barren.

Telus

Alberta Government Telephones (AGT) was the incumbent telephone company and owned by the province. AGT was headquartered in the building now named ATB Place, long Alberta's tallest building. AGT had been transformed from part of the provincial department of public works into a crown corporation in 1958 allowing it to raise its own money through financial markets. In 1990 the province chose to privatize by means of what became the largest IPO in Canadian history underwritten by a group led by Royal Bank of Canada. Residents of Alberta had the first opportunity to buy the newly issued shares and could obtain them at subsidized prices.[49] Alberta had prepared for the privatization by creating a new holding company named Telus to own the phone assets. Telus was already Canada's third largest telecommunications firm.[50] By 1992 Telus had North America's first completely digital phone network.

EdTel was the incumbent telecommunications provider in the city of Edmonton and was owned by the municipality. It was founded in 1904 after the city had purchased the privately held Edmonton and District and Telephone Company from Alex Taylor. The city of Edmonton long refused to merge their phone service with the one provided by the provincial government. By 1916 the city government of Edmonton was fighting with the province of Alberta over phone toll sharing. By the early 1970s the province-local dispute escalated into outright war. The city set about to purchase its own long-distance equipment and attempted to join the Trans-Canada Telephone System but was effectively blocked by Albert Government Telephones. The year 1984 was the year the conflict reached a crescendo beginning with a city media campaign attacking the provincial utility company. The city was ready to finally buy equipment to launch their rival long-distance equipment, but the province reacted with threats of lawsuits. At 12:07 AM on Valentine's Day in 1984 city employees reprogrammed their computers to block the province's long-distance billing and set up their own billing. Three days later the provincial government shut down direct dial service in Edmonton. In the end Edmonton prevailed with a favorable settlement. According to the Canadian political scientist James Lightbody, this was an extraordinary local grassroots campaign victory over the "constitutional omni-competence of provincial power."[51]

EdTel was an early adopter of fiber optics.[52] On the other hand, EdTel was criticized by Shaw Cable in its early days for restricting access to the telephone poles and underground ducts for the cable firm.[53] By Spring of 1994 the city had hired Nesbitt Thomson Inc. and Goldman, Sachs & Co as advisors on possibly selling the phone company by means of an IPO. By summer Telus had begun efforts to acquire the municipal phone company despite initially being rebuffed.[54] On November 22, 1994, the city of Edmonton authorized the sale of Edmonton Telephone Corp. to Telus.[55]

Telus subsequently merged with BCTel, the dominant carrier in British Columbia in 1999. While also a regional monopoly, BCTel was always private with American telecom GTE as its largest shareholder since one of GTE's American precursors had funded BCTel's telephone network back in 1927. GTE's ownership stakes in Canadian telecom were unique, due to its ownership positions preexisting later Canadian restrictions on foreign holdings in domestic telecom companies. This grandfather clause did not extend to cable television however to the delight of rival Rogers Communications.[56] BC Telecom developed leverage by agreeing to take part in the Federal Beacon Project to create a national fiber-optic network to power a Canadian information highway.[57] The Canadian Federal Cabinet carved out a new exemption for BC Telecom to allow them to create a cable service, despite GTE's foreign controlling stake.[58] Federal judge Marc Nadon ultimately ruled that the Broadcasting Act allowed the cabinet discretion to grant BC Telecom the right to start a new cable service.[59]

Merger talks between BCTel and Telus accelerated in October of 1998 at about the same time BCTel parent firm was engaged with merger talks of its own with Bell South.[60] The back story to this merger was a much larger fight between BCTel and Bell Canada. BCTel had rebelled against Stentor, the Bell Canada-led national long-distance association. Telus had unsuccessfully tried to merge with AT&T Canada Long Distance Services Co prompting Bell Canada to respond by starting its own national network which could potentially entice customers out west as well.[61] The merger between BCTel and Telus reduced GTE's stake in the firm to 26.7%, but it also solidified Telus as one of Canada's major telecom firms. Bell Atlantic's acquisition of GTE meant that Telus's American partner had become a much larger giant in the United States, Verizon. Bell South and GTE had picked the name Verizon by combining the Latin word for truth, veritas, with horizon.[62] Verizon kept its stake in Telus until 2004 helping cement a very powerful business relationship between Telus and Verizon.[63] Their partnership led to shared technology and cooperation on service but did not stop Telus from later joining BCE to vehemently fight prospects of a separate Verizon cellphone service in Canada in 2013. By 1999 Telus was challenging BCE by building out a nationwide fiber-optic network.[64]

Telus has spent over a billion dollars just to wire Edmonton with new high-speed fiber optics in hopes of transforming it into the "first, significant urban gigabit society in Canada."[65] A great deal of the capital expenditure undertaken by Telus is dedicated to building out its own fiber-optic network to support its backhaul for a small cell structure. While offering immediate enhancements to performance today, the small cell structure is going to be critical in implementing a rapid transformation to 5G. Much of the Telus infrastructure for 5G is being built out by China-based Huawei. This is going to likely raise increasing security concerns as Western national security experts grow concerned that Huawei could provide a conduit for Chinese intelligence or even military operations. Russia's attacks on the 2016 American elections make these concerns ever more real to politicians and even corporate leaders throughout the West. The 5G cellular technology with its ultrafast speeds and virtually nonexistent latency promises to offer the world virtual and augmented reality applications, remote medical surgery, and self-driving vehicles.

Telus Health is the division largely responsible for providing healthcare providers and first responders access to digital records and access to advanced communications facilities. Telus Healthcare has formed a partnership with British start-up Babylon Health to offer patients the virtual care of physicians over very large distances. The huge size of Canada provides a unique arena to really exploit Babylon's potential. Babylon combines creating virtual patient visits with physicians with state-of-the-art artificial intelligence to help facilitate developing diagnoses and treatment plans.

The main aspiration of Telus Health is to utilize connectivity to transform healthcare. Home Health monitoring allows physicians to remotely monitor their patients every day, when the patients are home. On the flip side Telus also provides patients a personal health record, allowing the patient the ability to follow and take charge of their own healthcare.[66] The online record tool and a healthcare professional portal for the physician are built on software developed and provided by Get Real Health. Built upon this is the Telus Health Space which allows hospitals and clinics to seamlessly share and access patient records. Health Space utilizes Microsoft HealthVault software which was originally launched in the United States and United Kingdom. Other Telus Health products completely digitalize every other part of the healthcare administration virtually eliminating paper. Telus healthcare is partly built upon its purchase of Emergis.[67]

Rogers Communications

Rogers Communications was a cutting-edge firm from the beginning. Founded by Ted Rogers, its roots begin with Toronto's first private television station. Rogers's father had been an early North American pioneer in radio technology who had invented the first radio that could operate with the alternating current that homes are wired with. Rogers shifted into the nascent cable industry in 1967. By 1970 Wall Street and Bay Street started to recognize the huge potential of the cable industry, then often referred to as community antennae (CATV). The industry was created a bit on the backs of the phone companies. While it sought to bypass or complement the lines built of microwave relays and intercity coaxial cables, cable firms would require leasing access to telephone poles.[68] The lawsuit between Rogers and Bell Aliant in 2006 proves the telephone pole battles are not yet over.[69] He followed his 1979 acquisition of Canadian Cablesystems with an IPO on the Toronto Stock Exchange. In the mid-1990s Rogers launched the first cable modem service in North America. Rogers entered into the cellular business by acquiring Cantel in 1986. A partnership with AT&T gave Rogers wireless access to critical cellular technology in the 1990s. Rogers also led North America in the introduction of Blackberry, a portable device created by Canadian tech star Research in Motion.

Cantel was founded by David Margolese who would later go on to found Sirius satellite radio in the United States after a failed attempt at starting a new Israeli cellular provider. David Margolese had founded Canadian Telecom in 1978 at the age of 20. Canadian Telecom was originally a very successful paging firm, but Margolese realized the potential future for cellphones. He persuaded Ted Rogers to help found and finance Cantel, Canada's first cellphone service, with him. Ultimately, Margolese sold his stake to Rogers, and Cantel became Rogers Mobility.[70] Margolese moved to Israel and attempted to create Teletec, a much needed new competitor in Israel's heavily used cellphone networks. Even after enlisting both AT&T and Sprint for his project, Margolese still could not get a license in Israel to get his project off the ground.

Sirius XM Canada

After failing at launching an Israeli carrier, Margolese went on to create Sirius Satellite Radio in the United States. His objective was to beam pay radio programming to the customers on the ground primarily in cars. In order to cover the United States, Sirius chose to create a constellation of satellites with one always directly above the United States. In order to accomplish this, Sirius adopted the highly elliptical Molniya orbits first utilized for Soviet spy satellites.[71] The unusual orbit led to an unusual problem. Their high velocity led to their signals having a Doppler effect that put an additional challenge for the chips created to process the signal. The result was that the only other firm in the United States licensed to broadcast satellite radio, XM Radio, constantly ran ahead in receiver technology even after having a later start.[72] XM Satellite Radio had chosen to simply park its satellites in a geostationary orbit at the equator, meaning relative to our planet the satellites do not move, which eliminates any potential for a Doppler effect. The challenge was their position far south of any of XM's territory meant that many obstacles from buildings to mountains would easily block the signal even though these were the most powerful commercial communication satellites ever launched. XM's solution was to simply install 1000 repeaters throughout the United States.

What began as a disadvantage actually was in some ways a plus because it even allowed for substituting in local programming, a feature always opposed by local terrestrial radio stations.

Like with all media and telecom firms, Sirius and XM had to sponsor local affiliates, both of which ultimately got listed on the Toronto Stock Exchange. Sirius Canada was a partnership of Sirius, the Canadian Broadcast Corporation, and Slaight Communications. The launch of Sirius Canada initially without the most notorious personality of the American service, Howard Stern, triggered a major backlash for fans. The problem was that Howard Stern had already been banned by the Canadian Broadcast Standards Council for offensive comments made previously.[73] The uproar against Howard Stern's controversial remarks was greatly aggravated by several attacks against French. Unlike in the United States, the Canadian Radio-television and Telecommunications Commission (CRTC) felt satellite radio was largely bound by the same standards and regulations as regular radio. Ultimately, Sirius and the CRTC relented, and Howard Stern was made available to Canadian subscribers. Howard Stern has once again found himself a regular news item in North America, this time, for a former regular on his Sirius Radio show, Donald J. Trump.

XM Radio Canada was founded by John Bitove Jr. as Canadian Satellite Radio Holdings Inc. (CSR Holdings). An $11-million-dollar investment by Bitove had grown into a half a billion dollar company by the time of CSR's IPO.[74] John Bitove was a big figure in Canadian business having started the Toronto Raptors, Canada's first and only NBA basketball franchise. His father was a major operator of restaurants in Canada as well as a major advocate for Macedonian issues having formed the first World Macedonian Congress. The launch of XM Canada brought NavTraffic to Canada utilizing the XM signal to provide vehicle in dashboard systems the ability to display local weather and traffic data. The service was originally a joint venture of XM and Navteq, a Chicago-based digital mapping service. Despite all of the Howard Stern hype for Sirius, in the United States XM Satellite Radio seemed to have all the advantages. Sirius receivers were costlier requiring more expensive subsidies increasing the firm's cash burn. XM had stronger relationships with General Motors and Honda than the relationships that Sirius had with Ford and other car firms. XM successfully brought to market fully portable satellite radios, a feat Sirius could not match. Yet the selection of celebrity CEO Mel Karmazin as CEO of Sirius seemed to turn everything around for Sirius. Karmazin successfully engineered a merger of equals between Sirius and XM.

The merger of the two American satellite radio giants left their Canadian affiliates in a quandary. This situation created all kinds of conflicts and challenges for two rival Canadian firms required to heavily coordinate with one firm for all programming and for the most part the entire infrastructure. As a result, in 2011, after gaining the key Canadian regulatory approvals, XM Canada and Sirius Canada merged into one satellite firm. Coordination between Sirius Canada and Sirius XM in the United States began to fray even after the Canadian firms completed their merger. Naturally Sirius XM sought to just absorb it, but Canadian law prevents foreigners from taking a controlling stake in telecom and media firms. Sirius XM partnered with Slaight Communications and private equity firm Obelysk Media to take Sirius Canada privately. While Sirius XM gained a 70% stake in the firm, many of the shares it received came without voting power allowing Sirius Canada to remain under the control of Canadians as required by law.[75]

Rogers Media

Rogers Media represents one of Canada's largest media companies. Its flagship magazine is *Maclean's*, but it includes seven other magazines as well. Ted Rogers 1994 purchase of the parent company of *Maclean's* in 1994 was his attempt at creating a Canadian equivalent of Time Warner or Murdoch Corp.[76] Rogers owns CityTV, one of Canada's main television networks. The anchor station of CityTV is City-DT in Toronto. CityTV only really formed into a national network at the end of the last decade. Before the network was formed City-DT was one of the leading producers of local programming in North America. Also famous for the airing of soft core, it helped inspire the cult classic horror sci fi Canadian film *Videodrome*. In 2011 Rogers also launched CityNews Channel which offers 24-hour coverage of Toronto news which combines the news resources of CityTV's newsroom with *Maclean's*. One of Rogers' major Canadian Cable networks is FX, an affiliate of the American cable station of the same name, while its most lucrative networks is Sportsnet.

Bell Media

Bell Media is BCE's division for television, radio, magazines, and newspapers. In 2010 BCE bought back stakes from Woodbridge, Torstar, and Teachers' in Bell Media, resulting in it becoming a wholly owned subsidiary. In order to better compete with Netflix, BCE offers the streaming service Crave nationwide. Crave traces its roots to an early Canadian pay per view system. However, today it is also a streaming service accessible on the Internet through any service provider, and it has apps for every major smartphone platform. Rogers Communications and Shaw Communications had launched a rival service in 2014 named Shomi, but it had failed to gain any real traction in the Canadian marketplace and was canceled in 2016.[77] Despite these Canadian attempts to fight American video streaming services, Netflix and Amazon Prime remain the favorites. Yet Crave positively distinguishes itself by retaining a larger amount of domestic Canadian content.

CTV

The flagship TV network of Bell Media is CTV. Founded in 1961, CTV currently has 22 affiliate stations. The most interesting affiliate to ever belong to the network was Jamestown, New York-based WNYP-TV.[78] This was the first TV station ever owned by Bud Paxson. The stations record was pretty close to dismal. In order to save on the costs of having a direct connection, WNYP would pick up CTV broadcasts off the air from Toronto but was on occasion known to sometimes transmit the wrong station. Ultimately, the network affiliation was doomed by a lawsuit from local American network affiliates based on CTV's programming being heavily comprised of US network shows distributed in the United States exclusively to those network affiliates. Bud Paxson would go on to cofound Home Shopping Network and establish Paxson Communications. Ultimately Paxson Communications was taken over by NBC and Citadel but later acquired by vulture investor Black Diamond Capital Management.

The core content for CTV primetime are hit American series largely from the networks but also including cable hits like the *Sopranos*. Toronto-based flagship CFTO-DT is known for its especially strong local news programming.[79] Its sister cable network, CP24, covers local news all day and night. CP24 had actually originally been part of the CityTV network, but the CRTC had forced Bell Media to sell the CityTV stations after it acquired Chum Limited.[80] One daytime CTV show is the *Social* which is modeled after the American show *The View* on ABC. The *Social* is produced in house and filmed in front of a live audience at Bell Media headquarters. *Question Period* is aired on Sunday mornings and is one of

Canada's oldest shows having premiered back in 1967. It was hosted by iconic Canadian broadcast journalist Bruce Phillips.[81] *Question Period* did not appear on air for a decade as CTV stations began to broadcast a rival show produced by Canadian programming service Baton Broadcasting System (BBS). BBS would ultimately buy the CTV Network and replace Sunday Edition back with *Question Period*.

CTV also airs reality show *The Amazing Race Canada*. Contestants fly as part of two-member teams to various parts of the world and have to locate various clues and complete various challenges in order to complete the race. The Canadian crime series *Cardinal* is in its third season on CTV and is produced by eOne Entertainment, a publicly listed Canadian entertainment company listed on the London Stock Exchange. eOne joined the FTSE 250 Index on September 2013. *Motive* is a police drama that was briefly picked up by ABC in the United States and then carried by USA Network on American cable. The *Indian Detective* is an example of a Canadian broadcast TV show simultaneously made available to the wider Netflix audience globally.[82] The comedy was partly produced by Frank Spotnitz, the original show runner from Amazon Prime's award winning *The Man in the High Castle*.[83] A number of CTV affiliates were originally affiliated with the Canadian Broadcasting Corporation. CTV 2 affiliates CJDC-TV in Dawson Creek and CFTK-TV in Terrace were both CBC affiliates owned by the Astral Media. They both disaffiliated from the CBC last year a few years after Astral was purchased by Bell Media.

Bell Media's main sports network is The Sport Network (TSN) with 20% of the ownership held by ESPN. TSN was originally started by Labatt Brewing Company. Complimenting TSN's national network (TSN2) and the four regional networks is the Canadian version of ESPN Classic also with a 20% ESPN minority stake. Sports remains a powerful revenue driver for Bell Canada. Sunday night football and Thursday night football are simulcast on TSN and CTV. TSN also broadcasts many of the Major League games aired on ESPN on Monday, Wednesday, and Sunday nights. BCE and Rogers co-own NBA TV Canada and Canada's only professional basketball team, the Toronto Raptors, through their joint ownership of Maple Leaf Sports & Entertainment (MLSE). Raptors games are split between TSN and Sportsnet.

Chum Limited

Many of the Bell Media's current assets came from the acquisition of Chum Limited for around $1.7 billion in 2006.[84] As a condition of its approval of the deal, the Canadian Radio-television and Telecommunications Commission required Bell Media to sell the CityTV Network to Rogers. Many of the Canadians who had built the Chum Limited empire were very colorful characters. Chum's last CEO was Jay Switzer, the man who had created Much Music, Canada's music video station. He had grown up into the Canadian television business. His parents, Israel and Phyllis Switzer, along with Moses Znaimer had founded CITY-TV in Toronto. Born in Tajikistan to Jewish refugees fleeing the Nazis, Znaimer's family made it to Montreal. Znaimer had worked as an analyst at a venture capital firm. From the beginning it was a total struggle to keep the station afloat. On Friday nights they would air soft core porn movies. Ultimately, even this was not enough and they had to sell to Chum Limited. Znaimer would become the creative force behind Chum's Cable specialty channels.

The founder of Chum was Allan Waters, and his family retained control of the firm. Waters' death in 2005 put his company into play. A fight between his three children was pivotal in leading to the sale to Bell Media. Waters began his broadcast career by purchasing CHUM AM in Toronto which he switched to a 24-hour top 50 format popular in the United States. Subsequently in 1963 he launched CHUM FM originally with a format originally devoted to classical music, but within a few years it had switched to a very modern hip format consistent with the edginess that would define the company for its rest of time as an independent firm. In 1967 Waters listed Chum Limited on the Toronto Stock Exchange.

Shaw Communications

Shaw Communications was a cable company originally founded by JR Shaw in 1966 as a subsidiary of his father's oilfield services company, Shawcor. Shawcor originally was a construction firm in Southwestern Ontario which eventually found the oil pipeline business very lucrative. The Shaw family's original business, Robert Shaw's Hantsport Brickyard, is actually older than the state of Canada.[85] Shawcor's pipe coating division, originally named Bredero Shaw, is today the largest in the world and is a vital supplier to the world's offshore oil rigs. Halliburton owned a stake in Bredero Shaw until Shawcor purchased it in 2002 for $200 million (US). Halliburton had obtained this stake when it purchased Dresser Industries in 1998 with a $7.7-billion-dollar deal. In 2013 Shawcor eliminated the dual class share structure, and the last Shaw family members of the board, Ms. Virginia L. Shaw and Mr. Leslie W. J. Hutchison, retired. This leaves Shaw Communications and its spin-off Corus Entertainment as the two main companies the Shaw family still control. JR recognized the fairly sparsely populated province of Alberta desperately needed cable and acted accordingly. When JR split up responsibilities of the company with his brother Les Shaw, Les took over the pipeline business, and JR took over the cable division. Unlike Shawcor, Shaw Communications still has a dual-class share structure giving the family greatly disproportionate control. The Shaw family retains ownership of the bulk of the class A shares, while the bulk of shares in circulation are the nonvoting class B shares.[86] Shaw Cable was the first Canadian firm to bring digital cable to homes.[87]

Corus Communications

Shaw Communications spun off its media and broadcasting division to form Corus Entertainment in 1999, but it is still controlled by Shaw Cable and the Shaw family. Like with Shaw Communications the family held on to the bulk of the voting class A shares. Corus's WTN is a cable network entirely geared toward women. In 2009 Shaw had acquired *SexTV: The Channel* and converted it into W movies also geared toward a woman audience. These two cable channels are roughly equivalent to *Lifetime* and *Lifetime Movies* in the United States. Corus owns the Global TV Network, Canada's second most watched network. Before Shomi, Shaw Cable and Corus did make some noteworthy efforts to gain a presence on movies on demand. In fact, the very first movie-on-demand service in Canada, Movie Central Express, was launched in 2002.

Most of Corus's assets originally consisted of wide assortment of radio stations, and many of its cable specialty stations had a focus on children's programming. At the time of its initial public offering on the Toronto Stock Exchange, it owned Viewer's Choice, Super Channel, and Movie Max.[88] Corus also owned video on demand in partnership with Alliance Atlantis.[89] Corus was able to organically grow its cable offerings and was helped by Canadian regulations that required all cable and satellite operators to carry all stations designated as category one by the Canadian Radio-television and Telecommunications Commission. Corus Entertainment more than doubled from its acquisition of Shaw Media, which had come from Shaw's acquisition of Israel Asper's Canfield.

In 2010 Corus Communications moved into its new Toronto headquarters which consist of a huge office building named Corus Quay that sits on a 2.5-acre site and was financed by the city of Toronto to revitalize the Toronto waterfront. This beautiful state-of-the-art building looks far more like something you would find in Silicon Valley than the more conservative office buildings you would expect in one of North America's largest financial cities.

The broadcasting assets of Canwest were sold to Shaw Communications in 2010 to create today's Shaw Media division.[90] In 2016 Corus Communications acquired the Shaw Media Division gaining control of a number of radio and TV stations which came from Canwest. This was a mammoth $2.65-billion acquisition funded by taking on significant debt on the part of Corus Entertainment.[91] The deal gave Shaw Communications the money it needed to acquire Wind Mobile, potentially allowing for the creation of a fourth major cellular phone service provider in Canada. This allowed for a consolidation of TV and cable networks as well as content creation allowing Corus to rival Bell Media and Rogers Media in scale and scope. As a result, the Global Network came under the Corus Entertainment umbrella and became a stronger challenge to leading Canadian network CTV.[92]

Freedom Mobile

Shaw's 2016 acquisition of Wind Mobile represented the beginning of Shaw challenging Canada's dominant three cellular providers. Shaw's nascent mobile service is named Freedom Mobile. Freedom already has gained a sizable market share, and its prospects are bolstered by the federal government's repeatedly desired goal of having a viable fourth service provider for mobile telephony. Canadians pay more than residents of most other developed countries for their cell service. Ironically, the United States now only has four cellular carriers and almost lost one when AT&T attempted to purchase T-Mobile but was stopped by the US government.

Conrad Black

Hollinger was Conrad Black's Canada-based newspaper empire. At its height Hollinger was the third biggest newspaper company in the world. Conrad Black had inherited much of his wealth from his father, George Montegu Black II, who ran the family brewery company built up by George Montegu Black Sr., the grandfather. George Black Jr. created Ravelston Corporation with his business partner, John McDougald, as holding company for their stakes in Argus Corp.[93] George Black's stake stemmed from the sale of his brewing company to Canadian Breweries, a division of Argus. After George Black's death, Conrad Black was able to persuade under questionable circumstances McDougald's widow and sister living in retirement homes in Florida to sell their stakes, granting Conrad Black control of Ravelston and through it Argus Corp. At the time of George Black's death, Argus was one of Canada's most important conglomerates. Even in Black's early days as head of Ravelston, he was caught in controversial and possibly unethical practices.[94]

Over time he shifted out of his industrial holdings and set about to build a newspaper giant using the defunct mining division of Argus, Hollinger, as the main holding company. One of the divisions of Argus was Standard Broadcasting which was originally the radio firm created by Edward Rogers, Sr., the father of the founder of Rogers Communications. Black Sold Standard Broadcasting to Slaight Communications which it largely sold off to Astral Media.[95] Black's purchase of the London Telegraph in 1986 was his first major acquisition overseas.[96] In 1991 Hollinger took control of the Jerusalem Post, Israel's largest English language paper that was originally named the Palestine Post since it predated Israel's independence from the United Kingdom. Black's takeover of the Jerusalem Post led to an exodus of editors and authors as a result of a perception of editorial meddling from the new Canadian parent firm, Hollinger.[97] Conrad Black also took control of the Sydney Morning Herald and other Australian newspapers with local media mogul Kerry Packer and future Prime Minister Malcolm Turnbull in 1992. The establishment of Hollinger International as an American subsidiary and its listing on the New York Stock Exchange may have proven key to Black's downfall. It would ultimately be cases pursued by the US Securities and Exchange Commission and led by the US Attorney's Office for the Northern District of Illinois that would lead to his imprisonment and end his business career. However, the US government firmly established that

Black and his business partner were guilty of brazen fraud indirectly robbing shareholders of money that was rightfully theirs.

Canwest

Canwest has its roots from North Dakota station KCND purchased by Israel Asper in 1974. Asper was a lawyer and politician in Manitoba who had earned his law degree at the University of Manitoba.[98] KCND had actually gotten its license from the US Federal Communications Commission (FCC) in 1960. While operating out of North Dakota, its primary audience was in Manitoba. KCND was located in the US town of Pembina which had a population of only 625. Not surprisingly, KCND had trouble maintaining its relationship with US networks ABC and NBC given its limited American audience. However, KCND was still able to maintain solid advertising revenue by maintaining offices in Winnipeg. KCND's Canada-focused business was modeled after KVOS in the state of Vancouver that aimed its programming at Vancouver. Today KVOS utilizes HDTV technology to even broadcast Canadian Punjabi station Sur Sagar on one subchannel that provides unique programming for Canada's Sikh community. KVOS was established by David Mintz who would later help Canwest Global TV gain access to America's hottest network shows and ultimately became the president of Global TV.[99] Canada's income tax law was amended to end the deductibility of advertisements taken out on US TV stations, and regulators made other changes disadvantaging US network sales in Canada. The Western Manitoba Broadcasters and Communications Winnipeg Co-Op competed with Israel Asper to purchase KCND from the McClendon Corporation and gain a Winnipeg broadcast license from Canada's Canadian Radio-Television and Telecommunications Commission (CRTC). Asper ultimately won the contest to gain control of KCND. Asper's first Canadian TV station was aptly named CKND, and the old KCND transmitters would spend their last day active simulcasting this new Canadian TV station.[100] CKND gave new life to this now established station but also jumpstarted Asper's TV and media career.[101] Izzy Asper formally launched Canwest in 1977 in partnership with Gerald Schwartz who later launched Onex, one of Canada's largest private equity firms.[102] In 1991, Asper took Canwest public with an IPO on the Toronto Stock Exchange.[103]

In the late 1980s Izzy Asper began to expand overseas. In 1992 Canwest acquired Australia's Network Ten from the Northern Star

Holdings which had been forced into receivership. Canwest first invested in New Zealand's TV3 after the station had been put into receivership after a difficult recession. Despite Canwest's small stake the agreement also involved Canwest assuming management of the New Zealand station. In 1997 Canwest purchased another 48% of TV3 from Australian bank Westpac. That same year Canwest launched Ireland's first private national network also then named TV3. Today TV3 is controlled by Richard Branson's Virgin Group and is named Virgin Media One.[104] Canwest in conjunction with Goldman Sachs private equity wing GS Capital Partners purchased Alliance Atlantis, a big Canadian TV and movie studio which produced the hit TV series *CSI Las Vegas* in 2007.[105] Alliance also owned major Canadian specialty channels like *Showcase* but also was the major Canadian partner of many local versions of cable channels like BBC Canada, Discovery Health Canada, Food Network Canada, and National Geographic Canada. Alliance was Canada's largest film and television producer. In 1999 Canwest purchased Hollinger's Canadian newspapers. In the process Canwest ended up taking on significant debt that would prove fatal to firm's future solvency.

The financial crisis followed by the Great Recession proved too much for Canwest to endure. One early sign of trouble for Canwest was in November of 2008 it was forced to write down by a billion dollars its broadcast television assets.[106] The growing recession in Canada combined with the secular decline of the TV network business resulted in declining advertising revenue. While the American networks also were struggling at this time, the decline in Canadian television networks was probably worse than their American neighbors, since they were always the weaker siblings in English North America to the big three US networks. Amazingly, Rupert Murdoch had managed to propel the Fox TV Network into the ranks of major US networks just before the decline of US networks began to accelerate last decade.

GoldenTree Asset Management gained control of Canwest's print assets by picking up its distressed debt during the restructuring process and transformed the firm into Postmedia which has remained one of Canada's giants in newspapers and magazines to this day.[107] Goldman Sachs played a key role in the deal for Canwest's TV assets stemming from their previous ownership stake in the 13 cable networks Canwest had jointly purchased with Goldman from Alliance Atlantis Communications. The amount of money American private equity firms have managed to draw out of these traditional Canadian news sources has been a source of great controversy. Postmedia owns many newspapers throughout Canada, but it is led by its flagship *National Post* newspaper. Its flagship newspaper is the *Toronto Sun* but also includes Sun-branded newspapers in Calgary, Edmonton, Ottawa, and Winnipeg. Sun Media also included many community and local papers throughout the country. Postmedia relisted its stock on the Toronto Stock Exchange but in an unusual manner. First this listing did not involve an IPO where newly issued shares are sold to the public, and second special non-Canadian shares were issued to key sponsoring American hedge funds including GoldenTree to protect Postmedia's preferential tax status as a Canadian publisher. In 2017 Toronto-based private equity firm Torstar purchased many of Sun Media's local and community newspapers.

Global TV

The vision for Global TV came from Ken Soble, the head of Niagara Television. Niagara's first station CHCH came only after a big fight with the Canadian Broadcasting Corporation to even allow a rival TV station in Hamilton, so the compromise was that it would be privately owned and operated but function as a CBC affiliate.[108] The CBC sought to preserve its government monopoly in part by co-opting private broadcasters and other media firms. In exchange private stations got easy access to free domestic programming.[109] CHCH became Canada's first English independent channel in 1961 after breaking ties with the CBC.[110]

In 1966 Soble devised a plan to launch his own satellite in order to quickly link affiliates of a new network named NTV. Unfortunately, he died of a heart attack that year leaving his wife, Frances Soble, to run the firm. In 1968, NTV submitted an official application for a third Canadian network. However, in 1969 the Canadian Parliament passed a law creating the crown corporation Telesat Canada which would go on to launch a whole fleet of satellites that would fully cover Canada from coast to coast. This left Soble's plan economically unviable. Al Bruner, one of the architects of the proposed network, got fired in 1969.[111] Bruner formed a new investment team and created Global TV. His application to create a new Canadian TV network was approved in 1970, and it started with a brand new station named CKGN-TV. While his more ambitious satellite plans were foiled by Parliament, he succeeded in launching his network and is considered one of the leaders in Canada's use of satellites for television networks.[112] Last decade Canwest gradually consolidated its control of

Global TV.[113] In 2010 Shaw acquired Canwest's broadcast assets including Global TV. Today Global News produces both national and local news programming. Last year Shaw Communications started to redirect money previously allocated for local cable stations in Vancouver and Edmonton to Global News for its local programming.

Telesat Canada

Canada led the world in communications satellites and was even the very first to have deployed a domestic communications satellite. In 1969 the Canadian Parliament acted to create Telesat as a crown corporation but one in which private Canadians would be able to invest in along with the government. An earlier plan would have been led by the Trans-Canada Telephone System, the main long-distance service for Canada's telephone companies, as well as Canada's two main railroad companies.[114] Telesat Canada led the world in launching satellites to link Canada's telephone and TV networks.[115] Blasted from the Kennedy Space Center on NASA Delta rockets, Canada established itself as one of the great commercial space powers.[116] The first satellite, Anik, named with the Eskimo word for "brother," provided coverage to northern parts of Canada previously with only spotty radio and TV access. Radio Corporation of America (RCA) quickly signed up to use two of the channels on Arik, because Canada had beaten the United States by a couple years with its launch of communications satellites.[117] Another early prospective customer of Telesat was American Satellite Corporation, the subsidiary of Fairchild Industries that would become in the 1970s the leading provider of satellites linking American television channels.[118] The American Satellite Corporation would also get the contract for transmitting the *Wall Street Journal* nationwide. Telesat's ambitious satellite construction and launch schedule placed it in a strong position to remain a major technological leader into the 1980s.[119] However, the FCC also ordered RCA to switch its satellite service outside of Alaska to Western Union due to a new US-Canadian agreement not to compete for each other's domestic service.[120]

Telesat Canada was sold by the federal government to Alouette Telecommunications Ltd.[121] In 1992. Minority shareholder Canadian Pacific unsuccessfully sued to block the deal due to its ownership stake with Canadian National in rival phone company Unitel (formerly named CNCP).[122] Alouette was a consortium of companies which included BCE, satellite manufacturer Spar Aerospace Ltd., Canadian Pacific, and the

Ontario Northland Transportation Commission. The consortium was named after the Alouette 1, the first satellite manufactured in Canada, which was launched in 1962. Its mission was to study the ionosphere, but the satellite also provided Canadians an immense source of national pride. The launching of the Alouette 1 made Canada the third country to launch its own satellite beating the British who had used American-made satellites for their first couple space missions. In 1998 BCE took full control of Alouette, transforming it into a wholly owned BCE subsidy. BCE shifted away from a diversified strategy and sought to focus on core businesses. In 2007 Canada's Public Sector Pension Investment Board (PSP) and Boston-based Loral Space acquired Telesat from BCE for $3.42 billion.[123] The PSP manages the pension assets for members of Canada's public service, armed services, and the Royal Canadian Mounted Police. The deal left Loral with nearly two thirds of the ownership but slightly less than one third of the voting shares in order to comply with domestic control requirements. This has foiled Loral's goal to unload the Canadian satellite firm, despite representing most of Telesat's revenue. Loral had previously sold many orbiting satellites to Telesat in 2004 following Loral's bankruptcy, many of them purchased from AT&T's Skynet division. Today Telesat is the world's third largest operator of commercial communications satellites. Since CPPIB still controls Telesat, Loral is threatening to sue Public Sector Pension Investment Board (PSP) in order to be allowed to sell its majority stake.[124]

BLACKBERRY

Research in Motion (RIM) was initially started in 1984 by two Canadian engineers, Mike Lazaridis and Douglas Fregin, both graduates of Canadian universities. RIM's humble roots began in an office above a Waterloo bagel store. One of their early products was Budgie which served as a LED sign to keep General Motors assembly line workers on track. Their DigiSync film postproduction proved very popular with major Hollywood studios, and it became an industry standard. The product began with a project developing a digital film counter for the National Film Board of Canada. This project transformed Research in Motion into a major technology firm.[125] Research in Motion had its IPO on the Toronto Stock Exchange on October 28, 1997, followed by its listing on Nasdaq in 1999.[126]

Probably the very first wireless data network was at the University of Hawaii. ALOHAnet was built on radio transmitters, because linking the campuses on various islands by undersea cables was too expensive at that time.[127] The first real commercial player in wireless data networks was Illinois-based Motorola, whose products evolved into the best-selling pagers. It was Sweden's Erickson who started to really develop wireless data technology. Their first venture was created for first responders including ambulances in collaboration with the national telephone company Televerket. Interestingly, creating networks for fire, police, and paramedics remains a major priority in telecom even more so after 9/11. However, RIM ultimately came to be known for their two-way paging system like the RIM 900 Interactive Pager. RIM's early products relied on the Ericson's Mobitex wireless network built for Rogers Communications.[128] Ted Rogers realized early the revolutionary potential of highly interactive advanced mobile messaging devices.[129] Rogers was a very early backer and investor in Research in Motion's early products. The company developed the industry's best keyboard and rebranded their communicators as Blackberries inspired by their distinctive appearance which was said to resemble the oxidant-rich fruit. The success of Research in Motion's marketing and the huge appeal of the product in Corporate America led to extremely successful capital raising on both the Toronto Stock Exchange and on Nasdaq. Blackberry's demise came from a number of fundamental flaws to the system. The rapid evolution of mobile communications and Internet largely left Blackberry's proprietary network obsolete and unnecessary. The earlier decline of Motorola almost foreshadowed the fall of Blackberry. In today's world of highly clustered tech ecosystems, it is hard for geographically isolated tech firms to thrive over extended periods of time. Several spectacular system failures helped illustrate that Blackberry's proprietary network only left corporations with one additional potential vulnerability for critical communications. The launch of the Apple iPhone was the death knell for Blackberry. However, Blackberry's decline was also accelerated by poor execution and fumbled new product releases. Like with Nortel Networks, Blackberry raised hopes that Canada could one day become a major tech powerhouse like Silicon Valley or Israel. However, their respective crashes from the height of spectacular glory only illustrated how Canada's lack of depth and resilience in high tech has largely doomed the country as a very peripheral player in the high tech arena. Unlike Nortel Networks, Blackberry is still very much hanging in there. Last year Blackberry transferred its listing from Nasdaq Global Market to the New York Stock Exchange.[130] Blackberry continues to be listed on the Toronto Stock Exchange and remains included in the very important S&P TSX 60.

Conclusion

The tightly linked industries of telecommunications and media and entertainment are among the most protected by Canadian regulators. This has accomplished two objectives for Canadians. First, it has led to very strong and powerful private telecommunications giants in Canada. Second, it has amazingly succeeded to preserve a unique Canadian character to Canadian programming and movies, without which the Canadian national identity may have been that much weaker. The regulatory and market scheme in these areas appears to have achieved the best of all worlds. The four largest telecommunications companies are all cross listed on both the Toronto Stock Exchange and the New York Stock Exchange. This gives them access to the unrivaled global capital accessible from the American markets while allowing Canadians ready access to investing in these local giants. While protectionism has preserved the domestic ownership of these firms, Canada has also successfully retained access to all the top technology available from the United States and the rest of the world. Likewise, in respect to movies and TV shows, Canada has benefited from having its own uniqueness and diversity without missing out on world leading American entertainment. Despite the successful role of regulators in preventing Canadian telecom and media from being gobbled up by the giant to the south, like elsewhere in this book I have found that the key drivers of change and progress are market driven rather than state sponsored.

Notes

1. Curtis, H., Strahlendorf, U., & Wade, A. (1958). The Simultaneous Transmission of Television and Telephone Multiplex over a Single Microwave Channel on the Trans-Canada TD-2 System. American Institute of Electrical Engineers, Part I: Communication and Electronics, Transactions of the, 77(2), 185–190.
2. Bonneville, S. (1957). The Trans-Canadian Microwave System. *Electrical Engineering*, 76(11), 967.
3. MacDougall, R. (2007). The All-Red Dream: Technological Nationalism and The Trans-Canada Telephone System. Canadas of the Mind: The Making and Unmaking of Canadian Nationalisms in the Twentieth Century, 46–62.

4. Love, R. S. (2005). For The General Good: The Debate over Private vs. Public Ownership of Telephones And The Canadian West, 1900–1912. *The American Review of Canadian Studies.*
5. Langan, F. (1983, Mar 10). Ma Bell's Canadian Cousin Is Also Dialing A Big Spinoff. *The Christian Science Monitor.*
6. Alan Bayless. (1985). Daon Says Lenders To Ease Terms Of Restructuring. *Wall Street Journal*, p. 1.
7. Martin, Douglas. (1986). Rapid growth at Bell Canada. (acquisitions and diversification). *The New York Times*, p. 31.
8. Alan Bayless. (1986). BCE Development to Acquire $1 Billion of Real Estate Assets in Five U.S. Cities. *Wall Street Journal*, p. 1.
9. Pierre, B. G. (1990, Sep 11). BCE Agrees to Sell Stake in Transcanada — Company, Which Will Get $1.1 Billion For Holding, Exits Energy Business. *Wall Street Journal.*
10. Goad, G. P. (1990, Jan 26). BCE Posts Loss of $77.5 Million for 4th Quarter. *Wall Street Journal.*
11. Kara Scannell. (2002). Deals & Deal Makers: Ontario Teachers, KKR Complete Deal With BCE. *Wall Street Journal*, p. C.5.
12. Christopher J. Chipello. (2002). BCE Will Buy Back 20% Stake in Bell Canada From SBC. *Wall Street Journal*, p. B.4.
13. BCE announces completion of Bell Globemedia transaction. (2006). *PR Newswire*, August 30, 2006.
14. Austen, Ian. (2005). Sale Alters the Media Balance in Canada.(Business/ Financial Desk). *The New York Times*, p. C13.
15. Stewart, Sinclair And Jacquie Mcnish. (April 18, 2007 Wednesday). How Teachers raised the stakes for BCE. *The Globe and Mail* (Canada).
16. Investor Group Led By Teachers' Private Capital and Providence Equity Partners Enter into Final Agreement with BCE. (2008, Jul 04). *PR Newswire.*
17. Mehta, S. (2008). The Biggest Deal Ever. *Fortune*, 157(11), 74–80.
18. Gillies, Rob. (2008). Bell Canada agrees to record $35-billion leveraged buyout. (Ontario Teachers' Pension Plan and BCE Inc.). *Los Angeles Times*, p. C2.
19. Arleen Jacobius. (2007). Acquisition Of BCE A 'Leverage-Lite' Buy; Ontario Teachers Fund Says Less Debt was Deliberate Decision in Telecom Purchase.(Private Equity). *Pensions & Investments*, 35(14), 6.
20. Bell Canada Makes Effort To Save Buyout; The telecom hires PricewaterhouseCoopers to review its financials, to avoid an estimated $50 billion deal from falling through. (2008). *InformationWeek*, Dec 9, 2008.
21. Lattman, P. (2008, Dec 11). BCE Leveraged Buyout Deal Collapses. *Wall Street Journal.*

22. Erman, B., Sinclair, S., & Avery, S. (2008, Dec 10). BCE awaits its fate. *The Globe and Mail.*
23. Beltrame, J. (2008, Jun 21). BCE Clears Supreme Court Hurdle; Justices Unblock $52B Deal by Unanimously Overturning Quebec Court Of Appeal Decision. *Waterloo Region Record.*
24. The BNR story. (1991). *Telesis*, (92), 4.
25. Ian Mt. Mcavity. (1976). Bay Street vs. Wall Street. *Barron's National Business and Financial Weekly*, p. 9.
26. Mark Lukasiewicz; GAM. (November 7, 1979 Wednesday). MARKET PERSPECTIVE Northern Telecom system Gets Boost from AT and T. *The Globe and Mail* (Canada).
27. Lawrence Surtees; GAM. (November 29, 1985 Friday). Northern Telecom Goes South ...and East and West. *The Globe and Mail* (Canada).
28. McNair, J. (1987, March 30). Cellular Phone Company Talks Up Competition rates Compared light Users heavy Users. *Sun-Sentinel*, p. 10.
29. Friedman, T. L. (1982, Jan 17). Why Western Electric Has to Hustle. *New York Times.*
30. Kuhn, M. (1984). Telecommunications in Canada-A century of symbiotic development. *Communications Magazine, IEEE*, 22(5), 104–114.
31. Giniger, Henry. (1981). Ottawa: New Electronics Center. *The New York Times*, p. 21.
32. Mitel Makes Second Try at IPO. (2010, April 22). *Globe & Mail* [Toronto, Canada], p. B12.
33. Cover Story The Deal That Almost Got Away Competing Nortel's Bid to be a Global Player Was Pinned to a Crucial Chinese Contract. Here's How Nortel Outmuscled AT&T in Nightmarish Negotiations to Win Iis Dream Deal. (1995, July 28). *Globe & Mail* [Toronto, Canada], p. 26.
34. Neher, Jacques. "A French Giant Stalks U.S. Telephone Market." *New York Times*, 25 Nov. 1991.
35. Business Brief— Corning Inc.: Purchase of Some Businesses of Northern Telecom Closes. (1994, Mar 02). *Wall Street Journal.*
36. Corning Plans to Buy Northern Telecom's Optical Fiber Unit. (1993, Dec 16). *Wall Street Journal.*
37. Mehta, Stephanie N and Lee Gomes. (1998, Jun 16). Nortel Agrees To Acquire Bay Networks — Telecom Company To Swap $7.68 Billion Of Its Stock For Network-Gear Firm. *Wall Street Journal.*
38. Lawson, S. (1998). Nortel's Data Play. *InfoWorld*, 20(25), 1–116.
39. Northern Telecom Limited to Become Nortel Networks Corporation. (1999, Mar 11). *PR Newswire.*
40. Schiesel, Seth. (2000). Nortel Agrees to Buy Alteon for $7.8 Billion In Stock. *The New York Times*, p. B4.
41. For Roth, Success for Nortel Spells 'Acquisition'. (1998, 08). *Computing Canada*, 1, 34.

42. Taylor, Fabrice. (2001). The Story Behind Nortel's Fall.(Nortel Networks Corp.)(Company Profile). *Globe & Mail* (Toronto, Canada), p. B1.
43. (January 2, 2019 Wednesday). Bagnall: Ciena's Blowout Year - Built from the Ghost of Nortel. *The Daily Gleaner* (New Brunswick).
44. (March 17, 2014 Monday). Lessons from Nortel: Acquisitions Spree, Bad Management Calls Led to Tech Giant's Fall, Study Says. *Postmedia Breaking News.*
45. 'Culture of arrogance' felled Nortel. (2014, March 18). *Globe & Mail* [Toronto, Canada], p. B5.
46. James Bagnall. (May 9, 2012 Wednesday). Nortel Trial May be Unable to Solve Wilmerhale's Role. *Canwest News Service.*
47. Musgrove, Mike. (2009). Ciena Buys Nortel Unit to Expand Footprint: $769 Million Deal to Triple Maryland Tech Firm's Market Share.(Nortel Networks Corp.)(CIENA Corp.). *The Washington Post*, p. A16.
48. (January 2, 2019 Wednesday). Bagnall: Ciena's blowout year - built from the ghost of Nortel. *The Daily Gleaner* (New Brunswick).
49. Graves, K. (1990, September 4). Albertans Get Shot at AGT Shares. *Computing Canada*, 16(18).
50. Lamphier, G. (1990, Sep 13). Alberta's Offering of Phone Utility Draws Big Interest. *Wall Street Journal.*
51. Lightbody, J. (1989), With Whom The Tolls Dwell: The Great Edmonton Telephone Dispute, 1984–1987. *Canadian Public Administration*, 32: 41–62.
52. Ed Tel Prepares for Future with Fiber Drop In New Subdivisions. (Edmonton Telephone is Installing Fiber Optic Cable in New Residential Developments). (1990). *Fiber Optics News*, p. 1.
53. Peter Verburg. (1996). Promise of Peace on The Fibre-Optic Front: Cable Companies Say Ed Tel has Been Retarding Edmonton's High-Tech Infrastructure. *Alberta Report*, 23(8), 18.
54. Business brief — telus corp.: Firm Mulls Merger of Unit with Edmonton Telephones. (1994, Jun 20). *Wall Street Journal.*
55. Telus Corp.: Firm Gets Approval on Offer for Edmonton Telephones. (1994, Nov 22). *Wall Street Journal.*
56. Robert Williamson. (June 24, 1995 Saturday). BC Tel Fights Foreign Ownership Move Control by U.S. Parent Could Block Phone Company's Cable-TV Play under Rules Being Considered by Ottawa. *The Globe and Mail* (Canada).
57. William Boei. (April 25, 1996, Thursday, FINAL EDITION). BC Telecom may reconsider investment. *The Vancouver Sun* (British Columbia).
58. Boei, William. (October 23, 1997, Thursday, FINAL EDITION). Rogers hangs un-Canadian tag on BC Telecom. *The Vancouver Sun* (British Columbia).

59. Boei, William. (March 21, 1998, Saturday, FINAL EDITION). Ruling lets BC Telecom start cable TV service. *The Vancouver Sun* (British Columbia).
60. Surtees, Lawrence. (October 14, 1998 Wednesday). BC Telecom, Telus in merger talks Joining Canada's second- and third-largest phone firms would create a western powerhouse to battle Bell. *The Globe and Mail* (Canada).
61. Surtees, Lawrence. (October 21, 1998 Wednesday). BC Telecom-Telus deal 'a big game of leapfrog' TELEPHONE TAG When Bell Canada tried to move in on George Petty's Alberta turf, he trumped the eastern giant by forging a merger with his corporate neighbour in B.C. *The Globe and Mail* (Canada).
62. Schiesel, S. (2000, April 4). Bell Atlantic and GTE pick post-merger name. *New York Times*, p. C6.
63. Simon Avery and Andrew Willis. (December 1, 2004 Wednesday). Verizon reveals plan to sell $2.3-billion Telus stake in offering; Stock issue is expected by end of week. *The Globe and Mail* (Canada).
64. Greg Crone. (May 12, 1999 Wednesday). BCT.Telus challenges Ma Bell: Earmarks $260 M for cross-country fibre-optic network. *National Post* (Canada).
65. (June 19, 2015 Friday). $1 billion fibre optic investment will make Edmonton Canada's 'first gigabit society,' Telus Corp says. *Postmedia Breaking News.*
66. TELUS Health Unveils New Online Healthcare Hub. (2012, Sep 26). *Canada NewsWire.*
67. TELUS Acquisition of Emergis Creates Leading Electronic Health Care Solution Provider - Final. (2007, Nov 29). *Fair Disclosure Wire.*
68. CERTIFICATE of STOCK Cable Television: Birth of a New Giant? (1970). *Changing Times* (Pre-1986), 24(11), 19.
69. Austen, I. (2006, Oct 25). The Comma that Costs 1 Million Dollars (Canadian). *New York Times.*
70. Van Hasselt, C. (2010). *High Wire Act: Ted Rogers and the Empire that Debt Built.* John Wiley & Sons.
71. Trishchenko, A. P. (2016). Multiple-Apogee Highly Elliptical Orbits for Continuous Meteorological Imaging of Polar Regions: Challenging the Classical 12-H Molniya Orbit Concept. *Bulletin of the American Meteorological Society*, 97(1), 19-24-24.
72. Blum, S. (2001). Chips of a Different Flavor. *Satellite Broadband*, 2(3), 50.
73. Quill, G. (2004, Oct 30). Radio's Final Frontier; Will Satellite Kill the Radio Star? *Toronto Star.*

74. Brent, P. (2005, Nov 08). Bitove Files IPO for Canadian Satellite Radio. *National Post.*
75. Janjua, U. (2017). Sirius XM canada completes 'recapitalization go-private transaction'. *SNL Kagan Media & Communications Report.*
76. Konrad Yakabuski, T. S. (1994, Mar 09). With The Purchase Of Maclean Hunter Ltd., Ted Rogers Becomes. *Toronto Star.*
77. CRTC Chairman Blasts Rogers, Shaw for Shomi Shutdown. (2016, Nov 18). *Chronicle—Herald.*
78. Jon Ruddy (January 1, 1969). The Bountiful Booty-And Impending Fate-of a TV Pirate. *Macleans.*
79. Zerbisias, A. (2006, Mar 13). Viewers Winners In 6 P.M. War Tune in to Watch the War, Nightly at 6; The Gloves are off in The Long-Running Battle for Viewers of Dinner- Hour TV News. *Toronto Star.*
80. McDowell, A. (2008, Mar 22). Making the Most of a Merger; The Television Industry is Small, and Perhaps None Know This Better than Those Amicably Sharing the Crowded Citytv/CP24 Newsroom. *National Post.*
81. Fox, B. (2014, Dec 18). The Man Who Truly Understood Canadians; Phillips Helped Shape Political Discourse in This Nation For Decades. *Calgary Herald.*
82. Russell Peters' CTV Series Indian Detective Gets Premiere Date. (2017, Nov 04). *Telegraph-Journal.*
83. Brioux, B. (2017, Nov 21). Russell Peters On His 'Less Jokey' New TV Series 'The Indian Detective'. *The Canadian Press.*
84. Shecter, B. (2006, Jul 13). Deal Boosts Media Stocks. *National Post.*
85. ACOA Helps Shaw Upgrade Operations. (2017, Apr 27). *Chronicle—Herald.*
86. Reorganization of Shaw Family Holdings in Shaw Communications Inc. (2015, Nov 04). *News Bites—Telecommunications.*
87. Strachan, A. (2000, Dec 16). Television Goes Digital: Yes, Digital TV Is Finally Here, But What That Means in Terms of What You'll Be Watching Remains An Open Question. *The Vancouver Sun.*
88. McMurdy, D. (2001, Sep 17). Child's Play It's Not. *Canadian Business*, 74, 15.
89. Corus Announces Proposed Digital Television Networks. (2000, Apr 04). *Canada NewsWire.*
90. Friend, D. (2010, Oct 27). Shaw Communications Closes Purchase Of Canwest TV Assets, Rebrands As Shaw Media. *The Canadian Press.*
91. Press Release: Shaw Communications Inc. Announces Sale of Shaw Media To Corus Entertainment Inc. For $2.65 Billion. (2016, Jan 13). *Dow Jones Institutional News.*
92. Krashinsky, S., & Robertson, G. (2010, May 04). Shaw Shakes Up TV Sector With Canwest Deal. *The Globe and Mail.*

93. Slocum, D. (1982, Feb 18). MARKET PERSPECTIVE Dominion Sales Drop, But Market Share Up. *The Globe and Mail.*
94. Tombs, G. (2010). Robber Baron: Lord Black of Crossharbour. *ECW Press.*
95. Silverstein, S. (1985, Jul 03). Bidding War for Acquisition of Valley Cable Appears Over. *Los Angeles Times.*
96. Fraser, J. (1985, Dec 10). Conrad Black Gains Control of London's Daily Telegraph. *The Globe and Mail.*
97. Harvey, D. (1990, Jan 10). Paper's Heart Cut Out. *The Globe and Mail.*
98. Boswell, R. (2003, Oct 08). Israel H. Asper Leaves Major Legacies Behind. *The Gazette.*
99. Hustak, A. (2002, Feb 07). Mintz built global's stable of hit shows. *The Gazette.*
100. Bourette, S. (1998, Mar 24). 'Izzy Asper Never Gives Up' ISRAEL (IZZY) ASPER. *The Globe and Mail.*
101. Asper may be preparing for national TV network. (1987, Sep 09). *The Ottawa Citizen.*
102. Newman, R. (1984, Feb 15). Asper Takes over Control of Canwest. *The Globe and Mail.*
103. Hanlon, M. (1998, Nov 26). Izzy Looks Beyond the Small Screen. *Toronto Star.*
104. Urlocker, M. (1995, Jun 24). THE ASPER WAY: Izzy Asper's Take-No-Prisoners Ethic Has Made Canwest Global a Player Here. But How Will His Chutzpah Play Abroad? With Interests in Australia, New Zealand, Chile and Now Britain, Global TV Moguls Are About To Duel With The Boy From Winnipeg. *Financial Post.*
105. Shecter, B. (2007, Jan 11). Canwest Acquires Alliance in $2.3B Deal: Takeover Boosts Industry Consolidation. *Calgary Herald.*
106. Robertson, G. (2008, Nov 15). The new reality TV: Value erosion. *The Globe and Mail.*
107. Slater, J. (2010, Jun 10). How U.S. Investors Won a Canadian Paper Chase. *The Globe and Mail.*
108. Kohanik, E. (1994, Jun 04). The House That Ken Built Forty Years Ago, Kenneth Soble Put CHCH - And Himself -On The Air. *The Spectator Retrieved.*
109. Rutherford, Paul. *When Television was Young: Primetime Canada, 1952–1967.* University of Toronto Press, 1990.
110. Foley, D. (2004, Jun 05). CH Celebrates a Golden History; TV Station Nurtured By Visionary Ken Soble Proud To Be Hamilton's For 50 Years. *The Spectator.*
111. (1967, Jan 19)."Fired CTV Official Pilots Plans for a Third, Satellite-Based Network". *The Globe and Mail.*

112. Jack Miller, T. S. (1987, Aug 29). Al Bruner, 63, TV Innovator Global Network Founder Dies. *Toronto Star*.
113. Desbarats, P. (2000, Aug 05). The Truth About Global's Near-Demise and Izzy Asper's Rise. *The Ottawa Citizen Retrieved*.
114. Measure Would Allow The Public To Invest In Telesat Canada. (1969, Mar 25). *Wall Street Journal*.
115. A Satellite That Talks Canadian: Telesat System, The First Of Its Kind, Will Link All Of Canada In A Telephone And TV Network. (1969). *Business Week*, 50.
116. Allaway, H. G., & Lynch, J. (1972). Telesat-A: Press Kit (Synchronous Communication Telesat-A Characteristics, Launching By Delta 92, And Flight Plans). (No. NASA-TM-X-68636; *Pagination* 11P).
117. (1972, Dec 06). RCA Will Use Canada's Message Satellite. *New York Times*.
118. (1972, Dec 07). American Satellite Sets Interim-Lease Accord With Telesat Of Canada. *Wall Street Journal*.
119. Thorpe, D. (1977). Evolution of the Telesat Canada System into the mid-1980's. In 12th Annual Meeting and Technical Display (p. 220).
120. RCA is Told To Start Sending Messages In U.S. Via Western Union Satellite Link. (1974, Dec 30). *Wall Street Journal*.
121. Vardy, J. (1992, Mar 11). Alouette's Telesat Bid. *Financial Post*.
122. Canadian Pacific Ltd., Ontario Concern Sue Over Telesat Move. (1992, Apr 22). *Wall Street Journal*.
123. Loral and PSP Investments Complete CAD 3.25 Billion Acquisition of Telesat Canada. (2007, Oct 31). *PR Newswire*.
124. Telesat Second Quarter 2018 Conference Call. (2018). *GlobeNewswire*. July 26, 2018.
125. Strathdee, M. (1992, Apr 04). K-W Firm Helps Hollywood: Film-Measurement Device Makes Editing Easier. *Kitchener - Waterloo Record*.
126. BlackBerry ltd - Annual Report. (2000). Kuching: Acquisdata Pty Ltd.
127. Abramson, N. (1985). Development of the ALOHANET. *Ieee Trans. info.theory.*, IT-31(2), 119–123.
128. Grantham, T. (1992). Tune in and turn on to wireless portables. *Canadian Datasystems*, 24(8), 36–38.
129. McNish, J. & Silcoff, S. (2015). *Losing the signal: The untold story behind the extraordinary rise and spectacular fall of Blackberry*.
130. Press Release: Blackberry Announces Plan to Move to the New York Stock Exchange. (2017, Oct 03). *Dow Jones Institutional News*.

CHAPTER 11

Conclusion: Stock Markets in the Twenty-First Century

Much of the current North American stock market infrastructure was in place by the latter half of the 1990s, but several key developments have occurred in the past 30 years. The two developments that transformed the stock market the most in the late 1990s were the rise of online trading and the exploding dot-com boom. America Online had its initial public offering (IPO) in 1992, but the beginning of an actual dot-com bubble is usually traced to the Netscape IPO during the summer of 1995. Netscape stock doubled in its first day of trading even after the initial offering price itself had itself been doubled at the last moment. This despite the fact that Netscape was still far from earning an actual profit. The launch of E*TRADE's website followed by it going public in 1996 heralded the beginning of the mainstream era of online retail trading. Technically, Schwab had beaten E*TRADE with the launch of its trading website the year before. Strong competition soon ensued with Morgan Stanley Dean Witter Discover & Co. purchasing the small San Francisco online broker Lombard Brokerage. This became Discover Brokerage Direct.

Many of the dot-com stocks of the late 1990s in retrospect turned out to be garbage. Others like Cisco and Corning were vital technology infrastructure stocks but got horribly overvalued based on completely unrealistic inflated projections. It is at this time that Canada's Nortel fatally overexpands in an effort to compete with American telecom infrastructure firms like Cisco. Not that its American cousin from the old Bell System,

M. J. Szanto, *A Century of North American Stock Markets*,
https://doi.org/10.1007/978-3-032-22419-4_11

Lucent did much better. While Lucent was able to escape the throes of bankruptcy court, it also suffered from a harrowing stock crash from its heights in the late 1990s. Two noteworthy 1990s stock stars that remain prominent today are eBay and Amazon. Wall street incentivized research analysts to curry favor with listed companies causing many of them to become glorified cheerleaders for dot-com firms. Some blamed the 1975 end of fixed commissions for upending the business model that bundled quality research with higher commission rates.

The crash of the dot-com bubble caused many poorly worked out listed start-ups some with no semblance of a viable business model to lose all of their value. By October 2002 the Nasdaq index fell a staggering 77% from its peak. The terrorist attacks on 9/11 may have played a role. The discovery of the massive accounting frauds at WorldCom and at Enron certainly did not help matters. Rather than neutral assessors of value, many Wall Street research analysts turned into glorified used car salesmen selling some of the sketchiest public issues since the 1920s. WorldCom and Enron both presented themselves as major corporate successes but were nothing more than massive frauds. The collapse of Enron also took down the storied accounting firm Arthur Anderson, by thoroughly discrediting America's oldest leading auditing firm. Fortunately for Accenture, it had already completely separated itself from its former parent firm. The collapse of WorldCom also largely brought to an end the rise of Microwave Communications, Inc. (MCI) which it had purchased. MCI had successfully challenged the AT&T monopoly through courtroom victories and the construction of a nationwide network of microwave towers. MCI was an early stock star on Nasdaq as well as a leading telecom provider for the exchange. Thus, the collapse of WorldCom was a fitting but also tragic end to the Nasdaq-centered dot-com boom of the 1990s.

Despite the Tech Carnage of the early 2000s, technology stocks once again rose to the forefront of the stock market. Google which rapidly became the leading search engine with a better algorithm for searching the web had its IPO in 2004. The company has been incredibly successful ever since by leveraging its leadership in search to become the leader in online advertising. That same year a new social networking site, Facebook, would launch. While certain social networking sites had already existed, Facebook was the only one that really gained traction with masses in the United States and around the world. AOL had once offered social networking and even earlier online services such as CompuServe and Prodigy as well as before that bulletin board services, but none had struck the chord with

America's mainstream like Facebook. Facebook would successfully hold off with its IPO until 2012 with it gaining an unbelievable $104 billion valuation on its first day of trading instantly making it one of the world's most valuable publicly traded firms. This established a new pattern that holds true today that many start-ups choose to take their time in going public and instead rely on private markets for their financing needs for extended periods. This reflects a strengthening and broadening of the private debt and equity markets. Part of the rise of unicorns, start-ups with more than a billion dollar valuation, come from the lack of rush to go public.

The housing bubble was fueled by low interest rates, Wall Street banks aggressively competing with government-sponsored entities Freddie and Fannie, rampant housing speculation, and a legitimate effort to try to increasingly cater to nonconventional borrowers in the form of the mushrooming subprime credit market. The stock market would not play a central role in the development of the housing bubble, but all the key banks on Wall Street were directly hit, and the market majorly suffered indirectly. The unprecedented government intervention led by Treasury, the Federal Reserve, and the US Congress led to a fairly quick recovery and an extremely buoyant economy and stock market.

The central role played by over-the-counter (OTC) derivatives in leading to the nearly catastrophic financial collapse in 2008 revived the 1990s debate over their regulation and oversight. CFTC chairman Brooksley Born had fought an unsuccessful battle with leading Clinton Administration figures Larry Summers and Robert Rubin as well as Fed Chairman Alan Greenspan to force greater federal oversight and transparency over the OTC derivatives markets. The collapse of Long-Term Capital Management in 1998 was an early warning that Born may have been at least partly right, but her concerns nonetheless had been neutralized by the 1998 OTC derivatives moratorium snuck into a 1998 Congressional Appropriations Act. However, it is critical to realize that financial derivatives like credit default and interest rate swaps are critical for the efficient and risk-balanced operations of modern banks. In 2009, Brooksley Born was awarded a JFK Profile in Courage Award. Shortly after the Global Financial Crisis, the Atlanta-based Intercontinental Exchange (today's parent company of the NYSE) assumed responsibility for the clearing and trading of the bulk of the market for credit default and interest rate swaps.

The release of Apple's first iPhone in 2007 combined with the growing popularity of Netflix would lead to the tech stock run of the 2010s. The tech boom of the 2010s would be epitomized by CNBC's Jim Cramer's

FANG acronym consisting of Facebook, Amazon, Netflix, and Google. Cramer adjusted his acronym for investing to FAANG by adding Apple as a result of the exploding iPhone market. The 2009 Flash Crash was an absolutely stunning intraday market collapse on the US trading markets but proved to be little more than a hiccup in the US stock market recovery. The American stock markets would again be heavily tested by the devastating COVID pandemic and the subsequent shutdowns. However, all the people forced to stay home only fueled a growth in more retail speculation including Gen Z, which trading start-up Robinhood was able to capitalize on. While the emergence of Gen Z as investors led to questionable meme stocks highlighted on Reddit groups like Wall Street Bets, many of today's stock market leaders are fundamentally solid. Chip leaders like TSMC and Nvidia are immensely profitable as are the hyperscalers led by Alphabet, Microsoft, Meta, and Amazon. Today Apple remains an immensely profitable firm that merges hardware, chip design, and software, though questions remain about its long-term resilience and relevance as artificial intelligence increasingly drives technological advancement and innovations. There can be no question that stock market valuations by the beginning of 2026 are once again on the frothy side, and the near-term performance of the US stock market will heavily depend on how quickly the AI revolution can be monetized and how much monetary and geopolitical risk can be mitigated.

Index[1]

[1] Note: Page numbers followed by 'n' refer to notes.

M. J. Szanto, *A Century of North American Stock Markets*,
https://doi.org/10.1007/978-3-032-22419-4

D

The manufacturer's authorised representative in the EU is Springer Nature Customer Service Centre GmbH, Europaplatz 3, 69115 Heidelberg, Germany. If you have any concerns regarding our products, please contact ProductSafety@springernature.com

Printed and bound by CPI Group (UK) Ltd, Croydon, CR0 4YY
13/10/2026
02232331-0003